Authentic Learning Environments in Higher Education

Anthony Herrington, University of Wollongong, Australia

Jan Herrington, University of Wollongong, Australia

 Information Science Publishing

Hershey • London • Melbourne • Singapore

Acquisitions Editor:	Renée Davies
Development Editor:	Kristin Roth
Senior Managing Editor:	Amanda Appicello
Managing Editor:	Jennifer Neidig
Copy Editor:	Bernard J. Kieklak, Jr.
Typesetter:	Jennifer Neidig
Cover Design:	Lisa Tosheff
Printed at:	Integrated Book Technology

Published in the United States of America by
Information Science Publishing (an imprint of Idea Group Inc.)
701 E. Chocolate Avenue, Suite 200
Hershey PA 17033
Tel: 717-533-8845
Fax: 717-533-8661
E-mail: cust@idea-group.com
Web site: http://www.idea-group.com

and in the United Kingdom by
Information Science Publishing (an imprint of Idea Group Inc.)
3 Henrietta Street
Covent Garden
London WC2E 8LU
Tel: 44 20 7240 0856
Fax: 44 20 7379 3313
Web site: http://www.eurospan.co.uk

Library of Congress Cataloging-in-Publication Data

Authentic learning environments in higher education / Tony Herrington and Jan Herrington, editors.
    p. cm.
  Summary: "This book is made up of a collection of peer-reviewed chapters that reflect the construct of authentic learning--learning that is centred on rich, real-world, immersive and engaging tasks"--Provided by publisher.
  Includes bibliographical references and index.
  ISBN 1-59140-594-7 (hardcover) -- ISBN 1-59140-595-5 (soft cover) -- ISBN 1-59140-596-3 (ebook)
  1. College teaching. 2. Student-centered learning. 3. Effective teaching. I. Herrington, Tony, 1950- II. Herrington, Jan.
  LB2331.A898 2005
  378.1'2--dc22
                                                    2005004514

British Cataloguing in Publication Data
A Cataloguing in Publication record for this book is available from the British Library.

All work contributed to this book is new, previously-unpublished material. Each chapter is assigned to at least 2-3 expert reviewers and is subject to a blind, peer review by these reviewers. The views expressed in this book are those of the authors, but not necessarily of the publisher.

Authentic Learning Environments in Higher Education

Table of Contents

Section I
Guidelines for the Design of Quality Authentic Learning Environments
---

Anthony Herrington, University of Wollongong, Australia
Jan Herrington, University of Wollongong, Australia

Section II
Authentic Learning Environments Across the Disciplines

Adult Education:
Marilyn Laiken, University of Toronto, Canada

Architecture:
Di Challis, Deakin University, Australia

Section III
Enhancing Widespread Adoption of Authentic Learning Environments

Foreword

The problems that beset colleges and universities today are enormous. In the face of government budget cuts and increasing costs, many institutions have raised student tuition and fees, increased faculty work loads, and/or thrown open their doors to blatant commercialization (Bok, 2003; Kirp, 2003). In the USA, national surveys report dismal levels of student engagement in academic work (National Survey of Student Engagement, 2003), rampant grade inflation (Johnson, 2003), and the very value of the degrees issued by universities and colleges is being questioned (Lasson, 2003).

While lip service is paid to the importance of teaching in virtually all institutions of higher education, the reward system in most universities remains primarily based upon success with respect to publications, research funding, and entrepreneurial ventures (Amacher & Meiners, 2004). Instruction remains teacher-centered and textbook-driven, even in the most elite institutions. For example, after investigating the integration of educational technology at Stanford University, Cuban (2001) reported that "Lecturing still absorbs more than half to two-thirds of various departments' teaching practices… These traditional forms of teaching seem to have been relatively untouched by the enormous investment in technologies that the university has made since the 1960's" (p. 129).

Meanwhile, in physical as well as online classrooms, tenure-track faculty members are being increasingly replaced by adjunct instructors who have few of the rights or benefits of traditional academics (Dubson, 2001). Many of these part-time instructors are teaching face-to-face and online courses for such low pay that at least one authority has suggested that they would make more money selling burgers and French fries at fast food restaurants (Johnstone, 2004). Other adjuncts may attain a significant income, but only by teaching so many courses that the value of their contributions to student learning cannot possibly be substantive.

In the wake of these challenges, what does a book on authentic learning environments have to offer? The answer is a lot! I am convinced that a great deal of practical benefits for higher education will be derived from widespread adoption of the types of innovative teaching strategies described in these pages. After reading this book, you will likely share this conviction.

Although the need to adopt more student-centered, problem-based, and technology-enriched learning environments has been recognized for many years, few academics seem able to comprehend what it means to teach and learn in fundamentally different ways. To change their mental models of teaching and learning, academics need exposure to strong rationales and practical examples. This book provides just the right prescription through the clear description of underlying theories and the portrayal of realistic case studies.

The time for significant support for the development of more authentic learning environments throughout higher education is now. The critical characteristics of authentic learning described in Section 1 of this volume can be implemented in traditional classrooms, the real world, online, and through blended approaches. Furthermore, as so richly illustrated in the chapters of Section 2 and Section 3 of this book, they can be applied to virtually any discipline.

My personal experience of teaching undergraduate and graduate students for the past 25 years has been that the more authentic the tasks and activities in my courses are, the more students are engaged, the more they learn, and the more they retain. My own perhaps idiosyncratic style of designing learning environments boils down to: "It's the task that matters most — make it authentic."

In the 21st Century, most university and college academic staff members must continue to devote their energies to all three of their traditional roles of research, service, and teaching. We must continue to contribute to advances in science, provide our expertise in the service of social causes and the humanities, and provide our students with opportunities to develop the knowledge, skills, attitudes, and values required to lead meaningful, productive lives. There are many signs that while we in the professoriate continue to excel in research and service, our teaching role has been slipping. Fortunately, authentic learning environments provide an unparalleled opportunity to revive the precious practice of teaching.

References

Amacher, R.C., & Meiners, R.E. (2004). *Faulty towers: Tenure and the structure of higher education*. Oakland, CA: The Independent Institute.

Bok, D. (2003). *Universities in the marketplace: The commercialization of higher education*. Princeton, NJ: Princeton University Press.

Cuban, L. (2001). *Oversold and underused: Computers in the classroom*. Cambridge, MA: Harvard University.

Dubson, M. (Ed.). (2001). *Ghosts in the classroom: Stories of college adjunct faculty and the price we all pay.* Boston: Camel's Back Books.

Johnson, V.E. (2003). *Grade inflation: A crisis in college education.* New York: Springer-Verlag.

Johnstone, S. (2004, March). Personal communication. For more information, see the *Western Cooperative for Educational Telecommunications* Web site at *http://www.wcet.info/*

Kirp, D.L. (2003). *Shakespeare, Einstein, and the bottom line: The marketing of higher education.* Cambridge, MA: Harvard University.

Lasson, K. (2003). *Trembling in the ivory tower: Excesses in the pursuit of truth and tenure.* Baltimore, MD: Bancroft.

National Survey of Student Engagement. (2003). *Converting data into action: Expanding the boundaries of institutional improvement.* Bloomington, IN: Indiana University Center for Postsecondary Research.

Thomas C. Reeves
The University of Georgia, USA

Preface

The concept of authentic learning is not new. However, its practice in higher education is arbitrary and undefined. The purpose of this book is to define the approach through examples of good practice. We hope that the rich variety of examples of authentic learning environments found in this book will provide the reader with the inspiration to teach their own subjects and courses in ways that reflect authenticity. This book is made up of a collection of peer-reviewed chapters that reflect the construct of authentic learning — learning that is centred on rich, real-world, immersive and engaging tasks.

The book is divided into three sections. Section I provides guidelines for designing authentic learning environments and encompasses the theoretical notions on which these environments are based. Section II contains chapters that describe how authentic activities are instantiated in a range of discipline areas commonly found in university settings. These authors relate the practical designs of their learning environments to both discipline-based theories and situated learning theories, as exemplified in Section I. Section III chapters discuss generally how authentic learning environments can be implemented and sustained more widely across an institution.

The *Foreword* has been written by Thomas C. Reeves, Professor in Instructional Technology at The University of Georgia. His influence on raising the awareness of teachers in higher education worldwide, to employ more innovative and authentic approaches, is enormous. Throughout his career, he has sought not only to champion the effective use of technology in education, but also to set an exhaustive and socially responsible research agenda for the field. His substantial contribution to education was recognised in 2003 when he was awarded the inaugural *AACE Fellowship Award* from the Association for the Advancement of Computing in Education.

In Section I, the editors, Anthony Herrington and Jan Herrington, describe guidelines for designing authentic learning environments for higher education that can be applied across a range of disciplines and in a variety of modes. Characteristics of the approach are explored in depth, providing a practical framework for teachers wishing to break away from traditional, teacher-centred approaches in higher education, and who are willing to create learning environments where students are motivated to learn in rich, relevant and real-world contexts.

In Section II, Marilyn Laiken examines the creation of authentic learning environments in the light of adult education and transformative learning theory, using a graduate course as a case example. Through an analysis of the design and implementation of the course, the chapter provides specific ideas for how graduate education can contribute to significant personal change in the values, attitudes and behavior of adult learners.

Di Challis explores the synergies of an integration of the conceptual and practice worlds for students of architecture and construction. A case study is used as an illustration of curriculum design, including assessment aimed at creating learning experiences that were purposeful, rich in their complexity, and mirrored the demands of a profession fostering development in a supportive environment.

In her chapter, Annette Koenders describes the implementation of an authentic online collaborative assessment task implemented in an introductory biology course. The task required application of knowledge rather than simple summarising and had to be presented in a specific style. The study demonstrates that introductory students in a science course can achieve authentic learning.

Richard Ladyshewsky and John Ryan describe the use of peer coaching in the development of business managerial expertise. Peer coaching is one experiential learning method that can be used to enhance the depth of learning in managerial education. The experiences of students who participated in a peer coaching program as part of their post-graduate management education are revealed. Powerful learning effects are reported as well as characteristics of successful peer coaching relationships.

Greg Parry and Clive Reynoldson discuss a post-graduate economics program that forms a core part of a Masters of Business Administration (MBA) degree course. The program has been structured so as to create a learning environment in which students construct an understanding of economics through a semester-long, authentic learning task — specifically the development of a competitive strategy for a business in which they have a personal interest. The authors have observed that this approach has resulted in greater student engagement and a deeper conceptualisation of the role of economics in business as compared to the traditional approaches to teaching economics in MBA programs.

Shirley Agostinho describes a masters-level subject in the area of technology-based learning that uses an authentic scenario built around a fictitious consultancy company. This chapter describes a learning environment designed to create an authentic context for learning evaluation skills and strategies appropriate to technology-based learning settings. Students are given realistic jobs with realistic parameters, and in this way the subject is dealt with in a much more authentic manner than if presented in a decontextualized way. The rationale for adopting the approach is described together with a description of how it was implemented and evaluated.

Jennifer R. Jamison's chapter demonstrates how contemporary chiropractic education can use authentic learning opportunities to prepare students for the clinical practice. Safe professional practice requires a combination of factual knowledge and mastery of those thinking processes required to update and selectively utilize fresh information. This chapter demonstrates how three problem-solving formats can be used to help students achieve both these learning objectives.

Cate Jerram presents an adult educator's experience in teaching computer-mediated communication to undergraduate students. An "adult learner" profile is presented and compared to classroom experiences of undergraduate learners. The chapter discusses the application of adult education principles to the reshaping and new delivery and assessment of the subject. It outlines the fundamental changes wrought in the subject to meet adult education standards and approaches, including course program goals, learning outcomes, delivery format, method, and assessment activities.

Sue Bennett describes the design of a technology-supported learning environment in which small teams of students worked on authentic project tasks to develop a multimedia product for a real client. A key feature of the approach was the use of related cases to support authentic project activities. A rich set of data was collected, including student assignment work, discussion records and interviews. Analysis of the data provided insights into the role of the cases in supporting the collaborative project work.

In their chapter, Brian Ferry, Lisa Kervin, Sarah Puglisi, Brian Cambourne, Jan Turbill, David Jonassen and John Hedberg describe the development of an online classroom simulation that allows the user to take on the role of the teacher of a virtual kindergarten classroom (ages five to six years). During the simulation the user makes decisions about the organization of teaching and learning experiences, classroom management, and responses to individual students. The user is able to monitor and track the progress of three targeted students throughout the course of the simulation. An embedded tool has been developed to enable the user to plan and justify new decisions and reflect upon the consequences of previous decisions.

In his chapter, John Fitzsimmons uses the *Harry Potter* series to explore the basic proposition that those who read and teach literature have been speaking authentic learning all their lives, perhaps a little crudely — more Dr. Dolittle than Harry Potter — but speaking it nonetheless. The chapter concludes that some of the nervousness experienced by humanities academics when contemplating a more focused relation between their disciplines and the principles of authentic learning is misplaced.

Sandra Jones' chapter discusses how information technology can be used to augment the authenticity of the learning experience in student-centred learning environments. She argues that technology provides the opportunity to embed students in learning activity by bridging the gap between the "real world" and the classroom. The particular learning environment used to illustrate this is a restaurant complex with a number of outlets that was designed by the author to provide a common work environment.

Anthony Herrington, Jan Herrington and Evan Glazer describe design research conducted over four years, where pre-service teachers were immersed in an authentic learning environment using multimedia to learn mathematics assessment strategies. The first study was conducted with pre-service teachers in the second year of their degree, and then the second study followed up with the same people in their second year as practising teachers. The first study revealed several constraints for the participants on professional practice, including limited time and the influence of the supervising teacher. Later, as practising teachers, they faced cultural and practical constraints within the school environment that prevented them from fully operationalizing the pedagogical principles they learned as pre-service teachers.

Catherine McLoughlin and Joe Luca argue that while there are many frameworks that emphasise the cognitive aspects of learning, it is clear that the socio-affective aspects are of equal importance in creating a positive learning experience for students. By synthesizing findings from this area of research, this chapter provides a framework and a set of strategies that can be used to create an authentic learning climate, and illustrates a range of tasks that create positive social, learning experiences.

Karen Anderson provides an example of a performative assessment strategy for students in archives and records management studies. Students were required to find examples of policy documents and standards on the Internet, analyse and evaluate them, just as they would in the workplace. The use of online discussions helped to overcome the isolation felt by remote students.

Mike Keppell suggests that problem-based learning (PBL) may offer a means of providing authentic scenarios for assisting pre-service teachers before encountering teaching practice. The use of media-based educational triggers and authentic scenarios may form a bridge between their studies and real-world teaching practice. Five media-rich educational triggers are described in early childhood education, physical education, educational technology, project management and inclusive education. Reusable media-based educational triggers may also provide potential resources for other educators within teacher education.

In Section III, Ron Oliver outlines the high degree of energy and enthusiasm in the e-learning world being given to developing strategies and systems that support the reuse of digital learning resources. This chapter explores the potential impact this area will have for teachers developing authentic learning environments, and argues the advantages that teachers employing such learning settings will derive from the developments. The chapter suggests design and development strategies that are needed to ensure that potential advantages are realized.

Lynne Hunt describes models of work-based learning and outlines key features of the authentic learning pedagogy that informs its application. It contextualizes work-based learning in the political and economic imperatives driving curriculum change in universities in the Western world. In so doing, it refers to curriculum development based on generic skills and notes analyses of the role of universities in contemporary society, with particular reference to the relative importance of practical and theoretical training. Lynne describes innovative case studies showing practical examples of the implementation of authentic learning pedagogies through work-based university programs.

Jan Herrington and Ron Oliver examine the impact of the Internet on the teacher's role and explore the types of skills and strategies that teachers in higher education will need to be effective and efficient in online learning environments. The professional development needs for the new role of online teacher is discussed within the context of a *Graduate Certificate in Online Teaching and Learning* designed to encapsulate authentic approaches to learning.

Ron Oliver, Anthony Herrington, Sue Stoney and Jim Millar argue that teaching and learning in higher education requires institutional agreement on the benchmarks and standards by which its quality will be determined. This chapter provides a framework for conceptualising the elements of teaching and learning that need to be accounted for in any quality assurance process, with particular focus on teaching activities that reflect an authentic approach to learning.

Conclusion

The elements of authenticity presented in the introductory chapter comprise one framework for the design of effective and immersive learning environments that are appropriate for both face-to-face and technology-mediated courses, such as online subjects. However, not all the authors of the chapters presented here uniformly adopt these ideas. Different viewpoints and interpretations of authenticity are presented throughout, adding to a rich and diverse collection of perspectives and consequent learning designs. All the learning environments described in this book do, however, have one characteristic in common: they universally depict the work of dedicated and innovative teachers with a passion for excellence, and a desire to create inspirational learning experiences for their students.

Anthony Herrington
Jan Herrington

Section I

Guidelines for the Design of Quality Authentic Learning Environments

Chapter I

What is an Authentic Learning Environment?

Anthony Herrington, University of Wollongong, Australia

Jan Herrington, University of Wollongong, Australia

Abstract

Recent research and learning theory provides a wealth of thought, ideas and strategies to inform the design and implementation of learner-centered, realistic and effective learning environments. This chapter proposes guidelines for designing authentic learning environments for higher education that can be applied across a range of disciplines and in a variety of modes. Characteristics of the approach are explored in depth, and the chapters of the book are introduced as examples of authentic learning environments in diverse subject areas and contexts. The chapter provides a practical framework for teachers wishing to break away from traditional, teacher-centered approaches in higher education, and who are willing to create learning environments where students are motivated to learn in rich, relevant and real-world contexts.

Toward Authenticity in
Higher Education

Take a walk around most university campuses and observe what you see in the way of adult teaching and learning. If you are fortunate, you will find students engaged in motivating and challenging activities that require collaboration and support. The tasks the students do reflect the tasks seen in real professions and workplaces, and the problems they solve are complex and sustained, requiring intensive effort.

For most students at university today, the reality is very different. Large lecture theatres, centre-staged with discipline experts, continue to transmit theoretical knowledge in bite-sized chunks for passive learners to receive and consume. Collaboration is not encouraged or required. If it occurs at all, it is sought subversively among students away from the formality of the lecture halls.

So, why is the second scenario the more probable one to encounter?

The approach taken by many teachers in universities today is simply a result of the way they were taught. They are perpetuating a tradition of formal university teaching that has ignored the substantial insights gained from more recent theory and research into the way people learn. Typically, university education has been a place to learn theoretical knowledge devoid of context. Essentially, for students, this has meant that their teachers transmit the facts and skills that they are required to absorb and regurgitate on exams. Textbooks and lecture notes are the main resources for study, with the practice of "cramming" for exams a common learning strategy. Retention and transfer of knowledge was assumed but rarely assessed. For many students a "surface" approach to learning (Marton & Säljö, 1976) assured success. It is not surprising that a growing proportion of graduates now choose to follow their university courses with practical courses at vocationally oriented institutions (Golding & Vallence, 1999).

In the wider community it has become increasingly clear to employers of university graduates and governments that fund universities that university learning outcomes are lacking, and no longer meet the needs of a dynamic and changing workforce. What employers, governments and nations require are graduates that display attributes necessary for knowledge building communities: graduates who can create, innovate, and communicate in their chosen profession.

If traditional approaches to university education do not result in appropriate learning outcomes, what then are the teaching and learning approaches that universities should adopt? The growing influence of constructivism as a philosophical approach to learning, and a wide range of research studies and papers investigating alternative models of teaching and learning over the last decade, have prompted many teachers in universities to implement more "authentic" teaching and learning environments. The challenge they have faced is to align university teaching and learning more substantially with the way learning is achieved in real-life settings, and to base instructional methods on more authentic approaches, such as situated learning (Brown, Collins, & Duguid, 1989; Collins, Brown, & Newman, 1989; McLellan, 1996; Cobb & Bowers, 1999).

But what does it mean to be authentic? Some have argued that only real-problem contexts should be presented to ensure authenticity. For example, Savery and Duffy (1996) nominated two guidelines in developing problem-based scenarios for teaching and learning: firstly, that the problems must raise the concepts and principles relevant to the content domain, and secondly that the problems must be *real*. However, other research into the realism of learning environments has indicated that maximum fidelity, either in real situations or simulations, does not necessarily lead to maximum effectiveness in learning, particularly for novice learners (Alessi, 1988). Others argue, however, that in designing learning environments it is impossible to design truly "authentic" learning experiences. Petraglia (1998a, 1998b) contended that authenticity can be neither "predetermined nor preordained," and such attempts often result in little more than "pre-authentication," that is, "the attempt to make learning materials and environments correspond to the real world prior to the learner's interaction with them" (p. 53). Barab, Squire and Dueber (2000) have also argued that authenticity occurs "not in the learner, the task, or the environment, but in the dynamic interactions among these various components ... authenticity is manifest in the flow itself, and is not an objective feature of any one component in isolation" (p. 38). Smith (1987) in his review of research related to simulations in the classroom concluded that the "physical fidelity" of the simulation materials is less important than the extent to which the simulation promotes "realistic problem-solving processes" (p. 409), a process Smith (1986) describes as the "cognitive realism" of the task. Similarly, we would argue that it is the *cognitive authenticity* rather than the *physical authenticity* that is of prime importance in the design of authentic learning environments (Herrington, Oliver, & Reeves, 2003). Authenticity goes beyond mere relevance.

Characteristics of Authentic Learning

Recent research and learning theory provides a wealth of thought, ideas and strategies to inform the design and implementation of student-centered, realistic and effective learning environments. This chapter proposes guidelines for designing authentic learning environments in higher education based upon nine critical characteristics of authentic learning identified by Herrington and Oliver (2000) in their extensive review of literature and technology-based learning environments. The guidelines are based on constructivist philosophy and approaches, and specifically on situated learning theory.

Provide an Authentic Context that Reflects the Way the Knowledge will be Used in Real Life

The context needs to be all-embracing, to provide the purpose and motivation for learning, and to provide a sustained and complex learning environment that can be explored at length. It is not sufficient to simply provide suitable examples from real-world situations to illustrate the concept or issue being taught. It needs to encompass a physical environment which reflects the way the knowledge will be used, and a large number of resources to enable sustained examination from different perspectives (Brown et al., 1989; Hill & Hannafin, 2001; Honebein, Duffy, & Fishman, 1993; Reeves & Reeves, 1997).

Many courses ignore the rich potential of an authentic context by disembedding course materials from ordinary experience (Sternberg, Wagner, & Okagaki, 1993). Generalised, theoretical principles and skills are taught rather than the situation-specific capabilities, and textbooks often guide curriculum and context rather than the genuine practices of professionals. Such courses are often characterised by subject matter divided into weekly sections (reflecting textbook chapters), and usually presented in lectures/tutorial format.

By contrast, a course with a more authentic context is presented as a realistic problem preserving the complexity of the real-life setting. Students are able to access information resources as required, rather than have topics presented in a linear manner through weekly lectures and tutorials. Web-based courses might use an interface that comprises a metaphor representing the elements of the subject matter. For example, a course on marine biology might be represented by an image of a marina, or one on occupational health and safety by an image of a workplace, a teaching course by a classroom, a nursing course by a hospital ward, and so on. In any of its delivery forms, the context provides a realistic and authentic rationale for the study of a complex problem.

Authentic Activities

The tasks that students perform are arguably the most crucial aspect of the design of any learning environment. Ideally such tasks should comprise ill-defined activities that have real-world relevance, and which present complex tasks to be completed over a sustained period of time, rather than a series of shorter disconnected examples (Bransford, Vye, Kinzer, & Risko, 1990; Brown et al., 1989; Lebow & Wager, 1994; Reeves & Reeves, 1997).

University courses often require students to complete tasks and activities that are largely abstract and decontextualised (Lebow & Wager, 1994). They are formulated by others, well-defined and complete in scope (Sternberg et al., 1993), and often lead simply to an enculturation into the practices of universities and classrooms rather than real-world transfer (Clayden, Desforges, Mills, & Rawson, 1994). Such activities bear little resemblance to those of real practitioners (Brown et al., 1989).

In contrast to this fragmented and decontextualised approach, a situated learning approach promotes authentic activities that can create the focus for the whole course of study — the activity does not necessarily supplement the course, it can *be* the course (Herrington, Reeves, Oliver, & Woo, 2004). Lave and Wenger (1991) cautioned that the conception of situated learning was substantially "more encompassing in intent than conventional notions of 'learning in situ' or 'learning by doing' for which it was used as a rough equivalent" (p. 31). Instead, activities can be complex and ill-defined, and echo the same complexity found in real-world tasks.

Access to Expert Performances and the Modelling of Processes

To expose students to expert performance is to give them a model of how a real practitioner behaves in a real situation. Access to such modelling of processes has its origins in the apprenticeship system of learning, where students and craftspeople learned new skills under the guidance of an expert (Collins et al., 1989). Important elements of expert performances are found in modern applications of the apprenticeship model such as internship, and case-based learning (Riesbeck, 1996).

In many university courses, students are given no examples of experts performing tasks, or of expert comment, to enable them to model real-world practice. In order to provide such expert performance, the required skill or performance could be modelled within a real-life context. For example, if a scientific report is the required product, a similar report could be available to students. Video excerpts could show interviews with experts, or short clips of experts performing within their real environments. These allow students to observe the "social periphery" of relevant tasks as they are performed in the real world. Encouraging students to seek out expert opinion on the Internet and to subscribe to listservs gives them access to the ideas of experts and others at varying levels of expertise. The facility of the World Wide Web to create global communities of learners who can interact readily via e-mail, also enables opportunities for the sharing of narratives and stories.

Multiple Roles and Perspectives

In a more authentic learning environment, it is important to enable and encourage students to explore different perspectives, and to "criss cross" the learning environment repeatedly (Collins et al., 1989; Spiro, Feltovich, Jacobson, & Coulson, 1991a). Instruction which puts forward a single, "correct" interpretation, is according to Spiro, Feltovich, Jacobson and Coulson (1991b) not false, but inadequate.

Frequently, university courses promote learning compartmentalised and constrained by strict discipline boundaries (Relan & Gillani, 1997). Content is often discipline-specific, and presented in modules and sections, with little to offer students seeking alternative viewpoints. By contrast, providing a multitude of perspectives to enable students to examine problems from the point of view of a variety of stakeholders is more conducive to sustained and deep exploration of any issue or problem.

Collaborative Construction of Knowledge

The opportunity for users to collaborate is an important design element, particularly for students who may be learning at a distance (Brown et al., 1989; Collins et al., 1989; Hooper, 1992; Reeves & Reeves, 1997). Collaboration has been defined as "the mutual engagement of participants in a coordinated effort to solve a problem together" (Roschelle & Behrend, 1993, cited in Katz & Lesgold, 1993, p. 289). Forman and Cazden (1985) have suggested that true collaboration is not simply working together but also "solving a problem or creating a product which could not have been completed independently" (p. 329).

However, many university courses promote individual endeavour and cognition rather than collaboration, and students' activities are largely solitary. Students are given little opportunity to collaborate, despite the affordances of physical proximity and technology to enable it. In order to promote collaboration, group work can be facilitated with an appropriate incentive structure for whole group achievement. For example, activities and problems can be addressed to a group such as a board of directors, committee, interest group, department, and so forth. Collaboration can be encouraged through appropriate tasks and communication technology. For example, discussion boards and chat rooms can be used to encourage sharing and joint problem solving within and among groups.

Reflection

In order to provide opportunities for students to reflect on their learning, the learning environment needs to provide an authentic context and task, as described earlier, to enable meaningful reflection. Many theorists see reflection as both a *process* and a *product* (Collen, 1996), and that it is action-oriented (Kemmis, 1985). Knights (1985) contends that reflection is not the kind of activity that its name suggests — a solitary, internal activity — but a two-way process with the "aware attention" of another person. This view is strongly supported in the literature by others who point out that reflection is a social process (Kemmis, 1985), and that collaboration on tasks enables the reflective process to become apparent (von Wright, 1992).

In many learning environments, there are few opportunities to reflect because of an emphasis on pre-determined content that needs to be learned, and few opportunities to collaborate means students cannot reflect socially. In order to promote reflection, authentic and meaningful activities can be provided, together with access to expert performance and opinion to enable students to compare themselves to experts. Collaborative groupings enable students to reflect socially, and to engage in meaningful discussions on issues presented. Journals, portfolios and Web logs can provide a tangible outcome of students' reflections.

Articulation

In order to produce a learning environment capable of providing opportunities for articulation, courses need to incorporate inherent opportunities to articulate, and in particular the public presentation of argument to enable defence of the position (Edelson, Pea, & Gomez, 1996; Lave & Wenger, 1991). Baktin (1986) contends that "any true understanding is dialogic in nature" (Brown & Campione, 1994, p. 267). The implication is that the very process of articulating enables formation, awareness, development, and refinement of thought. Vygotsky has influenced the way educators see the role of articulation in learning (cf., Davydov, 1995). Vygotsky believed that speech is not merely the vehicle for the expression of the learner's beliefs, but that the act of creating the speech profoundly influences the learning process: "Thought undergoes many changes as it turns into speech. It does not merely find expression in speech; it finds reality and form" (cited in Lee, 1985, p. 79).

In many higher education courses, students are not required to articulate and justify their work to their peers. By contrast, more authentic tasks require articulation of ideas in one form or another. Students are required to present and defend their arguments in appropriate forums, such as in face-to-face classes, conferences and seminars, or by publishing on the Internet or on Web-based bulletin boards and listservs.

Coaching and Scaffolding

In order to accommodate a coaching and scaffolding role principally by the teacher (but also provided by other students), an authentic learning environment needs to provide collaborative learning, where more able partners can assist with scaffolding and coaching, as well as the means for the teacher to support learning, for example, via appropriate communication technologies (Collins et al., 1989; Greenfield, 1984). Coaching in a situated learning environment requires "powerful, but different roles for teachers" (Choi & Hannafin, 1995, p. 67), where the interactions with students occur mainly at the metacognitive level (Savery & Duffy, 1996).

In many university courses, the teacher's role is a didactic one, "telling" students what they need to know rather than a coaching role (Harley, 1993). The teacher controls the learning situation (Berge, Collins, & Dougherty, 2000; Jonassen, 1993) organising the order of content, activities, and assessment. A common approach used to present tasks and problems is to simplify the topic by breaking it down into its component parts. However, Perkins (1991) has suggested that oversimplification should be resisted, and instead teachers should search for new ways to provide appropriate scaffolding and support. A more authentic environment provides for coaching at critical times, and scaffolding of support, where the teacher and/or student peer mentors provide the skills, strategies and links that the students are unable to provide to complete the task.

Authentic Assessment

In order to provide authentic assessment of student learning, the learning environment needs to ensure the assessment is seamlessly integrated with the activity and provide the opportunity for students to be effective performers with acquired knowledge, and to craft products or performances in collaboration with others (Duchastel, 1997; Reeves & Okey, 1996; Herrington & Herrington, 1998).

Arguably, the majority of university learning continues to involve competitive relations and individual assessment. Particularly in online courses, students are frequently assessed with multiple choice or other tests that are easily marked, often revealing only whether students can recognise, recall or "plug in" what was learned out of context (Wiggins, 1990). An alternative approach is to provide for integrated assessment of learning within the tasks, where students present polished products.

Applying Authentic Principles
to the Design of Learning
for Higher Education

Authentic learning has found a place in the education agenda, as greater accountability in higher education grows. As technology continues to open up possibilities for innovative and effective teaching and learning opportunities, students and teachers are no longer happy to accept familiar classroom-based pedagogies that rely on content delivery and little else. While many teachers instinctively find the authentic approach appealing, many have difficulty envisaging how these principles could be applied across the disciplines, and how they might work both in face-to-face classes and Web-based environments.

As the title suggests, this book is made up of a collection of peer-reviewed chapters that reflect the construct of *authenticity* in teaching and learning as it is reflected in higher education institutions throughout the world. The book is divided into three sections. Section I provides guidelines to designing authentic learning environments and encompasses the theoretical notions on which these environments are based. Section II contains chapters that describe how authentic activities are instantiated in a range of discipline areas commonly found in university settings. These authors relate the practical designs of their learning environments to both discipline-based theories and situated-learning theories described in part one. Section III chapters discuss generally how authentic environments can be implemented and sustained more widely across an institution.

The elements of authenticity presented above comprise one framework for the design of effective and immersive learning environments that are appropriate for both face-to-face and technology-mediated courses, such as online subjects. However, not all the authors of the chapters presented here universally adopt these ideas. Different viewpoints and interpretations of authenticity are presented throughout, adding to a rich and diverse collection of perspectives and consequent learning designs. All the learning environments described in this volume do, however, have one characteristic in common: they universally depict the work of dedicated and innovative teachers with a passion for excellence, and a desire to create inspirational learning experiences for their students.

The concept of authentic learning is not new. However, its practice is arbitrary and undefined. The purpose of this book is to define the approach through examples of good practice. We hope that the rich variety of examples of good practice found in this book will provide the reader with the inspiration to teach their own subjects and courses in ways that reflect authenticity.

References

Alessi, S. (1988). Fidelity in the design of instructional simulations. *Journal of Computer-Based Instruction, 15*(2), 40-47.

Barab, S.A., Squire, K.D., & Dueber, W. (2000). A co-evolutionary model for supporting the emergence of authenticity. *Educational Technology Research and Development, 48*(2), 37-62.

Berge, Z.L., Collins, M., & Dougherty, K. (2000). Design guidelines for web-based courses. In B. Abbey (Ed.), *Instructional and cognitive impacts of web-based education* (pp. 32-40). Hershey, PA: Idea Group Publishing.

Bransford, J.D., Vye, N., Kinzer, C., & Risko, V. (1990). Teaching thinking and content knowledge: Toward an integrated approach. In B. F. Jones & L. Idol (Eds.), *Dimensions of thinking and cognitive instruction* (pp. 381-413). Hillsdale, NJ: Lawrence Erlbaum.

Brown, A.L., & Campione, J.C. (1994). Guided discovery in a community of learners. In K. McGilly (Ed.), *Classroom lessons: Integrating cognitive theory and classroom practice* (pp. 229-270). Cambridge, MA: MIT Press.

Brown, J.S., Collins, A., & Duguid, P. (1989). Situated cognition and the culture of learning. *Educational Researcher, 18*(1), 32-42.

Choi, J., & Hannafin, M. (1995). Situated cognition and learning environments: Roles, structures and implications for design. *Educational Technology Research and Development, 43*(2), 53-69.

Clayden, E., Desforges, C., Mills, C., & Rawson, W. (1994). Authentic activity and learning. *British Journal of Educational Studies, 42*(2), 163-173.

Cobb, P., & Bowers, J. (1999). Cognitive and situated learning perspectives in theory and practice. *Educational Researcher, 28*(2), 4-15.

Collen, A. (1996). Reflection and metaphor in conversation. *Educational Technology, 36*(1), 54-55.

Collins, A., Brown, J.S., & Newman, S.E. (1989). Cognitive apprenticeship: Teaching the crafts of reading, writing, and mathematics. In L. B. Resnick (Ed.), *Knowing, learning and instruction: Essays in honour of Robert Glaser* (pp. 453-494). Hillsdale, NJ: LEA.

Davydov, V.V. (1995). The influence of L.S. Vygotsky on education theory, research and practice. *Educational Researcher, 24*(3), 12-21.

Duchastel, P.C. (1997). A Web-based model for university instruction. *Journal of educational technology systems, 25*(3), 221-228.

Edelson, D.C., Pea, R.D., & Gomez, L. (1996). Constructivism in the collaboratory. In B.G. Wilson (Ed.), *Constructivist learning environments: Case studies in instructional design* (pp. 151-164). Englewood Cliffs, NJ: Educational Technology.

Forman, E.A., & Cazden, C.B. (1985). Exploring Vygotskyan perspectives in education: The cognitive value of peer interaction. In J.V. Wertsch (Ed.), *Culture, communication and cognition: Vygotskian perspectives* (pp. 323-347). Cambridge: Cambridge University.

Golding, B., & Vallence, K. (1999). *The university — VET transition.* RCVET Working Paper, UTS Research Centre for Vocational Education and Training, Sydney.

Greenfield, P.M. (1984). A theory of the teacher in the learning activities of everyday life. In B. Rogoff & J. Lave (Eds.), *Everyday cognition: Its development in social context* (pp. 117-138). Cambridge, MA: Harvard University.

Harley, S. (1993). Situated learning and classroom instruction. *Educational Technology, 33*(3), 46-51.

Herrington, J., & Herrington, A. (1998). Authentic assessment and multimedia: How university students respond to a model of authentic assessment. *Higher Education Research & Development, 17*(3), 305-322.

Herrington, J., Oliver, R., & Reeves, T.C. (2003). 'Cognitive realism' in online authentic learning environments. In D. Lassner & C. McNaught (Eds.), *EdMedia World Conference on Educational Multimedia, Hypermedia and Telecommunications* (pp. 2115-2121). Norfolk, VA: AACE.

Herrington, J., Reeves, T.C., Oliver, R., & Woo, Y. (2004). Designing authentic activities in web-based courses. *Journal of Computing in Higher Education, 16*(1), 3-29.

Hill, J.R., & Hannafin, M.J. (2001). Teaching and learning in digital environments: The resurgence of resource-based learning environments. *Educational Technology Research and Development, 49*(3), 37-52.

Honebein, P.C., Duffy, T.M., & Fishman, B.J. (1993). Constructivism and the design of learning environments: Context and authentic activities for learning. In T.M. Duffy, J. Lowyck & D.H. Jonassen (Eds.), *Designing environments for constructive learning* (pp. 87-108). Heidelberg: Springer-Verlag.

Hooper, S. (1992). Cooperative learning and computer-based design. *Educational Technology Research and Development, 40*(3), 21-38.

Jonassen, D. (1993). The trouble with learning environments. *Educational Technology, 33*(1), 35-37.

Katz, S., & Lesgold, A. (1993). The role of the tutor in computer-based collaborative learning situations. In S.P. Lajoie & S.J. Derry (Eds.), *Computers as cognitive tools* (pp. 289-317). Hillsdale, NJ: Lawrence Erlbaum.

Kemmis, S. (1985). Action research and the politics of reflection. In D. Boud, R. Keogh & D. Walker (Eds.), *Reflection: Turning experience into learning* (pp. 139-163). London: Kogan Page.

Knights, S. (1985). Reflection and learning: The importance of a listener. In D. Boud, R. Keogh & D. Walker (Eds.), *Reflection: Turning experience into learning* (pp. 85-90). London: Kogan Page.

Lave, J., & Wenger, E. (1991). *Situated learning: Legitimate peripheral participation*. Cambridge: Cambridge University.

Lebow, D., & Wager, W.W. (1994). Authentic activity as a model for appropriate learning activity: Implications for emerging instructional technologies. *Canadian Journal of Educational Communication, 23*(3), 231-144.

Lee, B. (1985). Intellectual origins of Vygotsky's semiotic analysis. In J.V. Wertsch (Ed.), *Culture, communication and cognition: Vygotskian perspectives* (pp. 66-93). Cambridge: Cambridge University.

Marton, F., & Säljö, R. (1976). On qualitative differences in learning. I: Outcome and process. *British Journal of Educational Psychology*, 46, 115-27.

McLellan, H. (Ed.). (1996). *Situated learning perspectives*. Englewood Cliffs, NJ: Educational Technology.

Perkins, D.N. (1991). What constructivism demands of the learner. *Educational Technology, 31*(8), 19-21.

Petraglia, J. (1998a). The real world on a short leash: The (mis)application of constructivism to the design of educational technology. *Educational Technology Research and Development, 46*(3), 53-65.

Petraglia, J. (1998b). *Reality by design: The rhetoric and technology of authenticity in education*. Mahwah, NJ: Lawrence Erlbaum.

Reeves, T.C., & Okey, J.R. (1996). Alternative assessment for constructivist learning environments. In B.G. Wilson (Ed.), *Constructivist learning environments: Case studies in instructional design* (pp. 191-202). Englewood Cliffs, NJ: Educational Technology.

Reeves, T.C., & Reeves, P.M. (1997). Effective dimensions of interactive learning on the World Wide Web. In B.H. Khan (Ed.), *Web-based instruction* (pp. 59-66). Englewood Cliffs, NJ: Educational Technology.

Relan, A., & Gillani, B.B. (1997). Web-based instruction and the traditional classroom: Similarities and differences. In B.H. Khan (Ed.), *Web-based instruction* (pp. 41-46). Englewood Cliffs, NJ: Educational Technology.

Riesbeck, C.K. (1996). Case-based teaching and constructivism: Carpenters and tools. In B.G. Wilson (Ed.), *Constructivist learning environments: Case studies in instructional design* (pp. 49-61). Englewood Cliffs, NJ: Educational Technology.

Savery, J.R., & Duffy, T.M. (1996). Problem based learning: An instructional model and its constructivist framework. In B.G. Wilson (Ed.), *Constructivist learning environments: Case studies in instructional design* (pp. 135-148). Englewood Cliffs, NJ: Educational Technology.

Smith, P.E. (1986). *Instructional simulation: Research, theory and a case study* (ED No. 267 793).

Smith, P.E. (1987). Simulating the classroom with media and computers. *Simulation and Games, 18*(3), 395-413.

Spiro, R.J., Feltovich, P.J., Jacobson, M.J., & Coulson, R.L. (1991a). Cognitive flexibility, constructivism, and hypertext: Random access instruction for advanced knowledge acquisition in ill-structured domains. *Educational Technology, 31*(5), 24-33.

Spiro, R.J., Feltovich, P.J., Jacobson, M.J., & Coulson, R.L. (1991b). Knowledge representation, content specification, and the development of skill in situation-specific knowledge assembly: Some constructivist issues as they relate to cognitive flexibility theory and hypertext. *Educational Technology, 31*(9), 22-25.

Sternberg, R.J., Wagner, R.K., & Okagaki, L. (1993). Practical intelligence: The nature and role of tacit knowledge in work and at school. In J.M. Puckett & H.W. Reese (Eds.), *Mechanisms of everyday cognition* (pp. 205-227). Hillsdale, NJ: Lawrence Erlbaum.

von Wright, J. (1992). Reflections on reflection. *Learning and Instruction, 2*, 59-68.

Wiggins, G. (1990). *The case for authentic assessment.* Washington, DC: ERIC Clearinghouse on Tests, Measurement, and Evaluation.

Section II

Authentic Learning Environments Across the Disciplines

Chapter II

Authentic Graduate Education for Personal and Workplace Transformation

Marilyn Laiken, University of Toronto, Canada

Abstract

The purpose of this chapter is to examine the creation of authentic learning environments in the light of adult education and transformative learning theory, using a graduate course as a case example. Authentic learning environments and authentic workplaces have much in common. They tend to be ones in which collaborative partnerships prevail over hierarchical power relationships; leadership is enabling rather than controlling; differences are viewed as rich resources for learning rather than challenges to be "managed"; reflection and critical thinking are encouraged through the development of vibrant communities of practice; conflicting ideas are surfaced through genuine dialogue; and wholeness is valued — both in the individual as a whole person, and in the understanding of groups and organisations as living systems. Traditional universities are challenging places in which to create learning environments that fit this description. Through an analysis of the design and implementation of Course 1130, the chapter attempts to provide specific ideas for how graduate education can contribute to significant personal change in the values, attitudes and behavior of adult learners.

Introduction

Authentic learning environments and authentic workplaces have much in common. They tend to be ones in which collaborative partnerships prevail over hierarchical power relationships; leadership is enabling rather than controlling; differences are viewed as rich resources for learning rather than challenges to be managed; reflection and critical thinking are encouraged through the development of vibrant communities of practice; conflicting ideas are surfaced through genuine dialogue, often leading to expanded thinking and revised world views; and wholeness is valued — both in the individual as a whole person (body, mind, emotions) and in the understanding of groups and organisations as living systems.

Probably the most important characteristic of these environments is the prizing of congruence between beliefs and behavior. However, this rarely describes the reality. Rather, an authentic learning or working environment is one in which participants may see themselves in a *process* of continuously striving for such congruence. This involves being clear at the outset about one's values and vision of an ideal, and then being willing to acknowledge instances in which the reality may be out of sync with that vision. The task then, is to conscientiously work toward closing the gap.

Graduate education programs in traditional universities are challenging places in which to create authentic learning environments that fit this description. Like the traditional workplace, they are generally hierarchically structured and tend to create power-over positions for those in leadership roles; encourage competition as opposed to collaboration through their funding and reward (i.e., grading) systems; use adversarial approaches such as collective bargaining or appeals procedures to resolve conflicts; and often implicitly allow and support critique which is judgmental and silencing as opposed to exploratory and inviting. Most significantly, genuine dialogue, honest expression of feelings and the opportunity to focus on process as well as content are clearly devalued — making it difficult, if not impossible to close the gap between espoused values and practiced behavior.

And yet, we learn what we live. In our graduate program, students in an Adult Education specialisation entitled *Workplace Learning and Change* are studying to be organisational change practitioners across work sectors. If these students are to help create authentic environments in their own work organisations, we believe that they must first experience such environments in their graduate education.

This chapter describes one course of many in our program that has been designed to teach the principles of authentic, transformative learning as it attempts to demonstrate those principles in action.

Authentic Learning as Potentially Transformative

I still suffer from perceptual vertigo. My point of view shifted continuously ... I am not the same person who started the journey. (1130 student, final paper)

This quotation is extracted from the final paper of a student in my course entitled *A Participant-Directed Seminar: Learning in Organisations* (or "1130," as it is usually called). The course provides an opportunity for students to create their own learning organisation, with my help as the instructor, in a facilitative role. The key concepts of systems thinking, personal mastery, examining mental models, team development and building a shared vision (Senge, 1990; Senge, Roberts, Ross, Smith, & Kleiner, 2000) provide a theoretical framework through which group members explore their learning experience. The group is helped to develop as a learning community through a residential weekend, which combines an "outward bound" approach with sharing personal goals and resources. Participants end their weekend by planning for their three-month future as an organisation with an action learning orientation (Revans, 1982).

Comments from students in course evaluations and term papers over a five-year period suggest that participants have often experienced what is described by many theorists as transformative learning (Mezirow, 1991; Jarvis, 1992; Brookfield, 1987). This concept is defined by Cranton (1994) as, "the development of revised assumptions, premises, ways of interpreting experience, or perspectives on the world by means of critical self-reflection" (p. xii). We believe that an authentic learning environment will result in this kind of learning, which in turn will influence how our graduates practice in the world of work.

Creating an authentic, transformative learning environment involves a great deal more than transmitting a body of content, or even helping learners to attain new skills. Educational theorists such as Cross, (1992), Knowles (1984) and Mezirow (1991) differentiate among subject-oriented, consumer-oriented and emancipatory or transformative learning. Subject-oriented learning involves the learner in acquiring new knowledge and skills. In consumer-oriented learning, the educator is attempting to directly meet the expressed needs of the learners. Although transformative or emancipatory learning may include the above, learners are also encouraged to develop their reflective judgment, in order to surface assumptions, and potentially revise their established world views. Cranton (1994) says: "If we view education as the means by which individuals and societies are shaped and changed, fostering emancipatory learning is the central goal of adult education" (p. 19). I would agree.

Many adult learners and educators who have experienced transformative learning also agree that it can be a difficult and often painful process. As one of my adult students has said, "It wasn't a balloon ride, but my view has certainly been altered." Cranton describes this type of learning as "probably the most complex and difficult experience from the learner's point of view, and the most challenging for the educator" (1994, p. 21).

How then, can adult educators meet this challenge in a way that both derives the benefits of transformative learning, and avoids some of the obstacles? The objective of the remainder of this chapter is to analyse the design and implementation of Course 1130, in an attempt to better understand what kind of learning environment may have an authentically transformative impact, and how we, as adult educators, might continue to successfully design such experiences for and with our adult students.

As a framework for this exploration, I have used Peter Senge's five disciplines for building a learning organisation (1990). As previously mentioned, these include: creating a shared vision; team learning; examining mental models; personal mastery and systems thinking. The chapter is organised around these ideas because they comprise a basic theoretical structure for Course 1130. Beyond such concepts, the participants themselves decide the remainder of the course content and most of its processes, to reflect individual and, ultimately, group learning needs.

Briefly, the general design of the course involves opening sessions, including the retreat weekend, which focus on introducing the learning organisation concepts, developing a vision, sharing resources, deciding on course content, and establishing learning teams. The body of the course is mainly comprised of learning team activities within and outside of class, including a "learning event" conducted by each team for the remainder of the group, focusing on content chosen by the class as a whole. Between these events are interspersed reflective sessions that help each team share their learning process with the class, and relate this to the learning organisation concepts that have been introduced by the instructor. The course ends with a group evaluation of the class' development as a learning organisation, using the initial vision to help members reflect on the problems and opportunities they have encountered. Thus, in a truly experientially designed format, the learners are helped to derive their learning from their lived experience — both from the process of the course itself, and through application of resulting insights to their lives at work. The following section explores in more detail each of the course components, combining descriptive data with an analysis of the participants' experience, supported by quotations from student papers and correspondence over the last five-year period in which the course was taught.

Developing an
Authentic Learning Environment

Creating a Shared Vision

Adult education theory has long acknowledged the importance of the emotional aspects of learning. Feelings such as self-doubt, concerns about "fitting in" and anxiety about having less (or more) to offer than others, often accompany adult learners into the classroom — frequently as a result of past experiences where humiliation and frustration have dominated the learning experience. A new student to our program reflects, in her final paper, on her feelings as she entered:

.... Little did I know what would be in store for me over the next three months. A slow start with a few bumps of self-doubt. Will I fit in? Will others share my interests or think them frivolous or unimportant? Do I have anything to offer here? How do I balance sharing my experience with a need not to be perceived as a 'know-it-all'? Can I struggle through another course, another learning experience? Do I really want to do this now? Have I made the right choice?

The challenge then, right from the start of the program, is to help the learner acknowledge such discomfort and begin to use it as a basis for learning. What is essential here is an environment that supports what I would call "optimal anxiety," where the learner is stimulated sufficiently to be open to learning, but not so anxious that he or she feels immobilised. Cranton (1994) describes such an environment as including three aspects — "trigger events" which stimulate critical reflection; a process that helps people become aware of and begin to question basic assumptions; and ongoing support and feedback from others.

The initial series of trigger events in Course 1130 is provided by a residential experience that includes negotiating a team climb through cliffs and caves, sharing personal learning goals ("gets") and resources ("gives"), and then based on all of this, envisioning the group's ideal learning organisation and, using this vision as a target, planning for the remainder of the course.

The purpose of an organisational vision is to align values, goals and action; to create a shared framework for decision making and problem solving; to inject a new level of synergy and creativity into day-to-day functioning; and to engage the commitment and unique resources of each individual member. It is a guide to action and, as such, it helps to create the culture and environment within which we do our work.

In Course 1130, we create our vision of excellence in response to the question, "What would our learning organisation look like if it were the best it could be?" Each member pictorially represents her or his response to this question and shares it with five or six others in a small-group dialogue. Each group then decides on the key components of the visions discussed, and finds a creative way to present these to the rest of the class. Through the use of skits, songs, poetry, collage, drawings, and so on, we evoke and unleash participants' creativity, as they articulate their dreams for an ideal learning experience. The combination of components from each group's presentation becomes the vision for the class. It is produced as a wall chart, as well as typed and copied for everyone, as the start-up for the visioning process.

However, this is just a start. During the following three months the group works continuously on the vision, through a process of defining behavioral indicators for each component; comparing the reality of members' behavior in class and in their work teams with these indicators; and problem solving to close the gaps between the vision and the reality whenever they arise. In this way we constantly monitor our actions to keep them consistent with the supportive, challenging, respectful environment that class members have envisioned as their ideal.

Enhancing Team Learning

A second set of trigger events in Course 1130 is initiated by the formation of learning teams. These teams evolve from the identification of specific areas of content about which participants wish to learn more. Through the use of a nominal group technique (Galbraith, 1990), the class identifies a number of areas of general interest, and then members vote individually on those that are most important to them in this course. The results indicate the whole group's priorities that are then refined into topic areas around which class members group to form teams. The task of each team is to plan and facilitate a two-hour teaching/learning experience for the remainder of the group. The specific goals for these events are based on needs assessments that each team conducts with the rest of the class. Members are encouraged to view the events not as a "performance" or "presentation," but as learning opportunities for all of us, and especially for the facilitating team. In order to support this notion, there is no grade attached to the event itself. However, there are several opportunities for feedback and reflection on learning — initially, immediately following each event, and again one week later, when team members have had a chance to read written comments from every other class member. In this manner, the learners, in a "consumer-oriented" approach, define a large portion of the course content. However, the focus of learning becomes transformative, as learners are encouraged to constantly reflect on their own processes as individuals, as a learning team and as an evolving learning organisation.

From the start, the team's formation and development is itself an opportunity for learning. Fairly early in the course, learners are asked to make their own decisions about how to form their teaching/learning teams. They are encouraged to "shop around," and make personal decisions based on their individual learning needs. The challenge of choosing and being chosen (or rejected) by others is not lost on these students. Immediately they are confronted with historical fears, doubts, feelings of inadequacy and issues of self-esteem. They are also challenged to be crystal clear about their own needs, both with themselves and others, and to be unafraid to represent their strengths and resources as well as their needs in the negotiation process. One student, in a final paper, describes her experience during the team formation period as "chaotic," saying:

Chaos ensued as small teams formed and reformed to focus on the identified interest areas. Our unconscious incompetence resulted in unfocused discussions and feelings of panic; where would this all lead? Chaos was uncomfortable.

The discomfort this student describes is the first step in creating an authentic learning environment. For the three ensuing months, learners are helped to examine the discomfort they may be feeling, as they ask themselves and each other such questions as: Why are we uncomfortable? What assumptions are we making? How does our behavior reflect these assumptions? What impact does this have on other individuals, teams, and the learning organisation as a whole?

What makes it possible to endure, and even to enjoy such an experience, is that the level of support offered to each learner equals the level of challenge.

Participants are helped to acknowledge their strengths and successes; to see obstacles not as failures, but as learning opportunities; and to celebrate each step of progress towards their vision. They consistently receive positive as well as constructive negative feedback from their instructor, team and classmates, and are taught how to offer such feedback effectively, as well as how to receive it graciously. The result is such insights as the following:

If I couple reflection with my need for harmony, I can become more patient and tolerant of differences, and be less intent on getting the world to adopt my approach.

Two members who conflicted early were able to successfully confront some of their assumptions about how "leadership" and "commitment" were defined. I have come to understand ... that this belief in my own "powerlessness" has had a large impact on my commitment and energy for organisation development work.

Mezirow (1975) refers to transformative learning as "perspective transformation." He outlines this as a process of experiencing a disorienting dilemma, followed by self-examination, critical assessment, relating to others' experiences, exploring options, building competence, developing a plan of action, acquiring knowledge and skills, making provisional efforts, renegotiating relationships and reintegration. This description quite accurately describes the experience of most 1130 participants as they design, facilitate, evaluate and reflect on their teaching/learning activities, both as individuals and as members of a learning team. One student says:

What happened was real learning — and with this learning came a shift of mind. A shift of mind to see that what was alienating me was not outside my control, but was in fact a series of structures that I had built and maintained for myself. Coming to understand these structures has made all the difference.

Examining Mental Models

Several design features of Course 1130 support the transition from emotional experience to integrated learning. One of these is a series of instructor-facilitated, reflective sessions that alternate with the student-directed "learning events." A key component of these classes is the opportunity for each team to reflect on their previous week's event. The reflection is often done in a "fishbowl" format, where team members talk with one another about their reactions to and perceptions of their own work, while the rest of the class listens in. Later, the dialogue is opened to include all of us, and usually involves questioning and challenging assumptions; requesting and providing feedback on behavior; confronting conflicting issues; and generally deepening the learning from the previous week's work. In this way, the teams are encouraged to debrief their experience publicly, so that every class member has an opportunity to learn from their insights. All of this is framed by theoretical content on the learning organisation, explored during part of the alternating sessions, and offered to the learners by the instructor and guest speakers, or through readings, discussions and films (Field & Ford, 1995; Laiken, 2002, 2004).

Mezirow's more recent writing on transformative learning, which evolved from his critical theory of adult education (1985), stresses the process of examining perceptions by questioning, validating and revising our assumptions, or "meaning perspectives" (1991). Many other educational theorists have addressed this notion, generating concepts such as Argyris' ladder of inference (1990); Argyris and Schön's left-hand column (1974); Senge's mental models (1990) and Ellinor and Gerard's approach to dialogue (1998). Cranton (1994) notes that unquestioned, unexamined, perhaps even unconscious, assumptions limit the learner's openness to change, growth and personal development. She believes that the role of the authentic adult educator is to help learners question these assumptions or mental models by developing their reflective judgment through such consciousness-raising activities as role-playing with skillful debriefing; examining critical incidents; engaging in dialogue; and participating in simulations to help learners view situations from alternative perspectives.

Course 1130 uses many such experiential learning approaches, both within the student-facilitated learning events and the alternating instructor-led sessions. An example of one approach is the use of Argyris and Schön's "left-hand column" (1978) to help learners explore how mental models limit us to familiar ways of thinking and acting, and allow us, in Argyris' terms, to be "skillfully incompetent" (1990). After an introduction to the concept, the class is asked to reconstruct a dialogue that has actually occurred in one of the sessions — preferably one in which there has been some tension among group members. Once the dialogue that took place is recorded on an overhead transparency, members are asked to offer their honest, unspoken thoughts as this dialogue was occurring, and this is recorded in the left-hand column opposite the actual spoken conversation. The level of authenticity and resulting awareness that this simple exercise engenders is often astonishing in its impact. An example of one class dialogue that was reproduced using this method is given in Table 1.

Table 1. Left hand column and right hand column thinking

LEFT HAND COLUMN (thoughts behind the words)	RIGHT HAND COLUMN (what was actually said)
	STUDENT A: 'We have changed the location of our next class to xxx'.
STUDENT B: What right did they have to change the location without consulting the rest of us?	STUDENT B: 'I have a problem with that. I need to be at another meeting just before class. I won't have time to get to the new location.'
STUDENT A: Oh god, she's all upset— let's just forget it, if it's going to be this much of a problem.	STUDENT A: 'We thought it would be nice to have a change of venue, but we don't have to do it.'
STUDENT B: I really feel manipulated into being seen as a 'spoil-sport' here.	STUDENT B: 'I'm not trying to be uncooperative, but I'm really in a bind.'
STUDENT A: Geez—you try to do something different, and there's always somebody who has a problem with it.	STUDENT A: 'O.K. forget it. We won't go—we didn't mean to upset anyone.'

Once the two learners represented here were willing to expose their left-hand column thinking, the class had a very productive dialogue about group consultation when decisions are being made. The actual problem was resolved by changing the starting time to allow for the extra travel involved in holding the class at the new location, and Student B was one of the first to arrive. Student B describes one insight resulting from this exercise in her final paper:

The change of venue for Team Two's learning event was, for me, a powerful example of Senge's mental models at work. Upon further reflection, I became aware of the influence of my values on my thoughts and feelings. My concern about the reaction of the class to my dissatisfaction with the decision-making process limited my ability to disclose my deeper emotional reaction to the situation and to the responses of my classmates.

Students in 1130 practice decreasing the limiting power of their mental models by learning to apply the following skills, originally described by Argyris and Schön (1978): recognising "leaps of abstraction" which take them from observation to generalisation; exposing and articulating what is normally deemed unspeakable (filling in the left-hand column); balancing inquiry and advocacy to sustain authentic interpersonal dialogue; and differentiating between *espoused theories* (what we believe) and *theories-in-use* (how we actually act out our beliefs).

Engaging in Systems Thinking
and Personal Mastery

Although Course 1130 represents the learning organisation as a systemic whole, in the end it is individual personal mastery that enables the system to flourish. I have juxtaposed *systems thinking* and *personal mastery* in this section because they are interdependent opposites — or, in Barry Johnson's terms (1992), "polarities to manage."

On the one hand, systems thinking holds that when placed in the same system, people, however different, tend to produce similar results — the structure is the key variable which influences behavior over time. On the other hand, personal mastery implies individual responsibility, and promotes the notion that we individually and collectively have the power to alter the structures within which we are operating. However, we often don't see the structures that are at play. Rather than seeing our role in isolation, we need to recognise how it interacts within the larger system. We need to learn how to perceive patterns and processes over a longer period, rather than as isolated moments in time.

In 1990, Mezirow claimed that individual perspective transformation must precede social transformation. Senge's *The Fifth Discipline*, written in the same year, exhorts us to sustain the tension between the two, identifying this as the essence of personal mastery. In Course 1130, systems thinking has been our greatest challenge. As the learning teams begin their work, the cohesion within these groups intensifies and becomes the main focus of participants' individual and collective experience. In the light of this, it is difficult to maintain a whole organisation perspective. One student grapples with this issue in her final paper:

As the weeks passed and the other teams facilitated their learning events, we did not use members of the first teams as resources on event planning. We also did not use later or earlier teams as sounding boards to prescreen programs and provide helpful design input to specific team events. In class, we did not suggest that team members from earlier teams become coaches for other teams. ...Throughout the process, it seemed that we gravitated towards operating from a mental model of the organisation as discrete operating units with no interconnection.

Although this may be the case, the opportunities for personal mastery in Course 1130 help make possible the foregoing insight. Personal mastery, according to Senge (1990), is the discipline of generating and sustaining creative tension in our lives. From the beginning, students in 1130 are challenged to manage the tension between polarities such as: individual versus group; team versus organisation; "gives" versus "gets"; and organisational vision versus individual behavior.

Learners also need to be respectful of a wide range of individual differences among their student colleagues — differences in learning, personality and cognitive styles; gender, race and class differences; differences in background, age, developmental stage; a wide range of differences in work experience and interests; and differences in openness to a self-directed learning opportunity. All of these differences hold the potential for creative tension, both intra- and interpersonally. The way in which these tensions are managed, and consequently, how learners experience the process, varies as much as the individuals do, themselves. After Course 1130, one student reflects:

My awareness of my own self and how I relate to others expanded considerably. I have become more sensitive to other peoples' needs, their perceptions, their issues, their processes, and have started to respect their right to it more than before.

The methods in Course 1130 which encourage individual reflection are not in any way new to the adult educator. They include the time-tested vehicle of personal journal keeping, a self-evaluation component for the course grade, and a final reflective paper. In the paper, students are asked to use any theory they have encountered of organisation design/development/learning to analyse their own experience as a member of our learning organisation. They can examine their experience generally, or pursue a particular area of interest that has been provoked by the course experience, and can also include case examples from their work lives. Many students report that writing the paper is an extremely important step in their reflective process, providing them with an individual opportunity for expression, in contrast to the team efforts required in class sessions.

Finally, the act of living the learning by applying it to "real-life" settings is the bottom line of personal mastery. It is one thing to experiment with new behavior in a classroom setting; it is quite another to apply the learning with colleagues and supervisors or clients at work, or with one's family and friends at home. It is in this arena that authentic learning can truly have an impact on social change. A student wrote, in an unsolicited letter three months after the course ended:

I would like to underline a very subtle, yet very transformative, organic and creative nature of this process of continuing to learn and change after the actual learning has happened in real time. There is a richness of insight and new behaviors which came to me later. I wonder how it is possible that all these delayed messages are so deep and meaningful, and how come it is that I wasn't aware of them before. It feels like the real process of discovery started after the course had ended ... "Professionally, whole new worlds opened for me, and I actually feel I leapt to a new and unexpected skill level, in what feels like 'overnight'. This has been confirmed by feedback from people I work with, and the success of my facilitation sessions. This is curious, because I didn't have much explicit knowledge about this area prior to starting your course.

Another student reflects on the impact of his learning in his final paper:

Seeing and feeling the power of a learning organisation has reminded me of why my work is so worthwhile on a human level, and how it can contribute to transformation in both our work and broader communities ... Specifically, I can contrast the practices of my (graduate) learning organisation with the practices of my home organisation. By holding up a working model of my vision against my current reality, I have been able to see opportunities and to discuss them in concrete terms with my partners.

The Facilitator's Role

"Sometimes I think that so many aspects of our group experience, including your facilitation, all spoken and unspoken dimensions and processes of group dynamics, all the subtleties of design, your incredible attention to detail ... everything mattered so much, though I didn't necessarily perceive it like that at the time. I think especially the power of the facilitator's behavior is enormous in this setting" (1130 student, final paper).

In order to foster personal mastery in organisations, Senge et al. (2000) encourage the building of organisational settings where: creating visions is safe; inquiry and commitment to truth are the norm; challenging the status quo is expected; and leaders at all levels model the behavior. This last point, the importance of organisational leaders "walking their talk" is emphasised consistently in leadership research (Block, 1987; Wheatley, 1992; Kouzes & Posner, 1991; Bushe, 2001). The implications for the instructor in a course such as 1130 are apparent, and must be included in a discussion on authentic learning.

Earlier in this chapter, a distinction is made among three approaches to adult learning: subject-oriented, consumer-oriented and transformative or emancipatory learning. Cranton (1994) notes that the power attributed to the educator's role differentiates these perspectives, with the power of the educator progressively decreasing as one moves from subject to consumer to transformative oriented roles. The notion here is that the more one works toward learner empowerment, the more likely that critical self-reflection and transformative learning will occur. Increased freedom and autonomy are both prerequisites for and anticipated outcomes of this process.

Of course, such challenges to the authoritarian status quo of our culture are not always easily met by even the most mature learners. One 1130 student astutely reflects on this issue:

During the class I saw the participants, myself included, looking to the facilitator for guidance and direction, even though care was taken to give the group choices in how things were done, what topics were covered and the pacing of material. We were again influenced by our mental models of an academic organisation; the teacher knows the answers and where we should go from here.

We were trying to live Senge's shifting the burden to the intervener archetype (Senge, 1990). The instructor did not allow us to do this. We were asked to make choices about our program content and flow. At times, having 20 people involved in a decision seemed unwieldy, especially since the mental model we were working from seemed to give power only to the facilitator. The quick fix would have been to have the facilitator make the choices. The systemic solution took longer to achieve and, in the longer term, will provide a more meaningful solution for all of us. Learning to set our own direction was important on two fronts. As individual learners we need to know where we want to go, and as members of organisations we need to understand how to help others set their own directions.

In order to aid in such self-direction, the educator's role changes from that of facilitator in creating a productive working environment, to that of co-learner, as students participate in discourse and decision-making, to that of provocateur to help learners think critically. The educator also assumes the role of counselor, friend and supporter to help people through what might be painful processes of change and finally, the role of resource person to help learners plan actions based on their revised assumptions (Cranton, 1994). In a classroom setting, the educator's efforts toward learner empowerment may include sharing control over resources, rewards, information and the environment by inviting progressively more participation in decision-making in all of these areas as the course unfolds.

In a graduate course such as 1130, informal, as well as formal feedback and evaluation/grading are the key extrinsic rewards available to learners. The 1130 course information outline specifies from the start that grades will result from a combination of individual, team, group and instructor evaluations.

Twenty-five percent of every student's grade is based on his or her own team's assessment of its success as a learning unit, supported by feedback from the rest of the learning organisation members. This assessment is designed by team members, based on their own goals and vision, and involves making such decisions as what criteria to use; whether to assign a team grade or grade every member individually; whether to provide feedback openly or anonymously; and whether or not to include a self-assessment component. Twenty-five percent of the grade is decided by members of the class as a total group, based on the goals and vision developed over the term, and how well the group has progressed towards these in functioning as a learning organisation. Again, the process is designed by the group as a whole, with little, if any content input (though much facilitative help) from the instructor. The remaining 50 percent is assigned by the instructor, based on a final written paper submitted by each student, as previously outlined. In this way, participants and instructor are equally responsible for each learner's final grade.

Another area in which the group shares control of resources is in the allocation of the course's $1,000 budget. This money is taken directly from program fees, and returned to the students as a resource to use for the purchase of relevant articles, books or other materials; film rental fees; honoraria for guest speakers, or any other expense that the group might encounter over the 13-week term. The allocation of this budget is entirely in the hands of the participants, and decisions regarding its use are usually an important focus of the group's planning activities.

Finally, the content of the course is essentially decided by the class members. Although the instructor provides a skeletal theoretical framework using basic learning organisation principles, each year's student group "fleshes out" this framework to include their own specific content interests. Each teaching/learning event is focused on a content area of interest to the group as a whole, and the alternating week's reflective sessions are guided by issues surfaced during these events. The planning involved in all of this activity constitutes an important part of the learning experienced by each member of the developing organisation.

References and reading materials to support this learning are initially provided by the instructor, but eventually all class members share this role as well. During

15 minutes each week allocated to resource-sharing, learners inform each other about upcoming conferences and other professional development opportunities; recommend Web sites, articles, books, films, and speakers; and offer myriads of other relevant data. The classroom itself begins to resemble a library, stocked each week with journal articles and books supplied by all members of the group. Finally, each participant contributes several entries to a class annotated bibliography, with brief comments on favorite books and articles, which are then compiled and distributed to everyone for further reference.

Although sharing control in this manner appears to be a critical component of facilitating authentic transformative learning, the final word on the facilitator's role needs to address the issue of personal authenticity. The key challenge for me as the instructor/facilitator in a course of this kind is to ensure that my behavior is unerringly consistent with the principles being taught and learned. This implies being willing to share my vulnerabilities and doubts, remaining open to being critiqued and to questioning my own thinking, and eliminating my investment in being right. Well beyond the design and facilitation of Course 1130, such personal challenges have been my learning edge. The opportunity presented to me in teaching this course is to continually hone my ability to be a reflective practitioner. Critical reflection is not something that is learned theoretically. In the end, I believe that the act of consistently making explicit one's assumptions and beliefs is the key to both promoting and experiencing authentic learning, for instructors and students alike.

Conclusion

The purpose of this chapter has been to examine the creation of authentic learning environments in the light of adult education and transformative learning theory, using a graduate course as a case example. Through an analysis of the design and implementation of Course 1130, the chapter attempts to provide specific ideas for how graduate education can contribute to significant personal change in the values, attitudes and behavior of adult learners.

Is the course described in this chapter truly an authentic learning environment that is transformative? This is difficult to judge conclusively, given the fact that many participants only begin to recognise the learning that they have experienced once the course is over. However, if *transformation* means "a change in form or disposition," as my Webster's dictionary defines it (p. 232), then a statement such as the following would lead one to believe that transformative learning is indeed a result, at least for some learners in Course 1130:

I am discovering new layers every day ... and I am taken aback by the richness and the sheer scope of new learnings. I felt differently right after the course. Although I felt I learned a lot about the process and design, and about the learning organisation, I didn't feel personally affected by that knowledge. And then, after about a month or so, after I interacted enough with the outside world to notice changes, I started feeling that I was influenced and changed far more than I expected. The mental and emotional images from the time of the course became more vivid and more often present in my mind. They were coming back to me forcefully and gently at the same time, and staying with me. I was getting new insights for the first time, and was able to see some things in a totally different light... Perhaps because my experience in the course was so rounded and full, and touched every aspect of my being, the actual transformation has been occurring. (from personal correspondence after participation in Course 1130)

References

Argyris, C. (1990). *Overcoming organizational defences: Facilitating organizational learning.* Needham Heights, MA: Allyn & Bacon.

Argyris, C., & Schön, D. (1974). *Theory in practice: Increasing professional effectiveness.* San Francisco: Jossey-Bass.

Argyris, C., & Schön, D. (1978). *Organizational learning: A theory of action perspective.* Reading, MA: Addison-Wesley.

Block, P. (1987). *The empowered manager: Positive political skills at work.* San Francisco: Jossey-Bass.

Brookfield, S. (1987). *Developing critical thinkers: Challenging adults to explore alternate ways of thinking and acting.* San Francisco: Jossey-Bass.

Bushe, G.R. (2001). *Clear leadership: How outstanding leaders make themselves understood, cut through organizational mush, and help everyone get real at work.* Palo Alto, CA: Davies-Black.

Cranton, P. (1994). *Understanding and promoting transformative learning.* San Francisco: Jossey-Bass.

Cross, P. (1992). *Adults as learners: Increasing participation and facilitating learning.* San Francisco: Jossey-Bass.

Ellinor, L., & Gerard, G. (1998). *Dialogue: Rediscover the transforming power of conversation.* New York: John Wiley & Sons.

Field, L., & Ford, B. (1995). *Managing organizational learning: From rhetoric to reality.* Melbourne, Australia: Longman House.

Galbraith, M.W. (Ed.). (1990). *Adult learning methods: A guide for effective instruction.* Malabar, FL: R.E. Krieger.

Jarvis, P. (1992). *Paradoxes of learning: On becoming an individual in society.* San Francisco: Jossey-Bass.

Johnson, B. (1992). *Polarity management: Identifying and managing unsolvable problems.* Amherst, MA: HRD Press.

Knowles, M. (1984). *The adult learner: A neglected species* (revised). Houston, TX: Gulf.

Kouzes, J., & Posner, B. (1991). *The leadership challenge: How to get extraordinary things done in organizations.* San Francisco: Jossey-Bass.

Laiken, M. (2002). Models of organizational learning: Paradoxes and best practices in the post-industrial workplace. *Organizational Development Journal, 21(1),* 8-19.

Laiken, M. (2004). The ecology of learning and work: Learning for transformative work practices. In E. O'Sullivan & M. Taylor (Eds.), *Learning toward an ecological consciousness: Selected transformative practices* (pp. 85-98). Palgrave Macmillan.

Mezirow, J. (1975). *Education for perspective transformation: Women's reentry programs in community colleges.* New York: Teachers College, Columbia University, Centre for Adult Education.

Mezirow, J. (1981). A critical theory of adult learning and education. *Adult Education, 32,* 3-24.

Mezirow, J. (1991). *Transformative dimensions of adult learning.* San Francisco: Jossey-Bass.

Mezirow, J., & Associates. (1990). *Fostering critical reflection in adulthood.* San Francisco: Jossey-Bass.

Patterson, R. (Ed.). (1989). *New Webster's dictionary.* FL: PSI & Associates.

Revans, R.W. (1982). *The origins and development of action learning.* UK: Brookfield Publishing.

Senge, P. (1990). *The fifth discipline: The art and practice of the learning organization.* New York: Doubleday Currency.

Senge, P., Roberts, C., Ross, R., Smith, B., & Kleiner, A. (1994). *The fifth discipline fieldbook: Strategies and tools for building a learning organization.* New York: Doubleday Currency.

Senge, P., Kleiner, A., Roberts, C., Ross, R., Roth, G., & Smith, B. (2000). *The dance of change: The challenges to sustaining momentum in learning organizations.* New York: Doubleday Currency.

Wheatley, M. (1992). *Leadership and the new science: Learning about organization from an orderly universe.* San Francisco: Berrett-Koehler Publishers.

Chapter III

The Music Room:
Translating Curricula into Real-World Professional Experience

Di Challis, Deakin University, Australia

Abstract

To explore the synergies of an integration of the conceptual and practice worlds, this chapter draws on part of an Australian Committee for University Teaching and Staff Development funded project for students of architecture and construction. Composing Architecture — The Music Room, involved 74 second-year students at an Australian university. The case study is used as an illustration of curriculum design, including assessment aimed at creating learning experiences that were purposeful, rich in their complexity, and mirrored the demands of a profession fostering development in a supportive environment. To support this aim the elements of the music room project were tested against proposed criteria for authentic learning. While recognising the differing views of scholars and challenging some claimed attributes, the case study indicates that, irrespective of discipline, there are some fundamental shared understandings of what an authentic learning environment entails.

Introduction

A compelling challenge for tertiary educators is to respond meaningfully to pressures to provide curricula that translate readily into real-world professional experience. As Berge (2000) recognises, employers are putting a higher value than ever before on the ability of employees to solve more complex and ill-defined problems. A recent Australian government funded project of employ-ability of skills for the future (McLeish, 2002) identified eight essential employ-ability skills: communication, teamwork, problem solving, initiative and enter-prise, planning and organising, self-awareness, and the ability to work with technology. Similarly, a U.S. study (Richens & McClain, 2000) found that 92.6% of 400 employers interviewed rated personal quality skills, interpersonal compe-tencies and thinking skills as most important. Tertiary educators, especially those who are preparing for the professions, are rightfully concerned to ground their teaching as far as possible within real-world situations and to provide students with opportunities to acquire, practice and demonstrate such skills. The chal-lenge is to find ways to do this effectively.

The term authentic in relation to learning experiences has been added to educational jargon because it resonates so convincingly with the notion that learning should be real and actual, as opposed to contrived and hypothetical (Challis & Langston, 2002). Traditionally, in much undergraduate teaching, and within the constraints of a normal semester's program, there is a propensity for theory and content to be privileged. There is forceful and compelling literature on assessment that claims much current practice in the higher education sector encourages surface learning where the extrinsic motivation is to focus on disaggregated selected details of content rather than intrinsically to seek deep understanding through constructing knowledge (Ramsden, 1992). With a recog-nized paradigm shift in higher education, one from a focus on teaching to a focus on learning (Barr & Tagg, 1995), more educators are seeking opportunities to link theoretical and applied knowledge. With assessed tasks as a driver, they aim to engage students in learning activities that are worthwhile and meaningful and which will pose challenges that are demonstrably relevant to, and aligned with, those that will be faced in the profession. In this context, theoretical and applied knowledge (the conceptual and the practice worlds) are never regarded as mutually exclusive. Rather, their linking, with its anticipated consequential synergies, is seen as an essential component of the learning experience.

Research suggests that students learn best in the context of a compelling problem (Ewell, 1997) and this is certainly what students in the case study discussed below found. Although the discussion is restricted to one cohort of students observed closely by the author throughout the semester, the author has had opportunities over three years to work closely with the lecturer involved and with other colleagues in the school, and to benchmark this project against other assessment tasks and approaches to teaching. Further, the author's experience as an educational designer over many years and within different disciplines indicates that the essential attributes of the project, and the approach to teaching and learning it demonstrates, is not restricted to architecture, but offers useful strategies for those in other disciplines to consider.

The Composing Architecture Project: The Music Room

Music, in its many forms, is something that is integral to most of our lives, something that we experience and enjoy every day; much like our architecture. You are asked to undertake the transition from listener to the role of composer or instrument maker in order to address one of two propositions that relate music to architecture. Firstly, that practitioners of music and architecture share similarities in compositional and design processes. Secondly, that musical instrumentation and architectonics are both products of 'making', reliant on intuitive and sensory interplay in order to produce a finely 'tuned' artifact. It is contended that architects have much to learn about architecture from the study of music ... Composing Architecture *studies the association of music and architecture in experiential terms through the design of a small-scale architectural masterpiece, the Music Room. The project then requires you to achieve thorough resolution at a detailed level of your conceptual design a means of allowing your design concept to transcend from the idea to the realizable [through 1:10 models and detail drawings] to be furthered through the construction of 1:1 models of selected schemes.* (Ham, 2001)

This case study, Composing Architecture — The Music Room, involved 74 second-year students at an Australian university over a nine-week period. Throughout this period the author closely observed the students and the teaching staff. Three interviews were conducted with the lecturer (at the start, mid-way and at the finish), with individual students at perceived key stages and by a focus group discussion with ten students at the end of the project.

This multi-faceted project required students first to create a piece of music or an acoustic musical instrument and then relate the musical composition or instrument in some way to the composition of architectural space. The design of a "Music Room," a space "specifically designed for the contemplation and/or composition of music" was undertaken individually. A second individual submission required students to construct a 1:10 model with detail drawings. Preparing such models is a customary part of architectural study. The significant difference here was that students, in groups of 10-13, then selected one of these designs and constructed it as a full-size piece (i.e., 1:1). In their groups, they presented their finished Music Room with associated posters and Web sites to their assessors and peers.

The Educational Challenge

The educational challenge was seen as threefold:

1. To provide meaningful and purposeful links with other disciplines
2. To bring together the worlds of design and construction
3. To move from the individual to the collaborative

This challenge was met by a learning task rich in possibilities and requirements and in this way it mirrored the complex interplay of issues that inform architecture and building.

1. *To provide meaningful and purposeful links with other disciplines*

Areas of high creativity, such as design, suggest private, often idiosyncratic spaces and there is an aura of the esoteric. The individual is foregrounded, as freedom to express oneself through the composition is an embedded expectation. Yet, in a discipline such as architecture, where the design normally requires making by others and has been commissioned by, and for, others, preparation for the profession entails that, while students have space and support to develop their creativity, they also gain experience of how the ideation underpinning their design is realised in its structure. The first area of concern for the lecturer, whose work is considered here, was to enhance the creative design element. His view was that, as architectural practitioners are composers of form, space, and materiality, students within this discipline have much to learn from the study of composers and their compositions in relation to philosophy and technique. Concerned by an increasing move towards specialisation within architectural education, he argued that this trend towards the insularisation of architectural education almost inevitably leads to designers less acquainted with "looking outside the realm" for inspiration. Hence, a deliberate association with non-architectural disciplines formed an integral element of the project.

The art chosen for the cross-fertilisation of ideas was music because of the lecturer's practical and research interests (as architect and percussionist) and its strong associations with architecture amongst scholars over the years (MacGilvray, 1992). Wanting students to consider the design and construction of the Music Room from multiple perspectives, the lecturer commenced with the purpose of the room. Alternative understandings of what constituted music were discussed and links to compositional Web sites provided opportunities for self-exploration. Translational associations with music, through free-form sketching whilst listening to musical pieces, allowed a guided entry into the generally unknown world of musical composition. In these ways students were encouraged to recognise that creativity is often underpinned and stimulated by the work of others and that professionals customarily seek, and have the skill of knowing where to seek, inspiration.

2.   *To bring together the worlds of design and construction*

The salient question to address was how to impart upon early students of architecture the importance of "designing construction" and "design making." Although final-year students had undertaken design and construction projects during the course of their studies, there was a shared concern within the school that they tended to slip back into the mould of "architect as concept designer," yet to realise that design *is* about construction. In terms of connectivity with professional reality, the fact was that the majority of projects within the undergraduate design curriculum operated entirely within the "schematic design" stage, yet this constituted only 15% of the fee basis of full architectural services (RAIA, 1996). The lecturer concerned contended that the importance of a tectonic approach to design (i.e., one incorporating the science or art of construction) is best realised when a design concept is actually constructed and an interaction between user and artifact occurs. This occurs infrequently at university. The problem is compounded by a tendency to oversimplify with flat and unidimensional problem situations or by setting unrealistic and unrealisable tasks, for example, the design of a school within the space of four weeks.

Such approaches lead students to believe that an architect designs in isolation and only to a conceptual level. Graduates are not prepared for the reality of architecture where design teams are composed of architects, consultants and project managers needing to reach satisfactory resolution requiring high detail, as well as construction viability. Issues such as responsiveness to the client and the influence of resource constraints, as well as the critical requirement for the designer to "sell" the design and the builder the finished product, are frequently disregarded elements of conventional projects set as student learning tasks. As Brown, Collins and Duguid (1989, p. 34) pointed out, there is the danger that, "By participating in such ersatz activities students are likely to misconceive entirely what practitioners actually do." A fuller contextualisation, such as found in this *Composing Architecture* project, combats such reductionist tendencies and allows students to realise that complex, multidimensional problems characterise the territory of real-world professional activity.

3.   *To move from the individual to the collaborative*

Students' first submission allowed them to operate entirely conceptually, knowing that the projects would be developed further. A second individual submission required students to explore the tectonics of their conceptual design, culminating in the construction of a 1:10 model with detail drawings. To link concept and construction (the designer and the builder), the next stage saw the transition from sole practitioner to collaborative team player and from design architect to construction manager and constructor. Six teams of 10 to 13 people (grouped alphabetically) were required to select a colleague's project to undergo the transition from concept to construction. This 1:1 construction task was obviously beyond the capacity of any single student and hence the requirement to work as part of a team was purposeful. Moreover, working collaboratively meant that the learning was embedded in social practice. For theorists such as Golomb (1995, p. 201), "... attaining authenticity is by no means a solitary pursuit. Indeed, what seems incontrovertible is that authenticity cannot be achieved outside a social context." While Petraglia (1998, p. 75) contends that "valuing collaborative learning for itself is only beginning across the academy," if we accept that knowledge is socially constructed this entails that authentic learning requires dialogue with others. Further, if tertiary study is seen as preparation for a professional life, as Bruffee (1993) asserts, collaboration is important because it mirrors the dynamics of doing business in the real world. The ability to work as part of a team is perceived as so important to most fields of work that, as Taylor (1993) claims, "Team building has become a vital management skill and a prerequisite for good management." Herrington, Oliver & Reeves (2003) claim that, to be characterised as an authentic activity, collaboration is integral to the task and this was demonstrably so for the building of the Music Room.

Was This an Authentic Learning Experience?

Some theorists (e.g., Wilson, 1993, p. 77), would argue that authentic activity requires "that learning and knowing always be located in the actual situation of their creation and use," and thus repudiate simulations. Kantor, Waddington and

Osgood (2000, pp. 211-12) claim that, irrespective of how realistic the case may be, or how authentic are the conditions or tools, this is not the same as the real work environment. This is uncontestable but, importantly, they add that such simulations mean "the participants tacitly agree to go along with an interpretation of job reality which we have crafted." Developing this notion further, Herrington et al. (2003, p. 61) contend that, once the fundamental basis for the simulated world is accepted and there is "a suspension of disbelief," the sort of immersion and engagement one would have with a film occurs and students recognise the complexity and value of such simulations. In this instance, while the actual work environment was simulated, it is important to note that the final product, the Music Room, was built full-scale.

Petraglia (1998, p. 72) suggests that the fundamental task facing educators is "to create the sorts of curricular environments that permit authentic learning to take place" and writes, "I would even go so far as to suggest that an understanding of contemporary education hinges on what we take *authentic learning* to mean and how we believe it is achieved" (p. 2). What then, is authentic learning? Bennett, Harper and Hedberg (2001) provide a compelling indication of the multiple perspectives and interpretations provided in the literature and reinforce Golomb's (1995) assessment that "the philosophical understanding of 'authenticity' is far more complex than its everyday use suggests" (p. 5), with the notion of authenticity signifying "something beyond the domain of objective language" (p. 7). However, in an attempt to understand more fully the concept of authentic learning environments, it is useful for the purposes of this discussion to delineate the essential characteristics of an authentic learning environment and, through a consideration of the Composing Architecture project, test both the project and the claimed attributes. Although there are several such lists extant (e.g., Jonassen, 1991; Young, 1993), Martin-Kniep's (2000) was chosen because it was relatively recent and, as a publication of the American Association for Supervision and Curriculum Design Development, carries implicit commendation from a relevant professional association. The more recent characteristics of authentic activities provided by Herrington et al. (2003, pp. 62-63) also provide a broad scholarly base for analysis.

1.   *Real purpose and audience*

Martin-Kniep (2000, p. 26) contends that authenticity "requires that students engage with real-life problems, issues, or tasks for an audience who cares about or has a stake in what students learn." This "invested" audience sits well beyond the classroom (p. 28). While, as discussed and demonstrated above, the Composing Architecture project had real purposes, there was no involvement with a client who had specific needs for the Music Room to be built, and in this way the true authenticity of the task was lessened. In the final presentations, the audience (which included invited members from the industry, other parts of the university and three core assessors who were all qualified architects with practice experience) certainly cared about what the students had learned, but they did not have the sort of stake that a client would have. In this regard the related criterion, "authentic activities have real-world relevance" (Herrington et al., 2003), is more accommodating as the activity matched "as nearly as possible the real-world tasks of professionals in practice rather than decontextualised or classroom based tasks" (p. 62). While this audience sat "beyond the classroom," the role of peers was more significant, given the intended learning outcomes of this project. In the early formative stages of this project, the students, as audience, assumed the role of the client. In all of the final presentations the connectivity of the roles of designer and constructors was explored.

Evidence of meaningful learning was reflected in the comment of one presenter that the group had learned "how designers need to specify very precisely and be prepared to link with the construction process." Designers also gained insights from how their concept had been realised with some being quite "stunned" by the scale of the finished products. While some designers were surprised by, and uncertain about some modifications, others recognised and appreciated the value adding of the changes the construction group had made. They were interested parties and represented the different perspectives from which the students' work would be judged in the professional arena, while providing students with some experience of how it felt to have one's creative output developed by others.

2.   Integration of content and skills

The project clearly met the requirement to build on prior knowledge and apply knowledge and skills from related areas. A nationally funded project had led to the development of a series of unit Web pages, resource pages, Virtual Galleries, digital projects and "games." This constituted a new mode of delivery of projects within the school and reinforced a major direction of the university. By the start of second semester, the lecturer believed that the students had achieved a high degree of mastery of digital technologies compared to that of previous years. This was evidenced in the group presentations where there was a high level of sophistication in terms of Web pages and digital presentation. The Composing Architecture project was seen as the natural extension of this continued exploration, and the work produced in the relatively brief timeframe evidenced that students successfully transferred skills. Herrington et al. (2003) claim that such integration encourages interdisciplinary perspectives and enables students to play diverse roles. Certainly this project took students far beyond one well-defined field or domain and in this way ensured that the tasks were: "ill-defined, requiring students to define the tasks and sub-tasks needed to complete the activity" (pp. 62-63).

3.   *Disciplined inquiry/academic rigour*

Tertiary teaching would seem to mandate a desire to provide learning opportunities that lead students to seek deep understanding. Martin-Kniep (2000, p. 28) links this with "systematic research and inquiry using a variety of primary and secondary sources." In this project, the sources were richly varied and, while the built piece was the culmination of the project, the crux of the learning was the explicit linking of the conceptual and the applied. Effective use of a variety of sources is undeniably important as it assists students to find information and also discriminate, a point Herrington et al. (2003) similarly recognise. However, to restrict "academic rigour" to this, as Martin-Kniep has done, seems reductionist. Here academic rigour was demonstrated principally by the skills that were required as students engaged in cognitive and physical activities that integrated and applied their theoretical learning in complex tasks as they conceptualised their music piece, instrument and space and realised it as a building.

4.   *Explicit standards and scoring criteria*

Martin-Kniep (2000, p. 28) claims that for assessment to be authentic, students need to participate in the identification of performance standards for the task and in the criteria that distinguish levels of performance. Negotiated assessment, along the lines suggested by Martin-Kniep, was not part of this project — in the professional world, judgements are often arbitrarily imposed. What *was* essential in this context was that these judgements were based on known reasonable criteria. In this regard, the Web site provided students with a clear listing of the issues to be explored and these were linked to explicit criteria that stimulated and challenged. The self-assessment criteria encouraged students to articulate how they had expanded their understanding and developed their design processes and the assessment criteria, while the craft and quality of the presentation, put as pre-eminent the qualities of the finished artefact, to be judged on Vitruvian qualities of "firmness, commodity and delight" (Ham, 2001). Further, the assessment was seamlessly integrated with the task in a manner that reflected real-world assessment through the review process (Herrington et al., 2003).

5.   *Elaborate communication*

Elaborate communication was a strength of this project's design, and Martin-Kniep's (2000, p. 28) explanation that this means that "students communicate what they know and can do and how they think through written, artistic, and oral performances and exhibitions, and through opportunities to teach others" was met fully. While the project included each of these elements, how the students dealt with these communicative opportunities was highly revealing. There was an undeniably high level of communication for nearly all projects as far as the presentation of the final "masterpieces" with their supporting posters and the Web sites were concerned. However, the oral presentations indicated, on the whole, that the students were far less accomplished in this area. Naïve honesty and openness in comment and the exposure of problematic elements within the experience indicated that these students still had much to learn. Sophisticated self-promotion is an important part of the repertoire of the successful architect yet is rarely explicitly taught. This is an area that the project aimed to address and this experience indicated that students generally have yet to recognise its importance and require further skill development and support.

6.   *Levels of thinking*

Martin-Kniep (2000, p. 28) explains levels of thinking as: "Students use basic and higher levels of thinking in a task that calls for a combination of skills and forms of knowledge." The project description at the start of this chapter provides compelling evidence that this is a highly complex task. While students were able to contribute to the teams that constructed the music rooms in many different ways, and the contribution and commitment at this stage were demonstrably variable, all students were engaged in a series of learning opportunities that incorporated the need for cognitive flexibility. Herrington et al. (2003) indicate that authentic activities comprise complex tasks undertaken over a sustained period of time, requiring significant investment of time and intellectual resources. Although this project was intended to be completed over an extended period, one less-satisfying element for some students was the brief time frame of three to five weeks for the construction. Successful project management meant that students contributed in areas of identified strengths, successfully reinforcing skills rather than exposing them to areas where they felt they had a lot to learn. With this caveat, because the learning design motivated students to explore a variety of sources, to reflect, to discuss, to seek solutions to real and immediate problems, and to apply developing understandings in meaningful ways — it supported a deep approach to learning.

7.   *Reflection, self- and peer-assessment and feedback*

Martin-Kniep (2000, p. 28) claims that in an authentic learning environment students "reflect on both products and processes through ongoing and specific questions, checklists, or rubrics." Coupled with this is formal evaluation of their own and other's learning "through ongoing, elaborate, and specific feedback from both their teacher and peers," leading to refinement and enhancement. Similarly, Herrington et al. (2003) characterise authentic activities as those that provide an opportunity to reflect, both individually and socially. The explicit self-assessment and mastery criteria prompted reflection. In the first stage, a roving bazaar review allowed students to peer review colleagues' design work, along with associated musical compositions. Students could draw on this critique, as the initial concept could be refined in response. During the construction period the lecturer arranged for solid support to be provided with frequent formal and informal contact so that students could receive feedback on their progress and receive assistance. The assessment of the Music Room, itself, was tied to a presentation by each of the groups to a panel of reviewers and this gave students the opportunity to engage in a conversation with their assessors and their peers. Here the feedback was immediate and, while the assessors deliberately posed evocative questions, the students engaged readily in the studio critique. Discussion with the evaluator reinforced that groups who chose to ignore advice from mentors and peers experienced the consequences and were made aware of the need to take responsibility for their decisions and actions. A further element was the incorporation of a group assessment form that gave students the opportunity to assess individual contributions to the team effort. This sought a numerical rating for judgements regarding contribution, time spent, attendance, innovation, enthusiasm, resourcefulness, motivation and team spirit and represented 20% of the final mark. The professional world requires constructive appraisal and, while it is not surprising that such peer assessment caused difficulties for some, it was an important learning experience.

8.   Flexibility in content, strategies, products and time

While the students had choices in terms of their original design and later their construction, the flexibility was more qualified than Martin-Kniep (2000) would consider necessary. Not only were student choices constrained in terms of subject area (the Music Room), but the brief total time span of nine weeks with a maximum of five of these allowed for construction of the 1:1 building meant the time allocation did not allow flexibility for different students and their needs, nor was there an explicit concern to accommodate differences among the products or performances, the two areas Martin-Kniep stipulates. However, the flexibility Martin-Kniep considers as an essential attribute of authenticity can reasonably be seen as denying the fundamental desire to represent, to the greatest extent possible, real-world conditions. As professionals, there are almost inevitably external constraints such as subject, time and work group and it is a critical aspect of the role of an architect that the completed work satisfies complex criteria — ranging from the aesthetic to the highly pragmatic, such as conforming to building regulations, and tight schedules with financial penalties for failure. Within the envelope of the Music Room and the guidelines provided, there was, as would be expected in the professional context, marked diversity in outcomes. Hence the qualified flexibility was a more reasonable representation of the professional world, and the learning environment was more authentic than if the types of accommodations stipulated by Martin-Kniep had been incorporated. Certainly, to return to Herrington et al. (2003), the culmination of the built Music Rooms as the final stage of the Composing Architecture project did create polished pieces that were valuable in their own right while demonstrably allowing for a range and diversity of outcomes.

Conclusion

Although theorists such as Petraglia (1998, p. 163) argue that, "…teacherly common sense tells us that life is multi-faceted and complex and that any attempt to prescribe what counts as real and authentic is doomed to failure," this complex series of tasks demonstrably meets accepted characterisations of an authentic learning experience. At the same time, as this discussion has attempted to reveal, it challenges some of the characteristic attributes but it also suggests that there are fundamental shared understandings of what is entailed in the provision of "authentic learning environments." This case study suggests that perhaps the most compelling requirement for those concerned with educating our under-graduate students as preparation for professional life is to be prepared to draw on one's own knowledge of the professional world to give students the opportunity to achieve excellence and to apply their conceptual knowledge and creativity. From his choice of the word *masterpiece*, this lecturer consistently sent the message that the professional world of architecture is demanding but, in a supportive environment, students could gain the experience to use resources to produce truly impressive outcomes.

From the outset, students were challenged and what they produced throughout these intensive nine weeks offers abundant evidence that all 74 were engaged in a rich learning experience. Underpinned by individual exploration and creativity, the rigour involved in the translation of architectural ideas to reality through the team construction of the Music Rooms quickly became apparent. Previous notions that architectural design occurred only in conceptual stages were, by necessity, overturned. Design and making were brought together as one with a curriculum that was readily translatable into real-world professional experience. This quality modelling of professional practice within the academy can be celebrated as authentic and can inspire and challenge tertiary educators.

Acknowledgments

The author expresses her sincere thanks for the experience of sharing the teaching of this project with the lecturer (Jeremy Ham) and his students and for their willingness to explore its contribution to their understanding.

Note: This is an updated version of a paper awarded the Edith Cowan University Centenary Prize for the best paper on authentic learning environments at the 2002 HERDSA International Conference.

References

Barr, R., & Tagg, J. (1995). From teaching to learning: a new paradigm for undergraduate education. *Change, 27*(6), 12-25.

Bennett, S., Harper, B., & Hedberg, J. (2001). Designing real-life cases to support authentic design activities. In G. Kennedy, M. Keppell, C. McNaught & T. Petrovic (Eds.), *Meeting at the Crossroads. Proceedings of the 18th Annual Conference of the Australian Society for Computers in Learning in Tertiary Education* (pp. 73-81). Melbourne: Biomedical Multimedia Unit, The University of Melbourne.

Berge, Z. (2000). New roles for learners and teachers in online higher education. Retrieved March 2004, from *www.globaled.com/articles/BergeZane2000*

Brown, J.S., Collins, A., & Duguid, P. (1989). Situated cognition and the culture of learning. *Educational Researcher, 18*(1), 32-42.

Bruffee, K. (1993). *Collaborative learning: Higher education, independence, and the authority of knowledge.* Baltimore, MD: Johns Hopkins University.

Challis, D., & Langston, C. (2003). Collaborating to provide authentic learning: the Building 'T' CD-ROM. In C. Langston (Ed.), *AUBEA 2003: Working together* (pp. 187-190). Geelong: Deakin University.

Ewell, P.T. (1997). Organizing for learning: A new imperative. *AAHE Bulletin, 50*(4), 3-6.

Golomb, J. (1995). *In search of authenticity: From Kierkegaard to Camus.* London: Routledge.

Ham, J. (2001). SRD264 website. Retrieved March 2004, from *http://www.ab.deakin.edu.au/online/games/semester2_2001/srd264_2001/start.htm*

Herrington, J., Oliver, R., & Reeves, T. (2003) Patterns of engagement in authentic online learning environments. *Australian Journal of Educational Technology, 19*(1), 59-71.

Jonassen, D. (1991). Evaluating constructivist learning. *Educational Technology, 31*(9), 28-33.

Kantor, R.J., Waddington, T., & Osgood, R.E. (2000). Fostering the suspension of disbelief: The role of authenticity in goal-based scenarios. *Interactive Learning Environments, 8*(3), 211-227.

McLeish, A. (2002). Employability skills for Australian small and medium sized enterprises. ACT: DEST. Retrieved March 2004, from *http://www.dest.gov.au/ty/publications/employability_skills/SME_research*

MacGilvray, D.F. (1992). The proper education of musicians and architects. *Journal of Architectural Education, 46*(2), 87-94.

Martin-Kniep, G.O. (2000). *Becoming a better teacher: Eight innovations that work.* Alexandria: Association for Supervision and Curriculum Development.

Petraglia, J. (1998). *Reality by design: The rhetoric and technology of authenticity in education.* Mahwah, NJ: Lawrence Erlbaum Associates.

Ramsden, P. (1992). *Learning to teach in higher education.* London: Routledge.

Richens, G.P., & McClain, C.R. (2000). Workplace basic skills for the new millennium. *Journal of Adult Education, 28*(1), 29-34.

Royal Australian Institute of Architects. (1996). *Practice note.* AN02.03.100.

Taylor, T. (1993). Foreword. In P. Moxon (Ed.), *Building a better team.* Brookfield: Gower Publishing.

Wilson, A. (1993). The problem of situated cognition. *New Directions for Adult and Continuing Education, 57,* 71-79.

Young, M.F. (1993). Instructional design for situated learning. *Educational Technology Research and Development, 41*(1), 43-58.

Chapter IV

An Authentic Online Learning Environment in University Introductory Biology

Annette Koenders, Edith Cowan University, Australia

Abstract

An authentic online collaborative assessment task, implemented in an introductory biology course, posed several challenges for the students. The task required application of knowledge rather than simple summarising and had to be presented in a specific style. It took many students some time to become at ease with the online environment. However, they appreciated the benefits of asynchronous communication and reported feeling more at ease to express opinions. In addition, group work and co-assessment challenged students to develop learning and interpersonal skills. An additional benefit of using online discussion boards was the teacher's ability to obtain evidence of the way students interacted within groups that is not available in traditional group settings. Students actually found collaborating online difficult but satisfying. The study clearly demonstrates that authentic learning can be achieved by introductory students in a science course. Furthermore, the online environment enhanced the learning experience and student satisfaction.

Introduction

Modern graduates need to be reflective practitioners and life-long learners. University students can therefore be thought of as entering a cognitive apprenticeship. My students are learning to see the world through a biologist's eyes, learning the discourse of biology, learning the methods of enquiry (experimental design, techniques, data interpretation) and learning to communicate (Brown, Collins & Duguid, 1989). Biology graduates need to be self-regulated, independent thinkers with good communication and teamwork skills. They therefore need competencies in cognitive, meta-cognitive, social and affective skills (Dochy, Segers & Sluijsmans, 1999). Assessment practices need to reflect these graduate attributes and are tending to become more focused on formative, authentic assessment to enhance deep learning.

Situated Learning and Experience-Based Pedagogy

The learning activities described here are based on constructivist theory, where the student learns through meaningful activities in a social setting (Oliver & Herrington, 2000; Oliver, 1999). The activities were designed to incorporate the nine elements of situated learning described by Herrington and Oliver (2000), and the construct of experience-based pedagogy (Ip & Naidu, 2001).

Experience-based pedagogy starts from the observation that learning is based on experiences and stories about experiences (Ip & Naidu, 2001). People learn from their own (first-person) experiences as well as stories of others' (third-person) experiences. Both types of learning can be incorporated into authentic online learning environments. First-person experiences provide students with opportunities for developing problem solving, role-play and other skills in a safe environment. This chapter contains a description of a first-person learning experience in the form of online collaboration. An important consideration in the design of the learning activity was an awareness of transitional issues with a student body consisting predominantly of new university entrants. Several issues have been identified as important in making the transition difficult, including personal and academic factors (Evans, 2000). Learning communities have been demonstrated to be highly effective in easing the transition (Tinto, 2000) as well as the excellent communication and collaboration tools available in online environments (Jonassen & Roher-Murphy, 1999; Palloff & Pratt, 1999; Reeves, 2000).

In this chapter, background information about the culture of the institution and the student body is given. This is followed by a description of an online learning activity involving group collaboration, with reflections from students and teachers. This is followed by a description of current and future planned activities.

Background

Edith Cowan University (ECU) has a strong commitment to quality in teaching, including life-long learning, flexible delivery and innovation. With ECU support, several computer and online activities were developed and the introductory biology subject *Origins & Evolution of Life* was developed for online delivery. This subject has been offered in face-to-face mode for several years. It introduces students to the molecular, cellular and evolutionary basis of life on earth and has no other course prerequisites.

Students

Students in the biology program and some education programs are required to complete two introductory biology subjects. These are generally taken in their first year at university and have no prerequisites. Most of our students are school-leavers, but a considerable proportion is mature-aged and there are some international students. Class sizes range from 120 to around 150. A subset of the on-campus cohort (20 students) chose to take the course online.

The important characteristics of the student group are their lack of prior knowledge of biology and their lack of experience with university teaching and learning in general — and online learning in particular. These factors have informed the design of the learning activity by balancing prolonged complex tasks with relatively simple, frequent tasks to maintain engagement and by incorporating strategies for the development of a learning community. The development team consisted of an experienced instructional designer without a science background, several content experts and the author (the teacher of the subject).

Design

The learning activities for *Origins & Evolution of Life* were structured using a situated design incorporating online collaboration. Three forms of assessment were incorporated, each implementing a range of the nine elements of situated learning (Herrington & Oliver, 2000) and experience-based design (Ip & Naidu, 2001). Weekly discussion board activities ensured that students maintained engagement with, and progressed through, the content; students engaged in practical application of the content through rule-based simulations; and a group assignment provided opportunity for sustained activity in collaboration using role-play.

The tasks were designed to motivate students to engage with the content, to provide feedback on their learning (from peers and teachers), to assess their learning and to foster the development of a learning community. The tasks included several components of situated learning including alternative views, collaborative construction of knowledge, reflection and articulation. In addition, several strategies were incorporated to ensure regular engagement (Hiltz, 1994). The design is described more fully in Koenders (2002).

Online Collaboration

A major assignment designed to facilitate online collaboration was set up to include many elements of authentic learning (Herrington & Oliver, 2000). The authentic task required students to work in small online groups (up to five members) to prepare a proposal for funding to search for evidence of extraterrestrial life:

Grant proposal to search for life on a space mission to Europa

You have recently discovered that an international consortium is planning a mission to Europa. You cannot let this opportunity pass, so you and your colleagues get together to prepare a proposal to use this mission to search for life on this satellite of the planet Jupiter. The four of you have a special interest in the origins of life on earth and are keen to investigate the possibility of life occurring elsewhere in the universe. Your argument is that investigating other planets and moons will very likely deepen our understanding of the origins of life on earth.

Proposal structure

There are some rules about the structure of the proposal that must be strictly adhered to, or you will be ineligible. [Headings and word counts follow]. You have only limited time to prepare your proposal, and competition is fierce. You are aware of several other highly experienced research groups that are preparing similar proposals. The problem is that you all work in very different areas and cannot interrupt your regular work to fly to a common place. You therefore decide you will communicate via the Internet. This has several advantages: you can each work and contribute at a time and place that suits you. Once you post a message on the discussion board your group members will read it at a time that suits them. You therefore do not have to organise a time and place when all of you can meet. You have several means of communication at your disposal: e-mail, a private discussion board that is accessible only to members of your group and a digital drop box.

Students acted as researcher practitioners, preparing a research proposal for application to a particular granting body. The proposal was divided into four sections, each addressing a different aspect of the search for life. Each student acted as an expert in one of the four aspects to be addressed — physical evidence of life, chemical evidence, evidence of actual living organisms and fossil evidence — and prepared the part of the submission addressing that aspect. Groups were instructed to select one member as team leader. This student did not take on writing a content section but organised the work and wrote the general introduction and conclusion. This provided equitable workloads for groups of different sizes, or groups that lost members part way through. Groups with fewer than five members would be allowed to omit a section for each student less than five.

The assignment was designed to incorporate several key features. Learning was *goal-based*. In this case the desired outcome was to win a grant through the submission of a competitive proposal. The structure of the proposal was set out in a similar way to competitive research grant applications with mandatory headings and strict word limits. Students were not, however, required to supply descriptions of their methods and budget.

In this assignment, students acted as researchers in different geographical locations without the opportunity to meet in person. Online discussions were therefore an integral aspect of the design. Although each student took on a particular task, a *shared responsibility* was ensured by a requirement that the proposal was to be a coherent piece of work and that the coherence of the proposal was the responsibility of all group members. Before submission of the work the accuracy, style, formatting and referencing had to be organised so the proposal read as a coherent work. A proportion of the marks was allocated to this aspect.

The design ensured that students were also acting as *coaches and scaffolds* for each other within and between groups. Groups were kept small and given private discussion boards, accessible only to group members and instructors. Small, private group forums are important to reduce anxiety in presenting views to peers (Oliver & Omari, 1999; Palloff & Pratt, 1999). This was an important feature of the design, as the students were in their first year of university study. A class discussion board was also available for general discussion and communication among groups. A good example of coaching occurred when a student admitted knowing very little about the topic, and requested that someone please pass on the required information. It was good to see that no student provided this. However, other students did offer suggestions for how to locate relevant information.

Distance study, including online study, can be an isolating experience in the absence of online interaction between students, even for experienced graduate students (Koenders & Brook, 2003). Online communication therefore had the very important aim of fostering a learning community amongst students. *Learning communities* have been shown to assist online students who may be widely scattered geographically and diverse culturally (Jonassen, Carr, & Yueh, 1998; Jonassen & Roher-Murphy, 1999; Palloff & Pratt, 1999; Reeves, 2000). In addition, online group work was an important support mechanism to assist first-year students with transitional issues to university study. Learning communities have been shown to assist first-year students with the formation of self-supporting student groups, more active engagement with learning, improvements in learning quality and student retention (Tinto, 2000). Afterwards, students reported that they indeed felt part of a community, although they had not met face-to-face at any stage. The students indicated that they were more inclined to express themselves online than in a classroom:

Lot more freedom online able to have your say without feeling intimidated or not feeling that your contribution in a classroom is undervalued. ... Looking forward to an opportunity to do another online subject.

At first it felt very impersonal, but after a while it was good as you began to get to know people, and used the system the way it was intended.

[The assessments stimulated my interest in the topics] especially through the discussions with other students.

[The best aspect of the online environment was that] everyone was able to input their ideas. I think it was easier to contribute as I think a lot of students are held back in the classroom by thinking they maybe asking a dumb question.

Initially was very difficult, as everything had to be discovered/solved individually. In a class situation everything is spelled out in a group situation, also more visual/verbal.

Generally, students find group work frustrating (Swan, Shea, Fredericksen, Pickett, Pelz, & Maher, 2000), but in this case they reported that collaboration was difficult, but satisfying.

Finally the students also took on the role of *peer assessor* in the co-assessment of the final work. This was set up to promote improved awareness of the assessment process, self-reflection, communication and motivation (Dochy et al., 1999), reduce the incidence of plagiarism and incorporate an aspect of role-play. It was considered too onerous a task to require students to take complete responsibility for assessing each other's work, particularly at the first-year level. The assessment was therefore designed as follows. The instructor marked the assignment according to a marking key. All groups that obtained a credit or greater were offered the opportunity to distribute some of the marks among the group members according to set criteria, presented to students as follows:

Marks allocation

This assignment is marked out of 20. Because it was a group effort, you as members of the group have the best knowledge as to the relative contributions of the individual group members to the final work. This includes actual work produced, but also effort exerted in organizing the group and tying the work together. The total mark for your work comes to 17.5 out of 20. You each get the first 12 marks from me. The remaining marks are to be divided between you by you. Your task therefore is to divide 27.5 marks (5.5 times the number of students in the group) amongst the five of you. There is the proviso that no one can get a total score greater than 20. You are to use the group discussion board to discuss this. If you cannot resolve this amongst yourselves, I can be called upon as arbitrator. Please let me have your decision by [date].

The members of these groups were therefore assured of 60%, with additional marks divided amongst them. This method of distributing marks needed careful explanation but was a good guard against problems, such as "friendship marking" (Dochy et al., 1999). These discussions were to be conducted on the discussion board for monitoring.

Discussion of the relative merits of each other's contributions is a confronting and difficult task. There were several approaches by different student groups. Many groups chose to avoid discussion and allocate the same mark to all members. Others were able to come to an arrangement amicably, with members putting forward their view in a mature way. Occasionally the teacher was asked to arbitrate. This usually involved one member at odds with the rest of the group.

When arbitration was requested, several criteria were used that had been communicated to students at the start. The first criterion was each individual's contributions on the group discussion forum. Students were required to communicate via this medium and the frequency and quality of their contributions would be taken into account during arbitration. This is a huge benefit of online group work, and a most useful way for teachers to gain insight into group dynamics. The teacher would also take note of the co-assessment discussions on the group discussion forum. The final ruling was based entirely on these two lines of evidence. The quality of many discussions regarding the contributions of group members was highly varied, but generally not very useful. I have therefore amended this process so that each student is required to submit a confidential reflection on their own and other members' contributions. This process yielded more useful information, but many students still appear very reluctant to write critically about their peers.

Another issue was the process used to form the groups. When students with unmatched expectations and work ethics collaborated, there was generally discontent with the mark. This improved after aspects of group work were workshopped with students, and students self-selected groups on the basis of their desired grade. Even then, several groups still experienced significant problems. This is a difficult aspect of collaboration in general and assists with the development of interpersonal and communication skills such as listening and respect.

Applying the Authentic Approach

Through situated learning, students derived several general benefits, including improved confidence in their own ability, greater awareness of quality, more self-reflection and a greater responsibility for their own learning (Dochy et al., 1999). Situated learning can be examined through the use of several design elements

(Herrington & Oliver, 2000). The way in which each element was incorporated into the design of the online collaboration is briefly described below:

- **Authentic context and activities:** The search for extraterrestrial life is current and relevant. NASA is working on this and it is regularly reported in the mass media. The group assignment modelled a group of scientists located around the world collaborating on a joint grant proposal. This presented a complex task addressing an open-ended question that is current and relevant. Not only did students have to investigate a complex problem, they also had to frame it as an application for funding. Many resources were available, including the subject content sections, texts, professional journals, the Internet, peers and teachers, and NASA. The students were given broad outlines of the areas of investigation that had to be addressed in the work. Within this framework students had to define the task. My observations of students confirmed that the task was sufficiently unstructured to extend their learning. Several students had difficulty understanding that they were asked to apply current knowledge of Earth and Europa to an unknown scenario. Some expressed frustration at the lack of information on the life on Europa, while others approached the task as they would the writing of an essay, rather than a proposal.

- **Access to expert performances:** Students had access to expert thinking in the form of scientific publications and consultations with the instructors. Informal access to learners at different stages of development came from the diverse nature of the student body. There was ample opportunity to share learning experiences via online discussions. Practitioners could be observed by corresponding with NASA scientists and observing the teachers.

- **Multiple roles and perspectives:** Different perspectives could be presented on the group discussion boards and on class discussion boards on any issues from the group assignment. Students consistently reported feeling safer to express different views online than face-to-face. There were several points for revisiting learning: each group member prepared part of the final work individually, and then the parts were brought together to make a coherent whole. Each student was responsible for the entire work and therefore had to go over their own and others' work as part of ensuring there was no repetition or contradiction. In addition, the process of co-assessment provided another opportunity to reflect on their learning.

- **Collaboration:** Working within a group was an essential part of the design. Students were informed that their online discussions would be monitored and taken into account in the assessment of the work. Suggestions for effective group work were listed on the assignment sheet, and group work was also discussed online with the whole class. Forming small groups was done in an effort to reduce any fear students may have to express themselves formally (Oliver & Omari, 1999; Palloff & Pratt, 1999). Each group had a private discussion board and e-mail facilities also accessible to instructors. Finally, communication with the whole class about the assignment was facilitated with another discussion board. An additional benefit of working online was to enable the teacher to monitor group dynamics. The quantity and quality of discussion board contributions was used by the teacher as evidence of the contributions of individual group members to the final product.

- **Reflection:** Having an authentic topic and activity created opportunities for reflection. Putting together individual contributions into a coherent piece required reflection on parts of the activity and enabled comparisons with other learners. The discussion board tasks also provided the opportunity for comparisons. Finally, co-assessment necessitated reflection of, not only the work produced, but also on the process of collaboration.

- **Articulation:** Communication was a major part of the learning process. Students communicated with each other, not only about the content but also about dividing up various tasks and, finally dividing marks on the basis of their input. Additionally, the actual work submitted required students to articulate their learning in a highly authentic format, namely in the form of a grant proposal.

- **Coaching and scaffolding:** Instruction was kept to a level deemed necessary for beginning students. However, in the context of the group assignment, the instructions on the format of the work (grant application) were authentic. Granting bodies have highly specific requirements for the length and format of applications. The teacher did not provide direct instruction but monitored the discussion boards. Students were also encouraged to resolve problems with each other, rather than seek an answer from the teacher.

- **Authentic assessment:** The group assignment task presented complexity for students in an introductory subject. As the word limit was kept deliberately low, students had to make decisions as to what information could be presented and what to leave out. Students worked both in the group and individually. The assessment was seamless with the activity — the preparation of a grant proposal.

Conclusion

The experiences described here clearly demonstrate that authentic teaching and learning can be applied successfully to biology education at an introductory level in an online environment. The task of preparing a proposal to search for extraterrestrial life was current and engendered enthusiasm in students. The grant proposal format was well suited to introductory teaching, because it imposed a strict structure, which was appropriate at this level of learning. The use of small online discussion forums worked well for students who reported feeling safe in contributing as part of a learning community. The latter was deliberately incorporated into the design, as introductory students are at risk due to transition issues, particularly as online students. Some time must therefore be allowed for students to familiarise themselves with communication in this medium. Online collaboration stimulated the development of communication, articulation, collaboration and reflection skills. This was exemplified when students discovered the benefits of asynchronous online communication.

Students reported having difficulty understanding the task, working in a group and working online. Although students were fired up about the topic, they tended to take some time to get their heads around the grant application format, in particular the application of current knowledge to an unknown situation. Students also frequently complained about having to work in groups and co-assessment was also difficult for many. A benefit of discussion boards in online collaboration was that they maintained a record of interaction that was used as evidence of group dynamics and participation. Being able to verify students' contributions independently in online group work had several benefits. For the teacher it provided a monitoring and checking mechanism not available in traditional group settings. For students it provided peace of mind that the teacher was aware of the group dynamics. Although online group work and co-assessment caused the students some difficulty, they provided great opportunities for developing learning and interpersonal skills.

Currently the online collaboration task described here is successfully applied in on-campus teaching with some modifications. The assessment criteria are now workshopped with the students, which helps them understand what is expected. Some time is also spent developing strategies for group selection with students. This has reduced the incidence of complaints and requests for arbitration during co-assessment. In addition, students now complete detailed reflections on the relative contributions by group members and identification of areas for improvement. Similar arrangements are also used in other levels of undergraduate teaching.

The strategies outlined in this chapter can be adopted in other disciplines and at all levels of tertiary education. Not only does authentic learning work well with introductory biology students, but also, in an online environment, it can actually enhance the learning experience and the satisfaction for students. Furthermore, this type of learning activity is ideal for distant online students, but is also eminently suitable for face-to-face courses with access to online facilities.

Acknowledgments

I would like to acknowledge the Edith Cowan University Strategic Initiatives Fund and a Faculty Teaching & Learning Grant. I also gratefully acknowledge the contributions from the following people: instructional designers Clare Brook and Christy Pinfold; tutor in the online unit Tina Lamey; and content experts Associate Professor A. Kinnear, Dr. K. Lemson and Dr. A. Needham.

References

Brown, J.S., Collins, A., & Duguid, P. (1989). Situated cognition and the culture of learning. *Educational Researcher, 18*, 32-42.

Dochy, F., Segers, M., & Sluijsmans, D. (1999). The use of self- peer- and co-assessment in higher education: A review. *Studies in Higher Education, 24,* 331-350.

Evans, M. (2000). Planning for the transition to tertiary study: A literature review. *Journal of Institutional Research, 9*, 1-13.

Herrington, J., & Oliver, R (2000). An instructional design framework for authentic learning environments. *Educational Technology Research and Development, 48*, 23-48.

Hiltz, S.R. (1994). *Online communities: A case study of the office of the future.* Norwood, NJ: Ablex Publishing.

Ip, A., & Naidu, S. (2001, September-October). Experienced-based pedagogical designs for e-learning. *Educational Technology, 53-58.*

Jonassen, D.H., & Roher-Murphy, L. (1999). Activity theory as a framework for designing constructivist learning environments. *Educational Technology Research & Development, 47*, 61-79.

Jonassen, D.H., Carr, C., & Yueh, H.P. (1998). Computers as mindtools for engaging learners in critical thinking. *Technology Trends, 43*, 24-32.

Koenders, A. (2002). Creating opportunities from challenges in online introductory biology. *Research and Development in Higher Education: Quality Conversations, 25,* 393-400.

Koenders A., & Brook, C. (2003). Online learning: Student and tutor as one. *Research and Development in Higher Education, 26.*

Oliver, R. (1999). Exploring strategies for online teaching and learning. *Distance Education, 20,* 140-154.

Oliver, R., & Herrington, J. (2000). Using situated learning as a design strategy for web-based learning. In B. Abbey (Ed.), *Web-based education* (pp. 178-191). Hershey, PA: Idea Group Inc.

Oliver, R., & Omari, A. (1999). Replacing lectures with online learning: Meeting the challenge. In J. Winn (Ed.), *Responding to diversity: Proceedings of the 16th Annual Conference of the Australasian Society for Computers in Learning in Tertiary Education* (pp. 257-264). Brisbane: Queensland University of Technology.

Palloff, R.M., & Pratt, K. (1999). *Building learning communities in cyberspace: Effective strategies for the online classroom.* San Francisco: Jossey-Bass.

Reeves, T.C. (2000). Enhancing the worth of instructional technology research through design experiments and other development strategies. In *International perspectives on instructional technology research for the 21st Century.* New Orleans, LA. Retrieved September 2003, from *http://it.coe.uga.edu/~treeves/AERA2000Reeves.pdf*

Swan, K., Shea, P., Fredericksen, E., Pickett, A., Pelz, W. & Maher, G. (2000). Building knowledge building communities: Consistency, contact and communication in the virtual classroom. *Journal of Educational Computing Research, 23,* 359-383.

Tinto, V. (2000). Learning better together: The impact of learning communities on student success in higher education. *Journal of Institutional Research, 9,* 48-53.

Chapter V

Peer Coaching and Reflective Practice in Authentic Business Contexts:
A Strategy to Enhance Competency in Post-Graduate Business Students

Richard Ladyshewsky, Curtin University of Technology, Australia
John Ryan, Ryan Management Consulting, Australia

Abstract

The development of managerial expertise is a combination of acquiring further knowledge and integrating it with past experience and beliefs. To do so in isolation limits the potential for positive outcomes in one's management development. Peer coaching is one experiential learning method that can be used to enhance the depth of learning in managerial education. In this chapter, the experiences of 43 students who participated in a peer-coaching program as part of their post-graduate management education are revealed. Powerful learning effects are reported as well as characteristics of successful peer-coaching relationships.

Introduction

The achievement of competence as a manager is an ongoing process and may never be achieved given the constant change that takes place in the modern workplace. Hence, lifelong learning is a key component of effective managerial practice. Acquiring this mastery has been described by Quinn, Faerman, Thompson and McGrath (1996). Citing the work of Dreyfus and Dreyfus (1986), Quinn et al. (1996) describe a model of managerial competency that commences at the novice stage and moves through the stages of advanced beginner, competent, proficient practitioner and culminates at expert status. Achieving expert status is an ongoing learning process and requires a high degree of self-awareness. Adequate knowledge, cognitive skill and meta-cognition are the key ingredients leading to mastery. Weaknesses in any one of these three dimensions reduces the competency of the manager and interferes with further development. Authentic learning strategies that maximise the development of these key ingredients are important if managers are to improve.

The Role of Knowledge, Cognition and Metacognition

Knowledge as the first domain of competence can be represented as propositional and non-propositional knowledge (Higgs & Titchen, 1995a, 1995b; Higgs, 1997). Propositional (declarative) knowledge is derived from research and scholarship and is supported by the professional body. It encompasses book knowledge as well as abstract, logical, and formal relationships between constructs and contexts. Non-propositional knowledge is divided into two categories (professional and personal). Professional (craft) knowledge incorporates "knowing how" and the "tacit" knowledge of the profession. It encompasses the practical skills within the profession. Personal knowledge is influenced by the personal experiences and reflections of a manager and helps them to understand the perspective of their team. Personal knowledge, such as individual beliefs, values and convictions, also influence propositional and professional craft knowledge. These three forms of knowledge constitute a manager's unique knowledge base.

The unique knowledge of the manager is developed using a variety of cognitive strategies, which are a subset of the knowledge domain. These strategies have been described in the literature and illustrate how knowledge and cognition work hand in hand to develop the unique skill base of the manager (Boud, 1988). The strategies are: *association, integration, validation,* and *appropriation.* Association involves connecting ideas and feelings that are part of an experience and tying it to existing knowledge. Integration involves processing associations to see if there are patterns or linkages to other ideas. Validation and validity testing looks at evaluating the internal consistency of emerging concepts and again tying these to existing beliefs and knowledge. Lastly, appropriation involves making new knowledge an integral part of how one acts or feels. Through this process, the manager constructs higher forms of learning which influences his or her competency.

Metacognition is the third component of the professional reasoning framework used by managers. It has been defined in a variety of ways, making its interpretation broad and vague. For example, terms such as cognitive monitoring, self-communication, metamemory, metacomprehension, and learning strategies have been used to describe metacognition (Strohm-Kitchener, 1983; Pesut & Herman, 1992; Worrell, 1990). Pesut and Herman (1992) define metacognition as the self-communication one engages in, or the internal dialogue that one conducts before, during and after performing a task. Hence, metacognition includes such things as knowing what one knows, knowing when and how one comes to know it, being able to think and plan strategically, the ability to represent knowledge effectively and in ways that permit efficient retrieval, and the ability to monitor and consistently evaluate one's own competence. It is the application of metacognition that leads to expertise (Nickerson, Perkins & Smith, 1985) as it is used to self-evaluate the knowledge framework of the manager.

Flavell (1979) was one of the first people to formally describe the concept of metacognition. Flavell notes that novel situations offer numerous opportunities for thoughts and feelings to emerge about one's own thinking. The metacognitive processing that surrounds these experiences lead to new goals or to the abandonment of old goals and adds to one's personal knowledge base and expertise. Strohm-Kitchener (1983) argues that most adults are faced with ill-defined problems that are often rife with conflicting assumptions, evidence and opinion, all of which can lead to different solutions. Working through ill-defined problems, therefore, requires the use of higher order thinking or metacognition. Individuals, especially managers and leaders, need to monitor the nature of the problem and the truth value of alternative solutions. They need to understand the limits of their knowledge, the limits of knowing, the certainty of knowing and the criteria for knowing. This is often difficult to do in isolation.

Metacognition is also inextricably linked to the notion of constructivism. Constructivists believe that learners actively construct their own knowledge frameworks using personal experience to structure their rules, concepts, hypotheses and associations (Biehler & Snowman, 1997). This personalised knowledge is influenced by the learner's experiences, beliefs, gender, age, ethnic background and individual biases (Biehler & Snowman, 1997; Graham, 1996). Hence, each learner's concepts and meanings will be unique, and the learner's task, therefore, is to seek meaning within their own unique frame of reference (Joyce & Weil, 1996). Building knowledge, and checking it against the concepts of others, is also seen to be a major part of the process of education (Biehler & Snowman, 1997; Joyce & Weil, 1996). It is in this final comment that the value of peer coaching and reflective practice in authentic situations may enhance metacognition, and managerial competency.

Cognitive Development Theory

The benefits that emerge from peer coaching and reflective practice from the perspective of building mastery can be understood more readily by examining cognitive development theory. This theory provides a framework for understanding how critical cognitive conflict supports heightened performance and competency (Piaget, 1977; Sullivan, 1953; Vygotsky, 1986). These theorists argue that peer interaction is seen to promote cognitive development by creating critical cognitive conflicts. If a manager, through deliberations with another manager, and by engaging in deep reflective practices, becomes aware of a contradiction in their knowledge base, the experience creates a lapse in equilibrium. This instigates the manager to question his or her beliefs and to try out new ones. Hence, if a manager is seen to be following a certain line of inquiry, and his or her peer coach (who may be another manager) does not follow or agree with the rationale behind this inquiry, there is "disequilibrium." The parties, as a result, will initiate strategies to restore equilibrium, for example, by working together to find a solution that both can accept.

The management of critical cognitive conflict appears to be more amenable between peers because they speak on levels which can be easily understand by one another (Damon, 1984; Foot & Howe, 1998). For example, two peers who are at the "advanced beginner" stage of their professional development will more likely use language, experience and dialogue that both can process and understand. This situation would be quite different between an expert and a novice. The informal communications between peers are also less threatening than the advice from a senior manager or mentor because issues of evaluation, status and power are minimised.

Educators can apply cognitive development theory into their curriculum by creating planned controversy in their teaching and learning experiences. Reflective practices and peer coaching in authentic contexts is one method to enhance controversy and learning. By creating situations where learners experience conflict between their own ideas and the ideas of others, the motivation to resolve this conflict will increase. The formalised application of peer coaching in combination with reflective practices was a strategy used to develop managerial competency in post-graduate business students. This strategy was embedded in authentic contexts, which were real and relevant to the students' business practice.

Application of Peer Coaching and Reflective Practice Methods

Forty three post-graduate business students were involved in this application of peer coaching and reflective practice. Virtually all students were enrolled part-time and had positions in which they were able to exercise managerial and/or leadership skills in authentic situations. Peer coaching and reflective practices were integrated into their units of study. Students were required to establish personal learning objectives that related to the content being studied within the course that were in alignment with their authentic practice situations. This helped to provide structure to the learning experience and provided the peer coaching with a focus whereby they could support their peers more strategically. Learning objectives needed to be clearly stated, with clear resources and strategies outlined to achieve these objectives. Further, an evaluation strategy, along with key performance indicators, was identified to ensure one could measure whether the students were successful in achieving their objectives. Students were also required to maintain a learning journal in which they documented key learning events, problems, challenges and questions that arose as part of their participation in the unit. The learning objectives and journal entries were resources to support the discussion during peer coaching sessions. The peer coaches used this information to structure strategic questions that could be used to develop their peers further in their learning quest.

Students were also required to select a peer coach from within their course and to meet at least once a fortnight, although weekly contact was encouraged. In most cases a face-to-face meeting occurred but in some cases telephone or e-mail was used to maintain contact. The purpose of peer coaching was to discuss progress on learning objectives and to discuss key learning problems faced by the learner in their authentic situation. The coaching was reciprocal with both parties providing support to one another.

All students received a one-hour orientation to the concept of peer coaching and how it applied to their study and development as managers and leaders. Students also received a comprehensive guide on PC (Ladyshewsky, 2001) and directions on how to maintain a learning journal and how to write learning objectives. The duration of the peer coaching relationships ranged from 12 weeks in one subject to 24 weeks in another. All students were required to submit peer coaching reports that focussed on a series of questions (given below):

Questions for the Peer Coaching Report

- Did you achieve your learning objectives?
- How did the peer-coaching experience support you?
- What were some of the positive attributes of your peer coach that supported your development?
- What were some of the negative attributes of your peer coach that interfered with your development?
- Was the peer-coaching experience helpful in processing your critical learning events?
- Did you incorporate the learning journal contents into your peer-coaching sessions?
- Were there any attributes of the peer-coaching experience that were frustrating?

The report, along with their learning objectives and an excerpt from their learning journal formed a component of their overall grade (20 percent). An evaluation component was necessary to ensure that the teaching strategies that were embedded into the curriculum were aligned with the assessment practices for the unit.

A total of 71 peer coaching reports were received from participants providing ample perspectives. The peer coaching reports were entered into a qualitative data management software program for analysis. A series of codes relating to the metacognitive outcomes of the peer coaching and reflective practice experience were developed by the investigators. These were used to evaluate the content of the peer coaching reports. The codes and their associated definitions are described:

Metacognition Codes and Definitions

- **Expansion of knowledge:** coachee gains more knowledge through the dialogue of PC. This can be new knowledge or it can be knowledge that adds value to existing knowledge frameworks. It is constructed from the knowledge base of both parties.

- **Similar perspectives:** where both parties recognise that they have similar perspectives on issues, which serves to solidify knowledge.

- **Access to tacit knowledge:** one party gains knowledge or "know how" by being able to access the tacit knowledge or "know how" of the other party.

- **Verifies knowledge:** a situation where either party experiences a verification of knowledge they already possess.

- **Structured conflict-controversy:** a phenomenon of peer coaching whereby existing knowledge frameworks of both parties are thrown into question. There is evidence of questioning and uncertainty expressed by both parties around a specific knowledge set.

- **Alternative perspectives:** one or both parties gain a different perspective on a common theme from the other party's approach or background.

- **Coach gains more knowledge:** the coach gains more knowledge through the dialogue of PC. This can be a new knowledge or it can be knowledge that adds value to existing knowledge frameworks. It is constructed from the knowledge base of both parties.

The Impact of Peer Coaching and Reflective Practice on Learning

Expansion of knowledge was a positive outcome of the reflective practice and peer coaching curriculum strategies. By actively engaging in a dialogue with another learner about the state of one's own propositional and non-propositional knowledge, the possibility of expanding knowledge became real. Evidence of learners gaining further knowledge from the dialogue of peer coaching was evident in the transcripts of the reports. These were seen as value added aspects of the peer coaching process and enhanced metacognition by allowing students to build upon what they already knew or had learned as part of their formal study. This would facilitate the development of constructs that would inform their future managerial and leadership practice. Some examples illustrating the expansion of knowledge are highlighted below:

There were many more insights that came out of the structured reflective listening process that had not, and may not otherwise have come into awareness, creating ... value for the learner.

Peer coaching has not only resulted in an increase in information and knowledge about things, but also an increase in self-awareness and self-appreciation.

The experience of seeing similar perspectives was another metacognitive benefit that stemmed from the peer coaching experience. Through the process of evaluating one's knowledge base, and seeing that it is a shared view by another credible source, learners could construct knowledge frameworks that informed their practice as a manager and leader. This is an important process of developing mastery. Some examples illustrating how learners felt about discovering similar perspectives are highlighted below:

My peer coach does similar work to what I do (although at a lower level) and she understands my mode of operation.

I found that we were operating at a very similar level and had a lot of values, ideas and attitudes in common.

When working towards developing skill as a manager or leader, gaining insights into the practices of others can be a valuable experience (Bandura, 1997). Bandura discusses the concept of vicarious reinforcement as an important strategy to build competence and to access the tacit knowledge of others. This type of reinforcement occurs by observing the experiences of others and then modifying your own behaviour based upon the outcomes that have been observed. By experiencing the actions of another peer as they elaborate on how they go about solving a problem, the observer can use this experience to build up their own personal networks of knowledge. Having the metacognitive skill to recognise these insights and then to cognitively integrate them into new knowledge is a skill unto itself. Those with the skill will use the tacit knowledge that is being shared to build their own personal managerial or leadership mastery. Examples illustrating moments where access to tacit knowledge emerged are highlighted below (pseudonyms used):

Peer coaching discussions allowed me to gain insights into my own behavior and that of my work colleagues.

The main source of knowledge for this learning objective was from the ex-technical services manager in the region. This person is now in a contract management role although he sometimes assists in reviewing designs. By involving John in the design reviews, I was able to pick up some of the knowledge that he had. The knowledge transfer was both 'explicit' and 'tacit'. The 'explicit' knowledge transfer consisted of John pointing me towards past designs as examples of how things had been done previously. The 'tacit' knowledge related to some good tips on how John approaches design review.

While expanding and strengthening knowledge frameworks to inform manage-rial and leadership practices is important, so too is the verification of existing knowledge. Through the verification of propositional and non-propositional knowledge, learners can generate operational norms for their action. These operational norms are built using knowledge that is known to be true. The verification process is another important metacognitive skill that helps to build mastery. Some examples where learners were able to verify existing knowledge are described below:

John was pleased with the peer coaching I was able to provide as he felt my techniques helped him further explore his current thinking and he gained real value from the sessions.

In general our discussions verified my own feelings, thoughts and findings.

The coaching sessions helped me to clarify various issues and to make connections through discussion.

Cognitive development theory describes the benefits of conflict and controversy during discussion as it encourages learners to explore more deeply the nature of their knowledge frameworks. While the outcome of the conflict-controversy process may vary, it is the process itself that is metacognitively rich as it forces both participants to articulate "what they know," "what they don't know" and to discover "what they didn't even know they didn't even know." Through this dialogue both parties' understanding of the concept under debate is questioned and leads to fundamental shifts in one's perspective. Examples of structured conflict and controversy in action during peer coaching sessions are illustrated below:

By coaching each other through this difficult decision, we provided the necessary support to make a decision and stick with it. It was a true leadership learning experience for both of us.

A fundamental result of our peer coaching has been to encourage a balance between thinking in parallel and in deliberately provoking constructive conflict between us in an effort to further explore possibilities, and this has worked well for us.

On a number of occasions the peer discussions involved heated discussion on some aspects due to differing points of view. This reinforced my own learning experience by allowing me to see that others may have sharply opposing opinions or interpretations of events.

The process of dialoguing around key learning issues may also lead to insights that were not considered before. Access to alternative perspectives through the discussion that is part of peer coaching provides participants with the opportunity to reframe their knowledge. This enriches the metacognitive experience by requiring participants to retrieve what they know and compare and contrast it with what they are hearing in their conversation. Again, discoveries into "what one didn't even know they didn't even know" are a possibility. Examples of where an alternative perspective became apparent and valued are illustrated below:

Through the process of being coached by Jane, I had a major shift in my view on marketing and where it sits philosophically with my future.

By stating the problem in new terms simply, the coachee could see the way forward.

One of the most outstanding spin-offs from the sessions was the experience and information I gained from the other member's learning objectives.

While peer coaching positively benefits both parties, it is often the coachee who receives greater cognitive gains from the process. This has certainly been shown to be evident in research on peer tutoring (Gillies & Ashman, 1995; Griffin & Griffin, 1998). These cognitive gains occur because the tutor must re-organise and explain the material in a way that facilitates the tutee's understanding. In doing so, this leads to a better understanding of the material by the tutor. The same outcome can be seen in peer coaching with the coachee experiencing cognitive gains. The process of coaching requires the coach to evaluate what they know and what they don't know. From a metacognitive perspective, this is a powerful learning experience, as it requires learners to evaluate their knowledge and to manage it actively. This helps to ground knowledge and provides a platform for the building of concepts that inform managerial practice. Examples of this concept are illustrated below:

As a consequence of seeking solutions from the other party, each party has discovered more things for themselves, and about themselves.

To some extent I found the experience of being a peer coach to be more rewarding than being coached myself.

Participants in this authentic learning situation also emphasised the importance of a formal structure to support the reflective practice and peer coaching. An element of formality was needed to ensure the peer coaching sessions were focused and directed toward the achievement of learning outcomes. For example, regular meetings, an agenda, a focus on objectives and journal items, and purposeful communication were all part of the formal process needed to ensure success. They helped to define the scope of each coaching session and helped to keep the focus of the sessions on learning. It was important, therefore, that the course materials be well structured with clear guidelines on how to implement the peer coaching and reflective methods. Some examples illustrating the importance of formal structure are illustrated below:

The need to peer coach in a formal sense dictated that a simple framework should be adopted to obtain the best possible result.

Participants must be given the time to get to know the norms and adapt or adjust accordingly to encourage honest evaluation. A certain amount of ground rules, delegation of tasks must be set to enable equal contribution.

Dyads that did not follow a formal or structured framework during their peer coaching meetings noted that greater attention to this stage of the framework would have improved the process and learning outcomes:

There was a need for us to add a bit more formality to our discussions so that we can identify actions and responsibilities.

Even though the [peer coaching sessions] have been quite informal, we really need to have some structure there.

We may have missed out on opportunities to learn. This could be due to the lack of formality in our reflection and critical thinking on the when and why of our approach.

The personalised learning objectives and learning journals that were used to support the reflective process and peer coaching sessions were an important curricular strategy. Again, participants who employed these strategies fully were able to receive positive outcomes from the learning experience. Attributing marks to these efforts was also important to ensure participants invested an appropriate amount of effort. Examples are illustrated below:

Learning Objectives

John had felt that he had lost focus on this objective, but realized by talking his objectives through with me, how he can now move forward. We engaged and focused on his learning objectives in great depth over time.

An important breakthrough occurred when I asked the coachee, 'what did you hope to learn from your learning objectives and how did you wish to apply those learnings to your work?' ... Connecting the learning objectives in this way provided a break-through, confirmed by the non-verbal clues in her expressions ... without the peer coaching session this may not have occurred ... by the second session the coachee has moved forward enthusiastically with all of her objectives.

Learning Journals

The learning journals tended to provide a good input to the peer coaching sessions and were often the basis for our discussion by sharing what we had learned and forming an opinion on how relevant that information was to our own situation.

The peer coaching, in conjunction with maintaining regular journal entries regarding my development, was a very rewarding experience and was useful in processing my critical learning events.

The reflective practice and peer coaching curriculum strategies were a low cost, low maintenance activity that had great payoffs for the students with respect to their learning in authentic contexts. By providing clear guidelines on how to structure reflective practice and peer coaching and aligning them to the practice of the students in their authentic business contexts, powerful learning outcomes were achieved. Students were able to take their learning from the classroom and extend it into the actual workplace using the curriculum strategies that were embedded in the course. The opportunity to experience and reflect upon learning within the context of an authentic practice situation had positive payoffs for the students. The gains in knowledge, cognition and metacognition were evident.

Conclusion

In this teaching and learning strategy using reflective practice and peer coaching in authentic contexts, participants were able to expand their knowledge base and managerial competency. Participants were able to ground and verify their own knowledge and skills by evaluating them against the propositional and non-propositional frameworks of their peer coach. The structured conflict and controversy and exposure to alternative perspectives heightened learning. Intense debate, argument and disagreement, within an environment of trust and support, encouraged deeper reflection and learning and further grounded what participants did and did not know about their management and leadership skill. These experiences are metacognitively rich in that they require learners to think and plan strategically and to represent their knowledge effectively in ways that permit efficient retrieval. It also provides them with the ability to monitor and consistently evaluate their own managerial and leadership competence.

The road to becoming a more masterful leader and manager is a complex and reflective practice and peer coaching is a tool that can be applied to make the journey more successful. Unlike some of the more technical professions, where black-and-white solutions to problems are perhaps clearer, the manager is often faced with ill-defined problems. The pathway to a "correct" outcome is nebulous and more often than not there are potentially several "solutions." If solutions are reflected upon with adequate metacognitive depth, in a formal and structured manner, these experiences can be used to further build managerial competency.

The peer coaching experience, when applied to a group of post-graduate business students, was able to produce salient outcomes from the perspective of metacognition. Knowledge gains were evident for both participants. As a tool to enhance the development of mastery, peer coaching along with reflective practices such as journaling and objective setting, is a viable strategy that management and leadership programs should consider as part of their curriculum framework.

References

Bandura, A. (1971). *Social learning theory.* New York: General Learning Press.

Bandura, A. (1997). *Self efficacy: The exercise of control.* New York: WH Freeman.

Biehler, R., & Snowman, J. (1997). *Psychology applied to teaching.* Boston: Houghton Mifflin.

Boud, D. (1988). How to help students learn from experience. In C. Cox & C. Ewan (Eds.), *The medical teacher* (2nd ed.) (pp. 68-73). London: Churchill Livingstone.

Damon, W. (1984). Peer education: The untapped potential. *Journal of Applied Developmental Psychology, 5,* 331-343.

Flavell, J. (1979). Metacognition and cognitive monitoring: A new area of cognitive developmental inquiry. *American Psychologist, 34*(10), 906-911.

Foot, H., & Howe, C. (1998). The psycho-educational basis of peer assisted learning. In K. Topping & S. Ehly (Eds.), *Peer assisted learning* (pp. 27-43). London: Lawrence Erlbaum.

Gillies, R., & Ashman, A. (1995). Current developments in peer learning. *Unicorn, 21,* 77-88.

Graham, C. (1996). Conceptual learning processes in physical therapy students. *Physical therapy, 76,* 856-865.

Griffin, M., & Griffin, B. (1998). An investigation of the effects of reciprocal peer tutoring on achievement, self-efficacy, and test anxiety. *Contemporary Educational Psychology, 23,* 298-311.

Higgs, J. (1997). Valuing non-propositional knowledge in clinical reasoning: An educational perspective. *Australian New Zealand Association of Medical Education Bulletin, 24,* 7-15.

Higgs, J., & Titchen, A. (1995a). The nature, generation and verification of knowledge. *Physiotherapy, 81,* 521-530.

Higgs, J., & Titchen, A. (1995b). Propositional, professional and personal knowledge in clinical reasoning. In J. Higgs & M. Jones (Eds.), *Clinical Reasoning in the Health Profession* (pp. 129-146). Oxford, UK: Butterworth-Heinemann Ltd.

Joyce, B., & Weil, M. (1996). *Models of teaching.* Boston: Allan and Bacon.

Ladyshewsky, R. (2001). *Reciprocal PC: A strategy for training and development in professional discipline.* Jamison, ACT: Higher Education Research and Development Society of Australasia.

Nickerson, R., Perkins, D., & Smith, E. (1985). *The teaching of thinking.* Hillsdale, NJ: Lawrence Erlbaum.

Pesut, D., & Herman, J. (1992). Metacognitive skills in diagnostic reasoning: Making the implicit explicit. *Nursing Diagnosis, 3,* 148-154.

Piaget, J. (1977). *The moral judgment of the child.* London: Penguin.

Quinn, R., Faerman, S., Thompson, M., & McGrath, M. (1996). *Becoming a master manager: A competency framework.* New York: John Wiley.

Strohm-Kitchener, K. (1983). Cognition, metacognition and epistemic cognition. *Human Development, 26,* 222-232.

Sullivan, H. (1953). *The interpersonal theory of psychiatry.* New York: Norton.

Vygotsky, L. (1986). *Thought and language.* Cambridge: MIT Press.

Worrell, P. (1990). Metacognition: Implications for instruction in nursing education. *Journal of Nursing Education, 29,* 170-175.

Chapter VI

Creating an Authentic Learning Environment in Economics for MBA Students

Greg Parry, Edith Cowan University, Australia

Clive Reynoldson, Edith Cowan University, Australia

Abstract

This chapter discusses a postgraduate economics program that forms a core part of a Masters of Business Administration (MBA) degree course. The program has been structured so as to create a learning environment in which students construct an understanding of economics through a semester-long, authentic learning task — specifically the development of a competitive strategy for a business in which they have a personal interest. The curriculum, teaching and learning activities and assessment are aligned in such a way that they all contribute to the achievement of this task. The authors have observed that this approach has resulted in greater student engagement and a deeper conceptualisation of the role of economics in business as compared to the traditional approaches to teaching economics in MBA programs.

Introduction

The Exec kept asking me, So What? Why should I learn this? How can we use it? How do you know what you are telling us is true? How can it help us Execs make better decisions? (Maital 1993, p. viii)

In a not altogether tongue-in-cheek parody of the situation faced by economics teachers in modern postgraduate business education, Maital (1993) imagines a world made up of two tribes — the "Exec" and the "Econ." The former seeks rapid access to "useful" knowledge from whomsoever can supply it; the latter, traditionally providers of much of the knowledge required by the Exec, now finds it increasingly difficult to persuade the Exec that this transfer of knowledge is worthwhile. The Econ, although having an interest in retaining the Exec as students, nonetheless, sincerely believes that this transfer of knowledge is beneficial and should continue. Accordingly, the Econ must find new ways of distilling their knowledge and packaging it in a way that appeals to an increasingly sceptical Exec.

This chapter outlines the development of an authentic learning environment for postgraduate (MBA) students which has as its objective that, at the completion of the program, students should feel they "know how," rather than "know what" economics can contribute to the management of business enterprise. Economics is usually included in the MBA curriculum because, along with a number of other disciplines, it is perceived as somehow useful and relevant. However, MBA program designers often see this usefulness as axiomatic rather than something that has to be demonstrated. Traditionally, many students have achieved success in MBA economics programs by demonstrating that they have acquired decontextualised knowledge of economic definitions, models and techniques. Yet questions remain as to the extent to which they engage with (derive deep understanding of) the material they are presented with and are subsequently able to use in the work environment. Along with Maital, the authors have noted an increasing tendency for the Exec to question the time spent on economics in postgraduate business studies. Moreover, we have not been alone in meeting student resistance to the study of a subject that was once regarded as a *sine qua non* of a business education (Maxwell, 2003; Millmow, 2000; Marangos, 2002).

As members of the "Econ tribe," the authors were called upon to meet the challenges posed by the "Exec." Our overall aim has been to respond to the challenge by increasing the perceived relevance of economics for postgraduate business students and making the study of economics seem worthwhile in the sense that it delivers something of lasting usefulness to the students in their day-to-day working lives. Specifically, we have set out to provide a significant authentic component in our economics program and by this means foster student engagement in the learning of economics.

In our program, we require students to select a real-world business enterprise (usually their own or their place of employment, ranging in size from micro-businesses to public companies). We then present them with a progressively enlarging "toolbox" of economic concepts and techniques from which *they* select material that *they* apply to solving the problem of building the enterprise's competitive advantage — perhaps the single most important factor in the life and death of business organisations. The end-point for students is the presentation of a 5,000-word project. Good projects typically consider aspects of the economic environment such as the economic value which their firm is able to add; the characteristics of the market in which it operates; the nature and impact of the driving forces affecting the firm (Porter, 1985); and the extent to which macroeconomic variables such as the business cycle, government policy and exchange rate fluctuations pose risks for the selected strategy. The relevance of this task is at once apparent to students at the outset of their program of study. However, what often surprises them is the extent to which they master concepts and analytical techniques that have a reputation for being difficult and abstruse. Mastery of these concepts and analytical techniques is facilitated by a learning task that is both concrete and practically oriented, and by the motivation provided by "pay-offs" in the form of projects with real-world value. Proof of success is to be found in the quality of these projects, which remain the property of students, and which comprise a lasting source of value and testament to the importance of shifting the study of postgraduate business economics into authentic environments.

The following is an account of how the program outlined above was developed, the pedagogic and economic thinking that has underpinned its development and the program outcomes. The first section discusses the conceptions of learning that have informed our work. That is followed by a discussion of our principal pedagogic device — our own "take" on a well-known integrative approach to the analysis of the economic environment of business enterprise. Finally, we discuss the many and varied student outcomes from the program. In an important sense this economics program remains a "work in progress." The program described below has been five years in the making and has gone through successive iterations. It is still being developed, semester-by-semester since authentic learning environments in economics are, by their very nature, dynamic and always in need of new responses.

Conceptions of Learning

The literature seemed to provide a clear direction in our quest to design an engaging and meaningful program of study. A recurring theme was that we should design the course around a complex, multi-dimensional problem (typical of real-world problems faced by the Exec), yet keep the learning task sufficiently straightforward so that it could be tackled by students using the scaffold of concepts and problem-solving techniques provided by introductory economics.

Our review of the learning literature uncovered a range of conceptions on the learning process held by students (and perhaps by their teachers). Harper and Hedberg (1997) for example, described such a continuum:

- Acquiring and storing of facts, skills and methods for reproduction;
- Relating parts of subject matter to each other and making sense of that relationship; and
- Understanding and interpreting reality in a different way — comprehending the world by reinterpreting knowledge.

Gibbs' (1992) five-level scheme distinguished between surface learning (learning is given knowledge; learning is reproduction for assessment; learning is applying algorithms to problems) and deep learning (learning as making sense by abstracting meaning from the learning experience; and learning enables the student to see the world differently). According to Entwistle and Ramsden (1983) the deep learning approach involves a desire to relate learning to personal experiences outside study, to see it as part of personal development; to seek relationships which help integrate the parts into a whole and to integrate the underlying structure or intention of the whole task. Just what the Econ always knew about economics! Other taxonomies resemble these, for example, the "expert-novice" (Van Sickle, 1992); and Heath's conception of the ideal learner as being a "reasonable adventurer" (cf., Entwistle & Ramsden, 1983, p. 11).

The work of Reeves (1992) and Reeves and Laffey (1999) had considerable impact on our deliberations in establishing a set of "pedagogical dimensions" as the basis for the redesign of this subject (see Table 1).

For us, a rightward shift on each dimension meant "mov[ing] from a sponge view to a view that requires the learner to work actively to understand the evidence they receive from the world and be aware of any framework of process which they apply to its interpretation" (Harper & Hedberg, 1997, p. 3). Entwistle and Ramsden (1983) have something very interesting to say on this point. They argue that a student's motivation and approach to learning is not just a product of

Table 1. Pedagogical dimensions (Based on Reeves, 1992)

Dimension	Continuum
The objectives dimension - what defines important knowledge, concepts and skills in the curriculum?	Highly specific ⇔ generalizable
The pedagogical dimension	Objectivist ⇔ constructivist
The instructor role dimension	Didactic ⇔ facilitative
The teaching/learning activities dimension	Replication ⇔ generation
The motivational dimension	External ⇔ internal
The assessment dimension	Rote memorisation ⇔ authentic problem

personal traits, but is largely a response to a learning situation. This insight focussed our attention on the design of a learning environment and the specification of learning tasks that would create the "right hand" (authentic) learning situation. Much of the literature refers to constructivist learning environments — their characteristics, design and advantages (cf., Oliver, 2001; Jonassen, 2002). According to Oliver (2001), the strengths of a constructivist approach lie in its emphasis on learning as a process of personal understanding and meaning-making. Grabinger (1996) identifies principles that underpin learning in constructivist settings:

- To make learning outcomes transferable, learners need both content and context learning
- Learners are active constructors of knowledge
- Learning is in a constant state of growth and evolution
- Learners bring their own needs and experiences to learning situations
- Learners acquire skills and knowledge within realistic contexts
- Assessment is realistic and holistic

For us, there are significant similarities in descriptions of constructivist pedagogies and descriptions of authentic learning situations. We found support for this idea in the work of a number of authorities. Herrington, Oliver and Stoney (2000), for example, suggest that an authentic learning "must be all-embracing and provide a sustained and complex learning environment that can be explored at length"

(2000, p. 88). Moreover, Biggs (1999) makes the point that what the student does is more important in determining what is learned than what the teacher does. His notion of "constructive alignment" is that each of the components of instructional design should address the same learning agenda and support one another. Lack of alignment, he suggests, undermines achievement of the principal objective, that is, is to create a situation in which students are most likely to embrace a deep approach to their learning.

Economics and Strategic Thinking: An Overview

Having established what the blueprint should look like, we came across the problem of achieving constructive alignment within a framework that was practicable to organise, resource and operate. The conceptual vehicle used to link economic theory and business practice is one familiar to MBA students — strategy and strategic thinking. *Strategic thinking* is a high order, integrative activity which is best taught in a context when the examples are deliberately realistic and rich in information, yet also infused with strong organising conceptual frameworks (in this case, drawn from economics). In the context of business studies, *strategy* has been defined as an idea that links together the functional areas of a firm (or organisation) and relates its activities to its environment. The role of economics in modern strategic thinking is very important.

In the objectivist paradigm, students learn content in order to solve a number of strategic problems or cases provided along the way as examples of how theory can be applied to real-world problems. We decided to reverse the sequence — to use strategic thinking as a way of solving the problem of constructive alignment, that is, to make the task of devising a competitive strategy central to learning about economics. We wanted our students to manage complexity in the way that business practitioners do, except that our students would do this armed with a toolbox of economic ideas and methods to help them in this task. A major project, the parameters of which are established at the outset of the course, creates the authentic environment. Each student is required to devise a medium-term competitive strategy for an enterprise they have selected for study. The choice of enterprise is significant — the enterprise is always of direct interest to students (as employer or prospective employer, as owner, supplier, major competitor, or potential competitor). The project, 5,000 words in extent, remains an open-ended, loose-structured task (because each project enterprise, and each student's visualisation of the project enterprise, is unique). However, we have found that the authenticity and immediate relevance of the project creates a meaningful context for all teaching and learning activities in the program. The project clarifies program objectives and communicates the need for students to "get there," that is, to master economic techniques in order to solve a problem in which they have a real and immediate interest.

Jonassen (2002) says that for students to engage in meaningful learning, they must be able to manipulate the learning environment in some way. To create the "problem manipulation space" in which this could occur, we referred to the many models for strategic thinking that are available (cf., Harding & Long, 1998; Montgomery & Porter, 1991) selecting the well-known "five forces of competition" model (Porter, 1980). The model is based on a conceptualisation of the factors that drive change in competitive markets and to which enterprises must respond in order to build or erode enterprise "competitive advantage." The Porter model proposes that a winning strategy is built on objective assessment of the firm's economic environment. In its simplest form, this model is relatively straightforward to explain, but is capable of substantial refinements.

The Porter model provides a useful problem manipulation space and an ideal "scaffold" for the teaching learning process. Figure 1 illustrates how the model fits into the constructivist learning paradigm.

The Porter model provides the scaffold through which the central topics of a traditional economics curriculum can be developed in an authentic context. In our program it comprises the centrepiece of our teaching and learning framework.

Figure 1. The Porter model as a teaching/learning framework

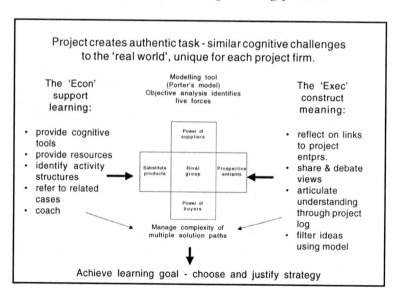

We make important extensions to the model both in the "lead in" and "exit" phases of its application that take it beyond its conventional textbook presentation yet retain its "core message" for students of economics (and strategy). In aggregated form, the model provides a framework for high-level systematic analysis of complex reality — a "cognitive apprenticeship" (Brown, Collins, & Duguid, 1989, p. 32). This is the really interesting part of economics but is difficult to master. In a real sense, the combination of the model and the task creates the curriculum for the student. Our role as instructors then becomes one of leading students through a process of discovery using items from the Econ toolkit.

Of course, this is where elements of a conventional approach creep into the instruction process. It is probably true that many instructors begin their programs with constructivist notions and authentic situations in their head but after a few weeks, fall back to the "old" objectivist teaching patterns. To avoid this possibility, we have consciously worked on creating tasks within tasks, emphasising questions that could themselves be projects to introduce further tools of analysis. Examples of such tasks are shown in Table 2, which also provides some comparisons with topics that might be covered in a more traditional economics course (i.e., what we used to do).

Those who have studied economics will recognise the basic theory of markets; price determination; elasticity; technology, production and costs; market structure; the business cycle; trade theory and growth theory in the sample above. But

Table 2. Authentic and traditional teaching/learning questions

Authentic learning environment – know how	Traditional learning environment – know what
How does my firm add value to the good or service we sell in the market?	What is profit?
What are the characteristics of my rival group?	What are the characteristics of markets?
How can I change my value proposition to improve competitive advantage?	How do I calculate and apply elasticity?
How can I use the cost drivers to improve competitive advantage?	What are my costs?
What are the driving forces at work in my firm's sector?	How do market forces change competitive equilibrium?
What risks may emerge from the external (macroeconomic) environment?	How do business cycles, government policies, fluctuating exchanging rates, globalisation and longer term "creative destruction" affect firms?

the presentation of the theory through the questions in the left column support and re-create the authentic context of student management of the firm and its strategic direction.

To enable collaborative learning and facilitate communication, we instituted a week-by-week progress log — a reflective diary that communicates how individual students have (so far) constructed their meaning. Students complete the log electronically by contributing to an online database module built into a Web-based information system. The reflective nature of learning established by the journal and the project finds us answering questions which are more of the "Where does this fit?" variety then the "What does this mean?" variety — our role as instructors has again shifted towards a more facilitative side.

We have also been encouraged to develop more authentic teaching resources which students can access as they develop understandings. We constructed approximately 20 questions that are similar to those in Table 2, except that they disaggregate the topics a little more. Short video clips, each of 30 or 40 seconds duration, record the responses of business people. The questions (and the answers) are timeless and central to the economics of corporate strategy. We as Econ have not been surprised by any of the answers the real Execs provided. We hoped the video clips would help us to prove that much of the world is, from an economic point of view, a reliable and simple place (and they do). They also help our student Execs to connect with the real world of business and acquire deeper and more authentic knowledge than they may have initially felt that the Econ could provide.

Those readers who have studied economics will know that its principles are typically presented in terms of mathematical and graphical models. Texts on managerial economics, for example, allocate much space to discussion and computations of marginal analysis based on the neoclassical view that the "best" result for any problem will be the point where the marginal benefits to be derived from any course of action are just equal to the marginal costs of carrying out that action. This is not wrong, or far removed from strategic thinking, but when expressed mathematically often tends to confuse rather than enlighten. This problem invited us to apply spreadsheets in an online environment as a rich teaching learning resource. The spreadsheets assist in the construction of understandings because they reduce the manipulation of algorithms and provide answers quickly and accurately. Graphs embedded in each spreadsheet enable students to see how changing parameters such as costs can affect profits, or how price elasticity affects consumer reactions to pricing decisions. We feel the videos and spreadsheet resources go some way to what Jonassen (1991) describes as "learner selectable information." There is no requirement for students to use this information, but it helps students to engage with the material and construct their own models of their chosen business.

Two tests are included in the program, but we have taken steps to ensure that these are aligned with the rest of the program. Test 1, in about Week 7, requires students to characterise and analyse the market in which their project firm is a participant. Test 2, in about Week 11, requires the manipulation of macroeconomic data to interpret the state of the economy and recognise its strategic implications for the project firm. Because the context of each test is the student's chosen firm, answers must reflect more than just the acquisition of information. Both tests are "take home" tests completed over a 36-hour period.

Student Perspectives

As with many postgraduate business study programs, our students are predominantly part-time local students or full-time overseas students based either at our university or offshore. Local students come to us from government departments, government business enterprises and businesses in the small to medium enterprise (SME) sector. In these organisations, they are mainly employed as middle managers or (in the case of SMEs) owner operators/managers. Most overseas students are also in employment but taking time out of their careers to upgrade their qualifications. Regardless of background, students generally study economics as part of a program of generic or professionally-oriented business studies, that is, few if any pursue the subject for its own sake. When asked about their needs, a consistent point made by these students was that knowledge of subject content (particularly in the guise of abstractions such as competing theories and the detailed workings of models) was much less valuable to them than explorations of subject applications (being able to use what was taught). Yet, students expected to experience little of the latter in their studies. Economics had a reputation for being too content driven, and economics textbooks (though claiming to be business-oriented and practical) were seen as lacking in verisimilitude. Over the past five years of its operation, the program has disabused many students of these perceptions. Small-to-medium business owners have used the major project to refocus their businesses using economics as both a handy tool for day-to-day management and a vital input into strategic thinking. Employees in large enterprises have challenged their organisation's "conventional management wisdom" and won respect and opportunities to progress their careers. Persons working in the not-for-profit sector (many of whom in our experience previously dismissed economics as entirely inappropriate to their concerns) have revisualised the operations of their organisations and now regard economics ideas as essential to their survival and development. Overseas students have been thrilled to discover that economic ideas are "portable" and applicable in diverse business environments. Projects have been used to acquire jobs (as convincing items in CVs) and to launch new careers and businesses. There are many individual stories along these lines to report.

The common element in all these stories is the mould-breaking acceptance of truly authentic learning in economics. It is difficult to do this in economics. The discipline has a highly organised body of knowledge, an accepted pedagogy that militates against what it sees as dilution and absence of rigour — and we admit that in some circumstance the traditional approach has much going for it. We do not recommend the approach described here for conventional post-graduate studies in economics leading to careers in the economics profession (to explain why would require another chapter). However, for the large number of post-graduate students who need to acquire what we refer to as economic literacy — the ability to understand basic economic ideas and use them in day-to-day business management — it seems to us that there is no alternative to employing a constructivist teaching methodology embedded in an authentic learning environment.

References

Biggs, J. (1987). *Student approaches to learning and studying: Study process questionnaire manual.* Melbourne: Australian Council for Education Research.

Brown, J.S., Collins, A., & Duguid, P. (1989). Situated cognition and the culture of learning. *Educational Researcher, 18*(1), 32-42.

Entwistle N., & Ramsden, P. (1983). *Understanding student learning.* London. Croon-Helm.

Harding, S., & Long, T. (1998). *MBA Management Models.* Aldershot: Gower.

Harper, B., & Hedberg, J. (1997). Creating motivating interactive learning environments: A constructivist view. *Proceedings of ASCILITE.*

Herrington, J., Oliver, R., & Stoney, S. (2000). Engaging learners in complex, authentic contexts: Instructional design for the web. In M. Wallace, A. Ellis & D. Newton (Eds.), *Proceedings of the Moving Online Conference* (pp. 85-96). Lismore, NSW: Southern Cross University.

Herrington, J., & Oliver, R. (2000). An instructional design framework for authentic learning environments. *Educational Technology Research & Development, 48*(3), 23-48.

Jonassen, D. (2002). *Constructivist learning environments on the web: engaging students in meaningful learning.* Retrieved March 2004, from *http://www.moe.edu.sg/iteducation/edtech/papers/d1.pdf*

Lewis, P., & Norris, K. (1997). Recent changes in enrolments in economics degrees. *Economic Papers, 16*(1), 1-13.

Maital, S. (1994). *Executive economics.* New York: The Free Press.

Marangos, J. (2002). A survey of the value university students place on studying economics. *Economic Papers, 21*(3), 80-93.

Maxwell, P. (2003). The rise and fall of economics in Australian universities. *Economic Papers, 22*(1), 79-92.

Millmow, A. (2000). The state we're in: University economics 1989/1999. *Economic Papers, 19*(4), 43-51.

Montgomery C., & Porter, M.E. (Eds.) (1991). *Strategy.* Boston: Harvard Business School.

Porter, M. (1985). *Competitive advantage.* New York: The Free Press.

Reeves, T. C., & Laffey, J.M. (1999). Design, assessment and evaluation of a problem-based learning environment in undergraduate engineering. *HERDSA, 18*(2), 219-233.

Reeves, T.C. (1992). Effective dimensions of interactive learning systems. *Proceedings of the Information technology for Training and Education, ITTE '92 Conference* (pp. 99-115). Brisbane, Queensland: ITTE.

Van Sickle, R. (1992, Winter). Learning to reason with economics. *Journal of Economic Education,* 56-64.

Chapter VII

Using Characters in Online Simulated Environments to Guide Authentic Tasks

Shirley Agostinho, University of Wollongong, Australia

Abstract

The use of characters to present tasks and critical information in a simulated environment has proven to be a useful strategy in the creation of more authentic learning environments online. Such characters can not only perform the role of setting and structuring tasks within the fictitious scenario, but also that of providing useful and realistic guidance. This chapter describes a learning environment designed to create an authentic context for learning evaluation skills and strategies appropriate to technology-based learning settings. The subject in which this approach was adopted was a masters-level course in evaluation of technology-based learning environments. The chapter focuses on the use of a fictitious CEO (chief executive officer) who requests certain evaluation tasks of "employees." Students are given realistic jobs with realistic parameters, and in this way the subject is dealt with in a much more authentic manner than if presented in a more decontextualised way. The rationale for adopting the approach is described together with a description of how it was implemented and summary findings of an evaluation of the approach.

Context of the Learning Environment

The postgraduate subject *Implementation and Evaluation of Technology-Based Learning* is designed to expose learners to the key concepts and issues in a complex and evolving content domain. Its set objectives mix practical skills development with theoretical perspectives, and the underlying pedagogical approach is to facilitate students' building of their own understanding of the processes and techniques of evaluation, particularly within the context of technology-based products and learning environments. The subject had been offered in on-campus mode for many years, and when it was decided to offer the subject in a fully online mode, a new approach was adopted (cf., Meek & Agostinho, 2003).

In a major revision of the subject, the underpinning constructivist philosophy adopted into the design included such principles as: learning is a process of construction; learning occurs through social construction of meaning; learning is contextually mediated; and reflective thinking is an ultimate goal (e.g., Duffy & Cunningham, 1996; Jonassen, Mayes, & McAleese, 1993).

Focus of the New Approach

The focus of the new approach was to adopt a design that was task-based rather than centred on a pre-determined scope and sequence of content related to evaluation. The subject was presented within a course management environment (WebCT), and many of the inbuilt features of the courseware were utilised, such as the discussion board and chat facilities. A new set of resource material was gathered and structured within the WebCT environment. Activities in all but the first phase led to production of an assessable product. A summary of each phase together with its rationale and the artefact produced by students is presented in Table 1.

Table 1. Five phase delivery plan

Phase	Activity and rationale	Artefact produced
Orientate	Discuss subject objectives, assessment requirements, content, delivery strategy, etc. Trial/test the technology (i.e., online access and tools). Explore initial perceptions about subject content.	• Learner profile stating initial perceptions about the subject content and expectations of the subject (non-assessable) • Company name
Do	Conduct a small usability evaluation (instrument supplied) to foster "learning by doing" to anchor thinking about evaluation issues. Reflect on initial task and propose an alternate approach.	• Usability evaluation results and reflection • Alternate usability evaluation approach and rationale
Explore	Examine other perspectives about evaluation by critiquing several evaluation studies.	• Critique of evaluation studies
Apply	Transfer "theory" into "practice" by writing an evaluation proposal.	• Evaluation proposal
Reflect	Reflect and assess overall understanding of content by constructing a concept map, considering initial perceptions, and reviewing a peer's evaluation proposal.	• Concept map and reflection • Evaluation proposal peer review

In designing the learning environment, two characters were devised to structure and organise phases of student work. A Chief Executive Officer (CEO) and an Academic Advisor (a role taken by the real teacher of the subject) were used to motivate and maintain student engagement, and a scenario of a fictitious evaluation company was used to provide a meaningful context to the learning tasks. To anchor the activities in an authentic environment, students were introduced to the subject by setting the parameters for the fictitious company and by inviting them to suggest a name for the new company (see Figure 1).

After the orientation to the subject, each evaluation task was initiated by distribution of an agenda set by the CEO. Unfortunately, the CEO is always "unable" to present this in person. He/she is somehow always absent in Rio, London, or Paris, lining up the next deal for the company. Instead, directions come in the form of minutes from a strategic meeting held between the CEO and the company recruited academic adviser (see Figure 2). In this way, realistic drivers for action are presented, and the subject moves along with an appropriate "agenda." Whenever a new task is given, the minutes also contain advice in the

Figure 1. An invitation to join the new company

A company has just been created by a "high-flying" CEO. Following the demise of several "dot-com" companies in which he was involved, the CEO identified educational evaluation as the "next big thing." Now, with the help of some venture capital, he needs to build a team to get into a marketplace where there is significant opportunity.

The CEO is looking for highly motivated and enthusiastic people to join the team. He is not concerned if they don't have extensive experience in evaluation because he is prepared to "groom" them as evaluation consultants. They need to demonstrate that they are keen and prepared to put in the hard work in order to make the company viable.

The CEO has many contacts worldwide and has found out ... about a group of "up and coming" evaluation experts - you! The CEO is a great believer in teamwork and he expects you to work together, to share your knowledge and discoveries to cement your collective future. He has placed a "carrot" in front of you all - if you work hard to win the business, there is an opportunity to buy into the company.

The CEO has recruited your lecturer of this subject in the role of "Academic Advisor." Her role has been delineated as follows:

Delegate tasks to you based on the CEO's directions;

Assist you to build-up your knowledge base - your evaluator's toolkit; and

Verify your credentials for the company.

The CEO has stated that his preferred working arrangement is to meet regularly with the Academic Advisor to discuss current world trends, business opportunities and actions to be taken. The minutes from these meetings will outline the actions required from you. These minutes will be distributed to you via the "Company Web Site" (which is the subject Web site).

The first action required is to come up with a name and motto for the company that reflects the ambitious nature of its team!

form of a study guide to give scaffolding and support, and this is always provided by the company's academic adviser. Students are presented with a range of "jobs" required by the company, given in much the same way they would in a real context.

Typically, students would create their assignment responses in a manner in keeping with the task requirements, that is, as a memo or report with covering letter to the CEO. Students were encouraged to adopt these pseudo-roles only in their assignment responses. In all other interaction with their online teacher and each other they did not assume a role, and this was not expected as it might in a true role-play learning design. The final and major task that students completed was an evaluation proposal, not unlike a tender or proposal document that evaluation consultants would submit (based on Reeves & Hedberg, 2003). Again, in the interest of an authentic and polished product, most students completed this proposal by writing as if they were employees of the fictional evaluation company.

Figure 2. Excerpt from initial strategic planning meeting minutes

Company Minutes: Strategic Planning Meeting 1

(Activity details for Week 1)

Date: 12 May

Present: CEO, Academic Advisor

Focus: Doing usability evaluation

Agenda: Present brief for the first company job - A Usability task

Actions required: Complete usability task by 19 May (Task 1)

Details:

The CEO has been busy marketing the potential of the company over the past few weeks and as a result, has managed to secure the company's first job. The CEO has been contacted for assistance by the developers of a prototype Web site. The prototype site is accessible at: http://www.examplesite.au/beta5

The developers have acknowledged that the site has some "issues." They are in need of advice regarding its usability before progressing further with its development. They would like frank and honest feedback from you and have thus stated that you need not be concerned about "offending" them with any of your advice.

The CEO acknowledges that there may be more to "usability" than this form of investigation implies however, this is what the client wants. He also realises that you are new to evaluation. But he is convinced that by leaping straight in and doing an evaluation, you will be able to learn from it. To help you, he has instructed the Academic Advisor to provide you with some guidance by introducing you to the topic of evaluation and directing you to some initial readings on usability. This guidance is provided below: ...

Evaluation

At the time of writing, the revised course has been implemented in four semesters with four different cohorts of students (ranging from 8 to 19 students). In the first implementation, the subject was fully evaluated (cf., Agostinho & Herrington, 2004). Seven of ten students agreed to participate in this evaluation. Six students were interviewed, three students completed a formative questionnaire and five students completed a summative questionnaire. Eight students completed an externally administered teacher survey. The data collected was analysed by using six questions that guided the evaluation as overall themes, and determining the issues that emerged relevant to each theme. These questions were formulated based on the guidance offered by Bain (1999) and Phillips, Bain, McNaught, Rice, and Tripp (2000):

1.   What were the students' perceptions of the use of scenario in this course in terms of facilitating their learning?

2.   What were the students' perceptions of the learning design (that is, the sequence of tasks, the resources provided and the support mechanisms supplied) in terms of facilitating their learning?

3.   Was the online implementation strategy effective in facilitating student learning?

4.   What learning outcomes were achieved?

5.   What were the students' perceptions about their learning experience?

6.   What improvements can be made to this course?

In summary, the evaluation found the majority of participants rated the use of the company scenario and use of characters as effective in facilitating their learning. Two students, however, concluded the scenario did not work for them. For one student, the scenario context was mostly ignored because he had his own authentic environment (his work environment) to which he was transferring what he was learning. For another student, the character roles and the role of the company itself created confusion when completing assessment tasks as she felt that as an employee of a "commercial company" she had a responsibility to "win the business." This caused a conflict for her as she felt she had to propose evaluation solutions that were not as comprehensive as they could be.

An aim of the course design was to facilitate students' construction of their own understanding of the content. Most participants concluded that the nature of the course did encourage them to construct their own understanding of the content. Students rose to the challenge of involvement in a fully online course. The synchronous and asynchronous discussions tools whilst utilised, were not used to the extent the teacher had intended. From the teacher's perspective, all participants in this evaluation achieved the intended learning outcomes as well as a range of unintended learning outcomes. From the students' perspective, the majority of participants felt that they had achieved the intended learning outcomes. Most students rated their learning experience as positive.

Students offered a range of suggestions to improve the course in terms of the tasks and the implementation of the scenario. This is invaluable feedback in reviewing and refining the course for future offerings. Some students, particularly those with a relevant work-related context, needed to be encouraged to engage in the fictitious world that has been created for them in the learning environment yet not take it too seriously. This suggests that the use of scenario could be used more flexibly, to allow students with appropriate real-life contexts to substitute their own evaluation needs while still fulfilling the requirements of the course.

Conclusion

The use of an authentic context, and simulated company and characters, appears to have been a most successful strategy for teaching complex evaluation strategies for technology-base learning environments. Observations and evaluations indicate students generally responded well to the imagined CEO and company driving their activities. The conscious choice to use no graphical cues for the characters, and to keep descriptions of the scenario to a minimum, kept development cost down in the current implementation. From a teacher perspective, this "low-tech" implementation was "doable" and manageable. From a student perspective, this may also have yielded benefits in the scope provided to students to imagine their own CEO. The majority of students who have responded to evaluations of the revised course have deemed it effective. Of more significance, however, is the richness of tasks and interactions that students have contributed, and the overall quality of their products. Most student work was written in-role and was judged of a high quality. A range of unintended learning outcomes has been evidenced, such as students' ability to self-regulate their own learning, their high degree of motivation to participate in the subject and their reflective skills. Overall, the level of student engagement (observed in terms of online activity and quality of assessable work) suggests that the delivery strategy has been successful, effective and enjoyable for both students and teachers.

References

Agostinho, S., & Herrington, J. (2004). An effectiveness evaluation of an online learning environment. In L. Cantoni & C. McLoughlin, (Eds.), *Proceedings of EdMedia 2004: World Conference on Educational Multimedia, Hypermedia & Telecommunications* (pp. 3476-3481). Norfolk, VA: AACE.

Bain, J. (1999). Introduction: Learning centered evaluation of innovation in higher education. *Higher Education Research and Development, 18*(2), 165-172.

Duffy, T.M., & Cunningham, D. J. (1996). Constructivism: Implication for the design and delivery of instruction. In D. H. Jonassen (Ed.), *Handbook of research on educational communications and technology* (pp. 170-198). New York: Macmillan.

Jonassen, D., Mayes, T., & McAleese, R. (1993). A manifesto for a constructivist approach to uses of technology in higher education. In T. M. Duffy, & D. H. Jonassen (Eds.), *Designing environments for constructive learning* (pp. 231-247). Berlin: Springer-Verlag.

Meek, J., & Agostinho, S. (2003). An online subject delivered with help from an 'absent CEO'. In G. Crisp, D. Thiele, I. Scholten, S. Barker & J. Baron (Eds.), *Interact, Integrate, Impact: Proceedings of the 20th Annual Conference of the Australasian Society for Computers in Learning in Tertiary Education* (pp. 658-661). Adelaide: ASCILITE.

Phillips, R., Bain, J., McNaught, C., Rice, M., & Tripp, D. (2000). *Handbook for learning-centred evaluation of computer-facilitated learning projects in higher education.* Retrieved March 2003, from *www.tlc.murdoch.edu.au/archive/cutsd99/handbook/handbook.html*

Reeves, T. C., & Hedberg, J. G. (2003). *Interactive learning systems evaluation.* Englewood Cliffs, NJ: Educational Technology Publications.

Chapter VIII

Constructing a Clinical Experience in the Classroom

Jennifer R. Jamison, Murdoch University, Australia

Abstract

This chapter demonstrates how contemporary chiropractic education uses authentic "classroom" learning opportunities to prepare students for the clinical practice. Safe professional practice requires a combination of factual knowledge and mastery of those thinking processes required to update and selectively utilise fresh information. This chapter demonstrates how three problem-solving formats can be used to aid students achieve both of these learning objectives. The first scenario describes how, by requiring students to formulate a personal nutrition program, they become aware of the impact dietary choices have on health. An example is then provided of how skills acquired in the area of nutrition can be expanded to incorporate the various dimensions of wellness and transferred into a situation in which a wellness program is negotiated with a client. The final scenario explores how simulated cases can be used in the classroom to create a cognitive environment that simulates and prepares students for the clinical consultation.

Introduction

With the restructuring of tertiary education in Australia, vocational courses are now frequently offered as university programs. Unlike vocational education, which has tended to rely on the acquisition of factual knowledge and skills in an apprenticeship type system, traditional university education has focused on abstract learning emphasising conceptual frameworks and underlying principles. While conceptual knowledge is fundamental to the development of a discipline, it does not in itself provide an adequate background for professional practice. Arising from the realisation that activity, concept and culture are interdependent and that understanding must involve all three, it has been suggested that learning, regardless of the method used, should be embedded in an authentic situation (Brown, Collins, & Duguid, 1989). The creation of authentic classroom learning situations would seem an essential pre-requisite to the undergraduate training of professionals who, upon graduation, are required to practice their craft in real-life situations. This is particularly true for those health professions who are not required to complete a supervised internship prior to registration. One such profession is the chiropractic profession.

Chiropractors practice as primary contact practitioners. In addition to providing manual care, chiropractors serve as portals of entry into the health care system. In order to fulfill the latter role, chiropractic students need to acquire and share the general clinical knowledge and skills characteristic of all primary health professionals. They need to competently screen for disease, treat or appropriately refer patients to other health providers, and serve as a health information resource for promoting wellness. The challenge facing chiropractic educators is to offer a training program that meets the specialist chiropractic and "medical" generalist objectives despite being denied ready access to the teaching hospitals and community health centres used by those involved in training medical students. The dilemma is to provide vocationally oriented learning experiences that produce clinically competent self-directed learners using the classroom, student clinics and the occasional practice. One approach to addressing this challenge is to construct problem-based learning formats in authentic learning situations.

Problem-based learning has emerged as a viable alternative to the traditional curriculum. Distlehorst and Robbs (1998) found that students in a problem-based curriculum perform particularly strongly in the clinical situation. Hmelo (1998) found they demonstrated enhanced reasoning skills in applying science-based concepts to their explanations, while Ozuah, Curtis and Stein (2001) — like Khan and Fareed (2001) — found they were more enthusiastic about self-study than lecture-based groups. Such skills are fundamental to continuing self-education. However, as clinical reasoning is based upon factual information there is concern that those in a problem-based curriculum may fail to assimilate sufficient factual information. Research suggests such fears may be groundless (e.g., Khan & Fareed, 2001; Enarson & Cariaga-Lo, 2001). Furthermore, Schmidt and Molen (2001) reported that graduates from a problem-based medical curriculum perceive their ability to work independently, run meetings, cooperate and solve problems as greater than that of conventionally trained colleagues. Problem-based learning would seem to be well suited to vocational education. It would seem to admirably meet the "concept" requirement and, when conducted in authentic learning situations, it is postulated to adequately fulfill the "activity" and "culture" pre-requisite for successful learning. Learning in authentic situations is perceived to provide a psycho-emotional dimension to the intellectually stimulating learning environment achieved by a problem-based approach. Problem solving in authentic learning situations makes experiential learning a classroom teaching option. Although ideally authentic learning occurs in the student or private practitioner's clinic, realistically carefully crafted classroom experiences and community learning experiences can complement, but never replace, this process.

This chapter explores three scenarios in which use of various problem-solving formats in three discrete authentic learning situations prepares students for their future clinical encounters.

Preparing for Clinical Practice in Non-Clinical Locations

Using the notion of the spiral curriculum, three authentic learning experiences are described in which the student progresses from promoting wellness to diagnosing disease, from self-assessment to patient evaluation, from client negotiation to peer consultation.

A Personal Nutritional Health Assignment

Students with a background in chemistry and physiology are eligible to embark on a journey of self-discovery within the framework of a nutritional health care assignment. The nutrition assignment initially takes the form of a problem-orientated learning exercise in which students are provided with information and protocols. They are provided with the information necessary to implement a balanced diet and made aware of globally accepted nutritional recommendations for minimising the risk of chronic disease. They are also provided with a detailed protocol of how to undertake dietary analysis and given access to a computer-based, dietary analysis program. The nutrition assignment requires that the students analyse their usual diet with respect to the Five Food Groups and undertake a detailed nutrient analysis using a weighed dietary approach and computer-based, dietary program. They are then required to compare their usual dietary habits and nutritional intake both with the Australian guidelines for dietary health and with global recommendations for reducing the risk of osteoporosis, heart disease and cancer. Starting from the lowest level of the problem-based learning format continuum described by Harden and Davis (1998), the learning experience then progresses to a higher level at which students are required to undertake problem-solving. The task is transformed into an invaluable psycho-emotional experiential learning exercise by challenging the students to identify and implement dietary modifications that conform to health recommendations. Learners are asked to report on the changes made and indicate how successfully they adhered to their new self-determined dietary changes. Solving the problem of how to modify their diet to meet health guidelines rather than merely gathering nutritional information transforms the learning outcome.

The real-life relevance of this assignment is well demonstrated in the following data. Based upon the Five Food Group analysis from the class of 2000, of the 55 students who completed the assignment 53% ate less than five or more servings of fruit and vegetables daily. This finding is similar to a recent study in which Jamison (2002) found that 50% of Australian chiropractic patients failed to eat five servings of fruit and vegetable daily. In view of the documented health benefits achieved from a diet rich in fruit and vegetables, the Australian recommendation for fruit and vegetable consumption, as reported by Miller, Pollard and Coli (1997) has been increased from the traditional five to seven servings eaten as two pieces of fruit and five average-sized servings of vegetables daily. As only 18% of chiropractic students and 19% of chiropractic patients met this recommendation, the nutrition assignment would seem highly relevant to the student as an individual and a future health professional. The nutrition assignment also is consistent with the principles of good case design in that the content of the nutrition assignment draws on knowledge acquired earlier in the program and invites students to apply this basic science knowledge in a personal and health promoting context. Students are required to interact with the information. By comparing their dietary behaviour with a health standard and applying this information to achieve a desirable health outcome, students actively integrate prior knowledge with new information. The student is provided with an opportunity to apply concepts acquired in their basic science subjects in a context that has immediate relevance to the clinical situation. In fact, not only is the learning experience readily transferred to the clinical setting, the knowledge and skills acquired can be easily modified to meet diverse dietary related clinical problems such as the management of overweight patients. Indeed, students who have personally experienced the challenge of changing dietary behaviour are likely to have an empathetic appreciation of the predicament facing their overweight patients.

Student assessment blends seamlessly with the learning experience in that the assignment constitutes a substantial proportion of the final grade for the subject. Rather than focusing on how successfully proposed changes were implemented, the learning outcome is assessed by evaluating the nature of the dietary changes recommended and how failures to implement intended changes are managed. Almost all students did implement new eating behaviours, however, very few report they had maintained the changes some two years later. This assignment provides students with a first-hand learning experience of how difficult it is to initiate and maintain health-promoting lifestyle changes. It is invaluable in that it offers a learning situation in which students are given the opportunity to develop a genuine understanding of the trials patients may experience in complying with professional admonitions.

The nutrition assignment provides students with a real life experience of the type of difficulties their future patients may be expected to face when asked to comply with their clinical management regimes. It creates a learning environment consistent with the program's objectives. Although providing an opportunity to influence student attitude toward their future patients, the nutritional assignment does not prepare students to interact with others. This task is delayed to the next phase of the program.

A Client Health Promotion Assignment

The health promotion assignment provides an opportunity for students to become more aware of the health needs of others. Students are directed to prepare a health management contract for a "client." They are obligated to approach a "relative stranger" and gain permission to undertake a health status assessment. This problem-initiated learning experience requires that students develop a management plan to reduce their client's risk of disease. This involves undertaking a health risk appraisal with respect to diseases prevalent in the community. Particular attention is given to screening for risk factors associated with ischaemic heart disease, cancer, diabetes and osteoporosis. As the learning experience is designed to expose them to wellness constructs, it also requires that the client be made aware of health actualising behaviours. In practical terms, this means that students need to identify their client's current health status, particularly with respect to lifestyle choices, and compare this to optimal health behaviours. Once the health "needs" of their client have been identified, the student catalogues strategies that may be implemented to meet these needs.

In addition to the intellectual activity of formulating a health promotion plan, important elements of this learning experience are engaging in dialogue with and motivating a client. This interaction captures the nuances of patient/client communication and accurately reflects the wellness consultation of clinical practice. This learning experience is furthermore readily converted to task-based learning by modification of the health management plan into a health management contract. The contract incorporates self-monitoring and motivating features such as deadlines by which particular goals should be accomplished and rewards for successes achieved. The learning contract and client monitoring report are submitted for assessment, both by the examiner and a fellow student. In their evaluation of another's wellness contract, students are advised to emphasise how the initial contract could be improved, that is, marks are allocated for constructive criticism.

The assignment provides a particularly good "clinical" learning opportunity for students during the pre-clinical phase of their chiropractic program. It also creates a learning environment conducive to self-directed learning. The require-ment that students consider various options for health promotion and identify acceptable strategies compatible with their client's lifestyle requires they actively gather and integrate information using resources such as the JamisonHealth Web site (n.d.).

Overall, this discovery learning task provides students with an opportunity to:

- Increase their awareness of the dimensions of wellness as opposed to health as the absence of disease,
- Use and expand their knowledge in a clinically relevant context while still in the pre-clinical phase of their program,
- Experience the reality of interacting with patients,
- Access, evaluate and selectively use health information in a clinically relevant context, and
- Participate in peer review.

Differential Diagnosis of Clinical Problems

While chiropractic students inevitably undertake task-based learning in the clinics when called upon to diagnose and treat patients, such learning is largely restricted to problems with the musculoskeletal system. Preparation for practice at the practitioner-health care system interface requires a broader knowledge base and different interpersonal skills to those previously learned. To meet these needs, a *diagnosis* subject that requires students to work in groups and differentially diagnose disease in students, who take the role of simulated patients, has been devised to create a safe, yet realistic, learning environment.

Students are invited to form groups of four and each student is given the chance to rotate through the role of simulated patient and clinician. A number of "diseases" are allocated. Students then prepare themselves as simulated patients using a standard text (e.g., Jamison, 1999). With only the student in the role of simulated patient being privy to their condition, the group is challenged to make a working diagnosis based on history taking. The provisional diagnosis is then refined and a definitive diagnosis determined by working through a system of "yes" or "no" responses to closed questions about changes detectable on physical examination and laboratory investigation. By selecting a number of related cases for any session, the instructor can embed the total learning experience in a problem-based learning format. The learning experience can be structured so that the student is given the opportunity to generalise their knowledge from case to case and identify shared principles underpinning diagnosis decision making.

Patient-practitioner consultation simulations provide a uniquely instructive format. Simulated case discussions create a learning environment that increases the probability that students will correctly identify early disease states in clinical practice. As diagnosis can lead to intervention that changes the clinical outcome, early detection of disease and appropriate treatment or referral of patients is a fundamental feature of competent primary practice. Simulated cases can be used to expand the students' the clinical experience by providing an opportunity for learners to be exposed to serious conditions rarely seen in chiropractic practice. Preparation as a simulated patient is a particularly useful experience as the learners attempt to "walk in the shoes of the patient." In contrast, learners assuming the clinician role are given an opportunity to experience the benefits of "professional" cooperation and peer case review. By structuring the exercise as a group learning experience, the student is exposed to a peer consultation process. The student discovers the value of conferring with colleagues. This theme is further developed when students are required, as part of their assessment, to advise fellow students on the differential diagnosis and management of one of their clinical cases.

Unlike the first two authentic learning situations described in which the outcome of the learning experience resulted in an assignment that contributed at least 50% of the final grade, this subject/student assessment is independent of the learning scenario. Assessment consists of a multiple choice examination paper based on presentation of various clinical scenarios, preparation of a detailed case study differentially diagnosing a clinic patient and a critique of two case studies prepared by other students. Although not an integral component of the exercise described, student assessment is fundamentally governed by the learning experience. Students reported the learning experience was advantageous, particularly insofar as it made their "book knowledge" more meaningful and enhanced their clinical perspective.

Principles for Developing Authentic Problem-Based Learning Exemplers

Curriculum planning traditionally seeks to expose the learner to a hierarchy of increasing complexity. Knowledge, skills and attitudes can be developed in a sequential fashion in a problem-based learning program, for which an 11-step continuum model has been described by Harden and Davis (1998). Starting from an information-oriented platform, the model evolves into a problem-based approach. In this model of the spiral curriculum, the learning continuum moves from theoretical learning, consistent with providing information in standard lectures or texts, through a variety of problem-based formats to task-based learning in which actions are undertaken as a result of the presenting clinical problem. Learning moves from a theoretical base to managing real-world problems. Between the extremes of theoretical and task-based learning, information processing evolves within a range of problem-based formats along a continuum from problem-oriented, through problem-assisted, problem-solving, problem-focused, problem-based, problem-initiated, problem-centred, and problem-centred discovery to, finally, problem-based learning. Experiential learning supersedes rote learning as students are increasingly challenged to solve problems in a real-world context. Previous learning is increasingly activated in a quest to discover new relationships.

In all cases the nature of student learning appears to be strongly influenced by the quality of the cases presented. The more authentic the clinical problem and the structure of the "classroom" activity, the more effective the learning process. Seven principles of case design that influence the efficacy of problem-based learning have been identified by Dolmans, Snellen-Balendong, Wolfhagen and Van der Vleuten (1997). These are:

- The content of the case should be relevant to the student's prior knowledge,
- The case should contains several cues that stimulate student elaboration,
- A problem relevant to the student's future professional role should be presented,
- Presentation of relevant basic science concepts should be couched in the context of a clinical problem,

- Self-directed learning should be stimulated,
- The learning experience should enhance the student's interest in the subject matter, and
- The case should meet the objectives of the faculty and/or program.

While adhering to good principles of case design ensures authentic content, the learning situation influences the authenticity of the learning context. In the first example, this was provided by the students themselves being required to undertake a lifestyle change. In the second, the focus shifted to changing another, while the third simulated interaction between patient and practitioner, and practitioner and practitioner. A problem-based approach provides a vehicle for acquiring relevant content, and selection of an authentic learning situation offers the opportunity for socio-cultural and psycho-emotional learning. Barrington, Latimer and Prideaux (1997) found students particularly valued the realism, practicality and clinical focus of their new learning format. Chiropractic students made similar comments about the examples discussed in this chapter.

All the learning experiences described have a common theme characterised by the shared objective of providing a student-centred approach in which the problem acts as a stimulus for real-life learning. Using diverse formats in a problem-based learning continuum provides students with disparate and richly varied learning experiences. As Charlin, Mann and Hansen (1998) concluded, student learning consistent with a problem-based learning approach is an active process that activates prior knowledge in a meaningful context and provides opportunities for elaboration or organisation of knowledge. When preparing health professionals for clinical practice, a meaningful context refers not only to the cognitive framework but also to the psycho-social environment of patient-practitioner interaction. When evaluating students, assessment should not be limited to judging subject content, but should also incorporate appraisal of "clinical" performance. Authentic learning environments create both a more memorable learning experience and an appropriate assessment milieu.

Conclusion

This chapter has described different scenarios in which chiropractic students were offered a variety of learning opportunities within a problem-based learning continuum. While the exact nature of the learning experience differs depending on the stage of the program, the learning objective and the subject content, all the formats discussed seek to enable students to assimilate and integrate information in a clinically relevant context. The benefits of this approach, regardless of the problem-based format used, are deep learning characterised by the vocational application of theoretical knowledge, improved integration of previous learning and a greater appreciation of the nuances of interaction in the clinical encounter. Once students overcome the initial concern of taking increased personal responsibility for their learning, many students consider this to be a useful learning approach. Contemporary chiropractic education is less concerned with the accumulation of facts and more with mastering the thinking processes required for updating and competently utilising clinically relevant information. Formulation of authentic learning environments using problem-based learning can significantly contribute to this process.

References

Barrington, D., Latimer, W.K., & Prideaux, D. (1997). Evaluation of a change from traditional case studies to patient-based, problem-based learning: A case study. *Medical Teacher, 19*,104-107.

Brown, J.S., Collins, A., & Duguid, P. (1989). Situated cognition and the culture of learning. *Educational Researcher, 18*(1), 32-42.

Charlin, B., Mann, K., & Hansen, P. (1998). The many faces of problem-based learning: A framework for understanding and comparison. *Medical Teacher, 20*, 323-330.

Distlehorst, L.H., & Robbs, R.S. (1998). A comparison of problem based learning and standard curriculum students: Three years of retrospective data. *Teaching & Learning in Medicine, 10*, 131-137.

Dolmans, D., Snellen-Balendong, H., Wolfhagen, I., & Van der Vleuten, P. (1997). Seven principles of effective case design for problem based learning. *Medical Teacher, 19*, 185-189.

Enarson. C., & Cariaga-Lo. L. (2001). Influence of curriculum type on student performance in the United States Medical Licensing Examination Step 1 and Step 2 exams: Problem-based learning vs. lecture-based curriculum. *Med Educ, 35*(11), 1050-5.

Harden, R.M, & Davis, M.H. (1998). The continuum of problem-based learning. *Medical Teacher, 20*, 317-322.

Herrington, J., & Oliver, R. (2000). An instructional design framework for authentic learning environments. *Educational Technology Research & Development, 48*(3), 23-48.

Hmelo, C.E. (1998). Cognitive consequences of problem-based learning for the early development of medical expertise. *Teaching & Learning in Medicine, 10*, 92-100.

Jamison, J.R. (2002) Fruit and vegetable consumption by chiropractic patients: An Australian case study. *Chiropr J Aust, 32*, 2-6.

Jamison, J.R. (2001). *Maintaining health in primary care: Guidelines for wellness in the 21st century.* Edinburgh: Churchill-Livingstone.

Jamison, J.R. (1999). *Differential diagnosis for primary practice.* Edinburgh: Churchill-Livingstone.

JamisonHealth (n.d.). Retrieved July 2004, from *www.jamisonhealth.com*

Khan. I., & Fareed. A. (2001). Problem-based learning variant: Transition phase for a large institution. *J Pak Med Assoc, 51*(8), 271-274.

Miller, M.R., Pollard, C.M., & Coli, T. (1997). Western Australian Health Department recommendations for fruit and vegetable consumption: How much is enough? *Aust N Z J Public Health, 21*(6), 638-642.

Ozuah, P.O., Curtis, J., & Stein, R.E. (2001). Impact of problem-based learning on residents' self-directed learning. *Arch Pediatr Adolesc Med, 155*(6), 669-672.

Schmidt, H.G., & Molen, H.T. (2001). Self-reported competency ratings of graduates of a problem-based medical curriculum. *Acad Med, 76*(5), 466-468.

Chapter IX

Applying Adult Education Principles to an Undergraduate Subject

Cate Jerram, University of Western Sydney, Australia

Abstract

This chapter is a presentation of an adult educator's experience in teaching computer mediated communication to undergraduate students. An "adult learner" profile is presented and compared to classroom experiences of undergraduate learners. The chapter discusses the application of adult education principles to the reshaping and new delivery and assessment of the subject. It outlines the fundamental changes wrought in the subject to meet adult education standards and approaches, including course program goals, learning outcomes, delivery format, method, and assessment activities. The specific methods applied and the student responses and some startling results are described and discussed. The account does not present a structured research project, and offers no empirical evidence, but is rather a presentation of an experience in "best practice," applying adult education principles of authentic learning to an undergraduate class, and depicting results that challenge a need to research potential for change in undergraduate subject delivery.

Introduction

A common dictum in adult education is that university teaching is *not* adult education. Certainly, the usual university approach to teaching does not reflect adult education research, beliefs or praxis. Despite decades of research regarding the needs of the learner and how to address learner needs (Knowles, 1990; Kolb, 1984; Boud, 1981), universities continue using pretty much the same practices that have formed university teaching praxis since the Middle Ages. Primarily, university teaching assumes that the lecturer "knows everything" and "imparts this knowledge" to the students (Bligh, 2000; Silberman, 1996; Pollio, 1984). It is assumed (unrealistically) that after the student has listened to the expert tell them over two hours a week for several weeks, the student will have "learned" what they "need to know" (Freire, 1986; Bligh, 2000; Knowles, 1978). Again, despite considerable research demonstrating the ineffectiveness of such assessment activities to demonstrate real learning, as opposed to rote "parroting" (Gardner, 1991; Bligh, 2000; Silberman, 1996), university assessment usually requires that students "demonstrate their acquired knowledge" by regurgitating the information given by sitting an exam. Research has also demonstrated a need for "authentic learning environments" and "situated learning" for higher level, lasting and transferable learning to occur (Brown, Collins & Duguid, 1989; Herrington & Oliver, 2000). But although these concepts have been adopted to some extent in adult education, they remain rare in university environments.

Adult learners, typically, are self-motivated learners who bring a background of experiential knowledge to their learning, and have the ability to transfer and apply knowledge. They exhibit a commitment to the requisite work for learning, despite the fact that they often have other commitments (such as work and family). They tend to link learning to meaningful life applications and have an awareness of the political and life-changing ramifications of learning (Kolb, 1984; Brookfield, 1986, 1996; Freire, 1973, 1992). Any experienced university teacher (two weeks' experience would do it) will recognise that this is *not* a characteristic profile for the average undergraduate student. It has been my experience, and that of my colleagues in a number of different universities that, despite their legal status as adults, most university undergraduates have an approach to learning that is in almost direct opposition to the classic "adult learner profile." Discussing this subject with many students over the years in a number of different degree programs, I have regularly received the same response as that quoted to me by a library staff member: "The students tell me that they're not here to learn, they just want to get the qualification that will get them a high-paying job."

After considerable experience as an adult educator, I was unprepared for my first experience of teaching undergraduates. Many of the students had to be "made" to attend classes, to the degree that many of my colleagues included mandatory attendance clauses in their subject outlines. Common staff room anecdotes included stories of how students tried to get out of attending even mandatory classes or handing in assignments. One example was: "Her grandmother died. I'll have to check, but I think that's her 7th grandmother to die this year." Staff who did not make attendance mandatory would report regular occurrences of classroom attendance of ten students out of 120 enrolled, although it must be noted that this is anecdotal, not statistically researched or verified. It was also my experience, and that of my colleagues that many students did not do preparatory reading or voluntary assignments, failed to meet deadlines, and often failed to hand in required work without which they would fail the subject. They often exhibited little apparent motivation to work or study, and many were indifferent to repeated failing grades. Almost all students wanted to be "spoon-fed" but didn't want to have to read or listen to the required "feeding." They frequently demonstrated a reluctance to think — preferring to be told what to "know" — and took a shallow approach to learning (Marton & Säljö, 1976; Cotton, 1995). Many were unable to transfer learning, and having acquired learning in a specific area in one subject, they were unable to repeat the exercise in another subject, not recognising that they already knew how to accomplish it.

Essentially, my first experience teaching undergraduate university students impressed upon me that they wanted me to do their learning for them. Colleagues informed me this was common. I became determined to apply adult education (AE) principles to my decidedly un-adult non-learners in a determined attempt to turn them into adult learners. I did, however, recognise that adult education principles would only have a chance of working if judiciously mixed with some acceptable controls such as mandatory attendance.

The Class

In Spring semester, I was to teach computer mediated communications (CMC) to a class of 84 second and third year undergraduate students. Prior to my arrival, the subject had been taught using the traditional delivery approach of lectures and tutorials with electronic tests and a project as major assessment activities. When I set about reshaping the subject, I did not approach it as a research project, but simply as enacting "best practice" according to my AE training and experience. Consequently this "case study" of the CMC class is limited as a research report, presenting only vignettes of personal experience with no empirical evidence to support the best practice changes made or the results achieved. However, the results of reworking the subject were so striking, it seemed important to report the understandings gained.

I first rewrote the class outline to comply with adult education principles and course program goals. Learning outcomes were formulated. Then delivery format, method, and assessment activities were reshaped to comply with the new primary outcomes. The approach was characterised by the belief that the teacher is not the sole repository of knowledge, but that every member of a class is able to contribute. Involvement workshops were developed in which inhibitions would be overcome and students would have opportunities to develop relationships. The opportunity was provided for students to nominate their desired grades and select their team-members based on commonality of desired grade and workload (Knowles, 1990; Malouf, 1994). Interactive seminars replaced lectures. An iterative process of formative assessment and feedback to develop skills and confidence preceded summative assessments, and learning journals were designed to develop reflective learning and help students develop an awareness of, and control over, their own learning. An electronic *peer help forum* was instituted, in which students asked each other (and answered) any and all questions they had pertaining to the class — from "When is that assignment due again?" to "Does anyone know the source of the communication theory we were discussing in class?" And finally, simulated "real-life" projects became the primary assessment activity. These projects recreated, as much as possible, authentic situations that students would face in their future careers and workplaces, thus providing an authentic learning environment, clear relationship to the goals of the class, and adding to marketable personal employment portfolios.

These changes to the subject delivery and assessment inspired exciting results from an early stage. Students became excited and positive, many exhibiting a totally new belief in their capacities, and undertaking unusually heavy workloads. The pre-selection of desired grade and workloads resulted in unusual harmony in teamwork. There was exceptional quality of output in student projects, with many students exceeding their own expectations and ambitions. Students who historically sat in *Fail* and *Pass* categories achieved *Credit* and *Distinction* quality work as they put in more effort, believing they "could really get more than a Pass this time." They were also encouraged by the conviction that the projects were an authentic reflection of the work they would engage in after graduation, making them more attractive to potential future employers.

An unfortunate repercussion of this success was that, as the university was still committed to a normal curve approach to grading, it became necessary to "raise the bar" so that what was previously a *Distinction*-level standard became the *Pass* level, with extra work required to gain a higher grade. When the subject was re-run, to "raise the bar" in a rational way, all but one of the assessment activities were included as the required assessment activities for a *Pass* mark, with exceptional quality acquiring a *Credit*. To achieve *Distinction* or *High Distinction*, students had to voluntarily undertake an additional essay. Fortunately motivation was still there. Most students achieved the grade they pre-selected, and again there was harmony in teamwork as students grouped according to desired grades. The main assessment activities were very vocationally geared to understanding and application of business, management and information systems skills. The learning journal and essay were the only "academic" assessment activities. As this was a weak point for many students in this degree program, even if they excelled in writing good business reports, few were able to do well in essays or journals, so very few students decided to go for the higher grades.

The Subject: Goals, Outcomes and Course Design

My primary goals in the reworking of the subject were firstly, to motivate the students to believe they could achieve quality work and good grades, then help them acquire the requisite skills to fulfil the belief, and secondly to contribute to their employability. This necessitated a balance of intrinsic and extrinsic motivation (Herzberg, 1966), where a vocational focus was the obvious goal, and any academic achievement was an incidental goal along the path. This was necessary, as many students had openly admitted that they had no desire for academic accomplishment — they were at university solely to gain qualifications that would get them good jobs.

The first step was to clarify the learning objectives, then the assessment activities were aligned with the stated learning objectives so that students recognised the relevance of, and need for, each activity. The most heavily weighted assessment activity was the team project. This was carefully constructed to reflect authentic business tasks. The students had to develop a specification list of the CMC required by a stated business, develop a research proposal, research a shortlist of the CMC "best-fits" available to match their specifications, download, test and report on a "best buy." They then had to extend their knowledge of the chosen product, test it, write a user manual for the program, present a promotional package selling their choice to the whole class, and teach another team how to use the product. The final component was writing a Business Report on the project, including evaluation reports on the conduct, effectiveness and professionalism of their own team. This series of assessment activities added up to 50% of the subject grade. Although the work invested deserves considerably more than 50%, the students undertook the work willingly, with passion, enjoyment and remarkably few traumas.

The reflective learning journals were less popular. A significantly weighted assessment activity, the majority of the students hated it, even when they recognised and acknowledged its value, feeling it required more effort than the value assigned. It had to be written and posted electronically on a weekly basis, and was meant to enable students to reflect on their own individual learning style, growth, recognition of learning transfer, development of understanding in content, process and higher thinking, and their writing skills (academic or business). At the end of four weeks, these were submitted anonymously for peer review, with two to four students reviewing each journal. The journals and their reviews were submitted to the teacher for feedback, and then returned to their authors. The significant factor observable from this process was the huge learning curve accomplished through the process of the peer review. Interestingly, students learned less from the feedback received by peers or teacher than they learned through the act of reviewing. Almost all students had written poor journals themselves, but were able to define with clarity what their peers needed to do to improve their journals to meet the criteria. In the process of defining the objectives and needed improvements for their peers, they learned for themselves.

The final two assessment activities were written. The first was an essay comparing two designated articles about CMC and the second a business report in which each student specified a business of choice, then wrote a "Purchasing Manager's Report to the CEO" specifying computing needs required to adequately meet and upgrade that business' CMC functions. Unlike the team project, this report was to include the underlying IT infrastructure that supports and runs the CMC applications.

Teaching Approach

Such comprehensive and radical changes in learning outcomes and assessment activities required equally comprehensive and radical changes in approach to content and delivery. Classes were designed to facilitate the students' learning and enable them to excel in assessment activities. High on my personal agenda were developing a "life-long learner" attitude, critical personal skills such as motivation to self-directed learning for research, with a tandem development of interdependent learning for teamwork, advancement of academic skills for writing excellence, and some preliminary skills to aid the development of reflective learning. There were still specific CMC content-focused classes such as could be expected in any modern CMC class: basic data communications training, hands-on use of videoconferencing and experiential learning of different types of software.

Other, more unusual lessons included: activity focused workshops for inhibition breaking and team building; mind mapping, presentation skills workshops, essay-planning and writing; algorithms and logic; listening skills; verbal and non-verbal communication; and the development and presentation of personal and PowerPoint presentations. Extensive use was made of WebCT, particularly the bulletin boards, the most important of which was the *Peer Help Forum*. A mandatory subject-specific library research quiz was created with the assistance of library staff to demonstrate to students that they did not know how to use the library effectively, which caused all of them to learn how, enabling them to pass the quiz. Interactive seminars replaced all lectures and tutorials were replaced with labs. Labs were given double time, with the first hour assigned to structured learning and hands-on work, and the second hour specifically free for student group-work — overcoming the difficulties of assembling teams outside class. This timetabling of student project time that other lecturers couldn't claim and team-members couldn't book elsewhere was one of the most popular features of the course.

Attendance was mandatory for all classes. In the first seminar, adult education principles were explained, as were the behavioural norms and standards expected from the students to enable the format to work in a university setting. I emphasised that students were responsible for their own learning, and were expected to research and find their own answers. If unable to do so, they could then turn to friends or refer to the *Peer Help Forum*, and if that failed, approach their tutor during labs. If they were still unsatisfied, they could then turn to me (as lecturer, outside of class) for help as the "last port-of-call." Everything stated in the first seminar was included on a handout and posted electronically on the bulletin board.

Discussion of Findings

Most of the outcomes I intended the students to achieve could be clearly explained as vocational needs to accomplish their life goals. A deep approach to learning (Marton & Säljö, 1976) would save them hours of revision of the same subject basics every semester, and would help them acquire the habit of learning quickly and permanently what was needed on the job. There were, perhaps, too many years of bad study habits behind the students to enable them to truly acquire these attitudinal and behavioural changes in one semester, but they understood the significance and made some efforts toward application of these changes of approach. Critical self-reflection (Kolb, 1984; Boud, 1995) through experiential learning (Boud & Pascoe, 1988) was acknowledged as desirable as the students identified how advantageous experiential learning was for them, although the critical self-reflection was harder to accept and to achieve. To be honest, I don't believe it was achieved by many of the students at all. This was the one area in which work submitted was consistently deficient. There was a tendency toward (and frequent lapsing into) journals as documentation of events. Where reflection was applied it was sometimes critical of others or the subject rather than of self — but *any* self-reflection at all was a significant gain to be valued, and critical self-reflection did emerge periodically, if inconsistently, through the journals. Self-directed learning (SDL) (Stockdale, Fogerson, & Brockett, 2001) came to be appreciated as the students gained confidence in their ability to identify what they needed to learn and how to go about learning it. The development of skills transfer between subjects and from school to "real life" (Ellis, 1965; Taylor, 1998) was recognised as a need very quickly and readily, but the students still found this difficult to access or practice. The reflective journals probably did more to develop this ability than any other tool used. The acquisition and application of critical thinking skills (de Bono, 1994) was another goal somewhat assisted by the learning journals, but mostly unsuccessfully as students made initial attempts, but were discouraged when they found they did not achieve instant change overnight.

Taking personal responsibility for domain-specific knowledge (Craigie, 1996) was accepted immediately. CMC does have an extensive area of domain-specific knowledge, but is identifiably a discipline that develops so rapidly that any domain-specific knowledge acquired is usually obsolete within a year or two. Therefore, the emphasis of the subject is to learn the principles of CMC and the research skills to always be able to learn the current domain-specific knowledge at any given time in their future. This is so obvious that students acknowledge and are grateful for this approach — to the degree that students who would normally avoid any research subject happily acquired fundamental research skills. They were delighted to learn that employers prize this skill.

The vocational focus of students requires that subjects not only equip and prepare them for work, but that they contribute skills and experience that potential employers will recognise as valuable contributions to their work force. To meet these student goals, the subject delivery and assessment reflected many of the components described by Herrington and Oliver (2000, pp. 25-26) as conducive to "authentic learning environments." The project in particular provides *authentic contexts* that reflect the way the knowledge will be used in real life, and *authentic activities*, as the project was work any graduate could well expect to be assigned in the workforce. *Multiple roles and perspectives* were considered, as students had to work through different facets of the work usually undertaken by different staff in the workplace. *Collaborative construction of knowledge* was supported through the teamwork and through the *Peer Help Forum*. The learning journal promotes both *reflection* "to enable abstractions to be formed" and *articulation* "to enable tacit knowledge to be made explicit," although I am not convinced this was successful in either year. The structure of the subject as a whole provided *coaching and scaffolding* by the teacher, as there was an emphasis on self-directed learning with a teacher on call at all times to assist when self-direction was inadequate. *Authentic assessment* of learning was provided through self-, peer-, and teacher-assessment. The only criterion that was not genuinely addressed by the subject delivery is: "Provide access to *expert performances* and the modelling of processes," though the peer review exercise incorporated some elements of this. I have not, at this stage, worked out a means to address this lack, but consider the overall efficacy of the subject thus far to deem it an acceptable candidate for the label "authentic learning environment."

In the first implementation, the *Peer Help Forum* was used regularly for everything from the most trivial to significant searching for help. Students who were quiet in class were frequently comfortable in contributing assertively to the forum, even though postings were not anonymous. In the following year, the forum was used less extensively as, after the workshops, students had formed e-mail networks and used these for the communications that I had intended to facilitate through the more formal forum.

The peer review formative feedback on journals was an important element for eventual success. In the second implementation of the subject, the formative feedback was conducted solely by peer review, eliminating the lecturer review. This was not as effective as it was with the additional feedback from the lecturer, but nevertheless students continued to express amazement at their accomplishment and enjoyment of their learning. In the peer review exercise, learning is acquired through doing, not receiving, the peer reviews. This didn't change, so the exercise was still very valuable, and much tutor-marking time was saved.

Formative assessment and feedback was a tool used throughout the subject. It was most blatantly applied in the submission of journals-to-date half-way through semester for specific review and feedback, allowing students to learn from the process of reviewing as well as from the feedback received, and still leaving half a semester to either change their journal writing from that point on (demonstrating learning in the significant change between "before" and "after" writing) or, if they wished, go back and rewrite the journal from Week 1. However all assessment activities had some degree of formative assessment or feedback before final submission.

All students presented in class every week or, at the least, every second week as any learning material presented by me then had to be discussed, analysed, summarised and a portion reworded to express their own understanding in three to five minute mini-presentations. Other times they had to bring their weekly research results to class, share, analyse, discuss, summarise then prepare for presentation. They received feedback not only on the content of the presentation but also on their presentation skills including selection of material to present, vocal skills, eye contact, poise, and other public speaking skills. At the beginning of semester most students were excessively nervous about public speaking and their presentations were appalling. By the end of semester, they were confident and capable in presentation and were less nervous conducting major presentations for significant marks than they had been presenting un-graded one-minute reviews of their group discussions at the beginning of semester. Because so much of the interactive seminars required group discussion time on shared weekly research and the pulling together of their week's learning for the group mini-presentations, and much of the student lab time was group work during which I was "on call" but not specifically engaged in imparting topical content to the students, I was free during seminars and labs to circulate the classroom. During these times students could submit first drafts of essays, sections of reports, demonstrate on their computers the PowerPoints they were building, the analysis they were conducting, and so forth. They would receive formative feedback during this preparatory time. By the end of semester, no assessment activity that contributed to their final mark was ever a "first off." Almost everything presented had already received feedback and the students were aware that, to a degree, their final summative mark would not only reflect the quality of the finished product, but a component would reflect the degree of applied learning demonstrated in the difference of quality of work from formative feedback to the state of submission for summative assessment.

Learning journals and feedback surveys recorded positive attitudinal and learning reactions to the workshops. All students stated that they enjoyed the workshops, which were predominantly run with "drama games" that worked toward specific goals such as inhibition breaking or team building, although comments such as "we played silly games" were common. These were usually followed, however, by positive comments like, "Now I see why…" as the students realised the many-faceted benefits received. Also receiving much positive comment in survey and journals were the presentation skills workshops, and the opportunities to exercise those skills. Almost every student commented on how they gained in confidence as well as skill, and how important they considered the skills to be for their future employment.

The major project was successful beyond expectation. The User Manuals submitted were mostly of a higher standard than I usually receive with brand-name proprietary software. By the end of semester, most of the PowerPoint-supported speaking presentations were of a standard acceptable in the corporate environment of client or executive presentations. When project teams had to teach their CMC software package to another team, they consistently demonstrated comprehensive competence in their own subject and excellent communication skills in helping their "students" understand and acquire the skills and software packages taught.

Classroom discussions and surveys by "counting raised hands" made it clear that most students had previously experienced miserable team projects for a variety of reasons, but team-review evaluations, journals and surveys expressed gratitude and praise for unusually successful teamwork projects in CMC. There were two exceptions to these harmonious teams in the first year. In one, a "social loafer" placed himself in the "want an HD" category to be with the only person he knew in the room, and the other was a self-selecting HD group member with major ego problems. Apart from these two exceptions, the self-selection means of matching groups by pre-determined grades successfully teamed together students who had agreed-upon visions for the degree of work they wished to invest for the grade they wished to achieve. Teamwork was harmonious, social loafing minimised, a majority of "pass-average" students aimed for a *Credit* rather than a *Pass*, and with so many students aiming for *Credit*, many "accidentally" achieved *Distinctions*. In the second year, the creation of an "extra-work" means of achieving *Distinction* partially eliminated this, but the other beneficial effects were still the same.

Because of the format of the class, particularly the inhibition-breaking workshops at the beginning of semester and the interactive nature of the seminars, each time the class was run there was a degree of coherence and collaboration within the classroom that a number of students commented upon as "unusual." One of the consequences of this coherence was the consistency of improved results and positive feedback from the students across the whole class. Although there was individual improvement and growth demonstrated in individual student work and apparent in even the most poorly written learning journals, there was a collective growth and improvement in the class as a body. This subject drew students from 12 different degree programs, but clusters of students came from Bachelor of Information Systems and three other closely related programs. In subsequent semesters some of these students would return to tell me that they found they had continued applying some of the aspects of their CMC classes in other classes with fellow students who had also taken CMC.

The results were positive in the first year, but the cost was high in terms of time and money. There was also disapproval from university authorities for having grade results that defied the normal curve. I was told that in future, I would not be allowed such a high percentage of *Distinctions* and *Credits* for a single class. Nor would I be permitted such heavy costs in casual assistants for tutoring and marking. So in the following year, I removed the lecturer feedback component from the journals and reduced marking time significantly without affecting quality of delivery too severely. Splitting *Pass* and *Credit* work from *Distinction* work also reduced marking, as less than ten percent of the students undertook the additional work. This also met requirements to lower the grades for the subject to something equivalent to a normal curve, as even exceptional quality work did not rate *Distinctions* unless the additional work was also undertaken and produced with high quality. Many students now commented that the workload seemed excessive for the attainable grades, but few seriously complained, as they were still very happy with the subject, their learning and their grades.

Conclusion

Although two experiences are not enough to make absolute claims, the results are encouraging. In the first run, the subject structure achieved excellent results but at great cost in time and money. Minor changes in the subsequent implementation did not appreciably affect the results, but did reduce time, money and an over-abundance of *Distinction* grades. Primarily, however, a valid claim can be made that adult education principles can reasonably be applied to a university undergraduate setting, resulting in an authentic learning environment that can significantly increase student learning and enjoyment, and stimulate in the students a genuine interest in life-long learning and vocational pursuits.

References

Australian National Training Authority. (1995). *Participant's workbook for workplace training.* Melbourne: Australian Council for Training Resources & Curriculum.

Bligh, D. (2000). *What's the use of lectures?* San Francisco: Jossey-Bass.

Boud, D. (Ed.). (1981). *Developing student autonomy in learning.* London: Kogan Press.

Brookfield, S.D. (1986). *Understanding and facilitating adult learning: A comprehensive analysis of principles and effective practices.* San Francisco: Jossey-Bass.

Brown, J.S., Collins, A., & Duguid, P. (1989b). Situated cognition and the culture of learning. *Educational Researcher, 18*(1), 32-42.

Cotton, J. (1995). *The theory of learning.* London: Kogan Page.

DeBono, E. (1999). *New thinking for the new millennium.* London: Viking.

Ellis, H. (1965). *The transfer of learning.* New York: Macmillan.

Entwistle, N.J. (1988). *Styles of learning & teaching: An integrated outline of educational psychology for students, teachers and lecturers.* London: David Fulton.

Freire, P. (1974). *Cultural action for freedom.* MA: C. Nicholls & Co.

Freire, P. (1998). *Teachers as cultural workers, letters to those who dare to teach.* Boulder, CO: Westview Press.

Gardner, H. (1993). *Multiple intelligences: The theory in practice.* New York: Basic Books.

Herrington, J., & Oliver, R. (2000). An instructional design framework for authentic learning environments. *Educational Technology Research and Development, 48*(3), 23-48.

Herzberg, F. (1966). *Work and the nature of man.* Cleveland, OH: World Publishing.

Knowles, M.S. (1990). *The adult learner: A neglected species.* Houston, TX: Gulf Publishing.

Kolb, D.A. (1984). *Experiential learning: Experience as the source of learning and development.* NJ: Prentice-Hall.

Marton, F., & Säljö, R. (1976). On qualitative differences in learning 1: Outcome and process. *British Journal of Educational Psychology, 46,* 4-11.

Malouf, D. (1994). *How to teach adults in a fun and exciting way.* Chatswood, Sydney: Business & Professional Publishing.

Pollio, H.R. (1984). What students think about and do in college lecture classes. *Teaching-Learning Issues.* No 53. Knoxville, TN: Learning Research Center, University of Tennessee.

Silberman, M. (1996). *Active Learning: 101 strategies to teach any subject.* Needham Heights: Allyn & Bacon.

Stockdale, S., Fogerson, D., & Brockett, R. (2001). *Revitalizing the study of self-directed adult learning. AERC proceedings 2001.* Retrieved January 28, 2002, from *http://www.edst.educ.ubc.ca/aerc/2001/2001stockdale.htm*

Taylor, E.W. (1998). *The theory and practice of transformative learning: A critical review.* Columbus, OH: ERIC Clearinghouse.

Chapter X

Using Related Cases to Support Authentic Project Activities

Sue Bennett, University of Wollongong, Australia

Abstract

This chapter describes the design of a technology-supported learning environment in which small teams of students worked on authentic project tasks to develop a multimedia product for a real client. The students were enrolled in an advanced-level subject offered in a postgraduate education program, with most studying part-time, and many located a distance from the main campus. Jonassen's (1999) model for a constructivist learning environment was used as the framework for the design of the subject. A key feature of this approach is the use of related cases to support authentic project activities. The specifics of the design were informed by the research and conceptual literature, and by pilot testing with two class groups. The implementation of the subject was the focus of a qualitative case study that investigated learners' experiences of the environment. A rich set of data was collected, including student assignment work, discussion records and interviews. Analysis of the data provided insights into the role of the cases in supporting the collaborative project work.

Introduction

The gap between the knowledge and skills gained through formal learning and their application in real-life has long been of concern to educators (Dewey, 1938; Whitehead, 1929). Preparation for the world of work involves not only developing an understanding of the knowledge base of a discipline, but also how it relates to real-world practice. Furthermore, changes to the nature of work mean that roles and tasks are less narrowly defined than they once were, leaving traditional approaches to education inadequate for preparing students for the modern workplace (Berryman, 1993).

Engaging learners in authentic activities of the kind that reflect the ways in which knowledge and skills are used in the real world offers a means to bridge this gap between theory and practice. The rationale for authentic activities comes from the belief that knowledge is context-dependent, and therefore should be acquired in realistic contexts (Duffy & Cunningham, 1996). The aim of an authentic task is to encourage learners to "think like practitioners" as they face cognitive challenges similar to those experienced in the work environment (Savery & Duffy, 1995). Authenticity is not inherent in a task, but comes from its real-world relevance (Honebein, Duffy, & Fishman, 1993), and the context within which the activity is set should reflect as much as possible of the characteristics and complexity of the real-world setting (Barab & Duffy, 2000).

Case-based learning has been suggested as one instructional strategy that might be used to support authentic activities. Duffy and Cunningham (1996) proposed that case materials be used as a stimulus for problem-solving activities in a particular domain, similar to the approach used in medicine (see Barrows, 1994). By analysing the cases learners would come to understand the conditional application of knowledge within its context of use (Jonassen, Mayes, & McAleese, 1993). Jonassen (1999) extended these ideas, proposing a model of a constructivist learning environment in which related cases are incorporated to support learners as they solve a problem or work on a project. Such cases present solutions to past problems that can compensate for learners' lack of experience, and help them develop an understanding of concepts and strategies that might be useful in similar situations.

This chapter describes how Jonassen's (1999) model was used as the framework for an advanced-level subject that aimed to develop learners' skills in instructional design. The next sections describe the design and implementation of the subject, including its theoretical underpinnings; an overview of the research study into learners' experiences of the subject; and a summary of the key outcomes for learners.

The Learning Design

The Learning Context

The learning design described in this chapter involved the redevelopment of an existing subject in which student teams designed CD-based multimedia products to meet the educational or training needs of real clients. The teams were required to prepare a design statement that detailed their proposed solution and then develop a prototype that demonstrated key features of the product, seeking feedback from their client throughout the process. This task sought to mimic characteristics of a real-life instructional design problem, and to provide students with an opportunity to take on the roles and responsibilities typical of members of a multimedia design team.

Instructional design problems by their very nature are complex and ill-structured, being influenced by a diversity of interconnected factors that vary from one circumstance to another (Jonassen, 1997). Such problems cannot be solved using well-defined rules or models (Goel & Pirolli, 1988). Instead the designer must be able to assess the specifics of the situation and select the most appropriate solution, applying different approaches in different contexts (Visscher-Voerman, Gustafson, & Plomp, 1999). Experienced designers do this by drawing on their knowledge of theory in conjunction with their experience of past problems (Le Maistre & Weston, 1996). Being able to work in collaboration with others is also an essential skill required by an instructional designer, as many projects involve working in multi-disciplinary teams in which each member brings a different perspective and set of skills (Blum, 1995).

Traditionally, the preparation of instructional designers has combined conceptual and technical coursework subjects, and project experiences. This, however, does not always provide graduates with the contextual knowledge they need when faced with their first real project in the workplace (Milheim, 1996; Rowland, Fixl, & Yung, 1992). The integration of cases into instructional design courses has been suggested as a way to "bridge the gap between the complex reality of the design world and the design principles taught at university" (Ertmer & Russell, 1995, p. 25). A variety of case-based methods have been developed to provide instructional design students with access to a greater array of settings and problems than they might experience through project work or internships (Ertmer & Quinn, 1999; Julian, Kinzie & Larsen, 2000). These approaches have focused on the analysis of written cases as a stimulus for discussion or problem-solving.

While there is only a limited body of research literature on the effectiveness of case-based learning, a long history of use has resulted in a wealth of conceptual and anecdotal reports based on the practical application of various case-based methods (Carlson, Quintero, & Karp, 1998; Ertmer & Dillon, 1998; Morine-Dershimer, 1996). The two most commonly cited reasons for using a case approach are to develop professional expertise by involving learners in complex, job-related situations, and to help learners understand the relationship between theory and practice (Lynn, 1999). It is thought that by analysing and interpreting cases learners develop a range of skills that allow them to: diagnose particular problem situations; identify the range of issues relevant to a specific context; make decisions and develop solutions; and formulate principles for handling future situations (Knirk, 1991; Stolovitch & Keeps, 1991). Practitioners and designers of case materials across a range of disciplines emphasise the role of case-based learning for supporting higher-level objectives such as judging, evaluating and problem-solving.

The redevelopment of the subject discussed in this chapter built on these ideas in seeking to enhance the learning experience through the integration of cases with a collaborative project activity. This required the design of a learning environment and sequence of activities that drew together the essential characteristics of a real-life design project and gave students the opportunity to build on the conceptual and technical knowledge they had developed in prerequisite subjects.

Design of the Learning Environment

Jonassen (1999) described a model for a learning environment based on constructivist principles, which provides a framework for using cases to support authentic activities. The model centres on a focal learning activity, which may be a project, problem or case the learner must solve or resolve. These should be authentic activities that reflect the tasks undertaken by real-world practitioners in the discipline. For this subject the focal activity was the collaborative project task described above. The model also provides guidelines on the range of resources and tools that learners will need to support them in their task. Table 1 explains the role of each element of the model and describes its implementation in the learning environment developed for this subject.

The creation of suitable case materials was a significant part of the subject's redevelopment. The aim was to present cases that would illustrate the nature of multimedia design problems as ill-structured and ill-defined. With this consideration, the design of the materials was informed by three guiding principles: (1) the cases should present realistic situations that reflected real-world practice (Stolovitch & Keeps, 1991); (2) the cases should incorporate multiple perspec-

Table 1. Resources and tools provided

Role of element in model	Implementation in learning design
Related cases describe solutions to past problems similar in nature to the focal challenge, which learners can adapt to their own task.	The materials included richly detailed case materials that described two real-life design projects from inception to completion, from the perspectives of the key designers.
Information resources help learners to develop an understanding of concepts and principles relevant to their task.	Information resources included suggested readings from the conceptual and research literature, technical documentation, and templates and examples.
Cognitive tools assist learners to represent the problem, represent their knowledge and ideas, and/or automate low-level tasks.	Software tools were made available to assist learners represent their project ideas with text and graphics using concept mapping and storyboarding techniques, and to help them organise content.
Conversation and collaboration tools allow learners to share their ideas and interpretations, and aid group negotiation and organisation.	Asynchronous and synchronous online tools supported interpersonal, small group and whole class communication. Server space was available to all groups for file exchange and storage.
Social/contextual supports are tailored to suit the physical, social, cultural, organisational and technical characteristics of the learning context.	Face-to-face sessions and access to computer labs and meeting rooms provided social support. Sessions were tailored to the particular needs of the project teams.

tives and preserve complexity (Spiro & Jehng, 1990); and (3) the cases should provide richly-detailed information to encourage exploration (Shulman, 1996).

Two cases were developed, describing in detail the development of *Exploring the Nardoo* and *StageStruck* — educational CD-ROM products developed at the University of Wollongong (see Harper, Hedberg, & Wright, 2000 for more detail). Each case traces the project from its initiation through to completion. The materials include interviews with the key designers, original design documents, product reviews and research papers, prototypes and mock-ups, and the final CD-ROM product. This provides learners with a rich set of resources that they can explore to discover the multiple perspectives and the range of issues that are part of a real-life project. As such the cases serve to illustrate the ambiguities and contingencies inherent in the real world of design and development.

Technology supports played an important role in the learning environment. A key consideration was providing access the types of technology tools used by real-life designers to carry out their work. This included the kinds of software packages used to design and develop a project, and also to communicate with other team members and coordinate production tasks. Asynchronous and synchronous online communication tools were vital as nearly all of the students in the class studied part-time and many were located away from the main campus in Wollongong. These tools also allowed students to maintain contact with the rest of the class group between the four class meetings held over the semester. Web-authoring tools were used to create the case materials. This allowed the creation of a rich set of multimedia materials that included text, graphics and video, which was larger and more diverse than could be delivered in print form only. The use of hypertext links throughout allowed simple presentation and easy navigation through the large number of files.

Design of the Learning Sequence

Jonassen's (1999) model highlights the importance of activities that support learners in their analysis and exploration of the problem situation, the articulation of their solution, and later reflection on the final outcomes. These ideas were incorporated into the learning design for this subject as a three-stage sequence as represented in the diagram below (Figure 1).

Figure 1. Representation of the learning sequence

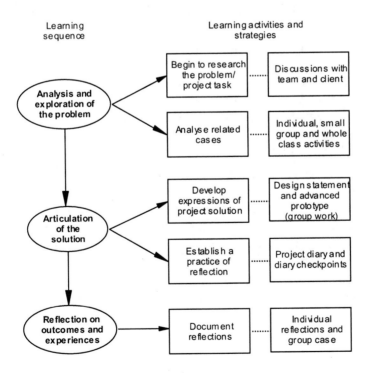

At the first class meeting students form project teams, and choose a project from the options offered by the instructor or those suggested by class members. Eligible projects are those that involve a real client needing a solution to an education or training problem. This process encourages students to develop ownership over their projects (Honebein et al., 1993).

The students then start to explore their project problems through discussions with the client and amongst the team, and negotiating the distribution of roles and responsibilities amongst team members. At the same time students begin to analyse the cases and prepare individual responses to a series of analysis questions. This is followed by small group discussion of the cases conducted in the project teams at the next class meeting, and then a full class discussion of the major issues. This process encourages learners to develop their own interpretations of the specifics of the situations presented (Christensen, 1987; Hazard, 1992). This understanding is developed further through discussion activities that encourage learners to share their ideas about the cases and bring them into contact with alternative views (Carlson et al., 1998; Levin, 1995). The analysis activities also encourage learners to relate their understanding of the cases to their own experiences, concepts from the literature and their own team's project problem. These activities help learners to move beyond the confines of the case contexts to consider issues more broadly (Miller & Kantrov, 1998).

In the second phase of the learning sequence, students concentrate on their collaborative project tasks. This begins with the preparation of a design statement that describes their proposed solution and then requires the development of an advanced prototype that demonstrates their design ideas. By working as a team with a client on a realistic design problem students encounter design and management issues relevant to their project. It is through these activities that learners face cognitive challenges similar to those present in the real-world context (Savery & Duffy, 1995). Learners are also encouraged to keep a project journal and contribute brief progress reports, called diary checkpoints, to the class discussion forum. This helps to establish a practice of reflection and continues the sharing of ideas.

Through the activities in the final phase of the sequence, learners evaluate and reflect on the outcomes of their projects and their experiences in two ways. They first prepare an individual response to a series of focus questions, and then develop a case that "tells the story" of the project in collaboration with the other members of the team. These two activities encourage learners to develop their own account of the project and negotiate a shared meaning. The activities also encourage learners to reflect on alternative approaches and lessons they have learned that might be of use in future situations (Schön, 1987).

The design of the learning environment and sequence were refined through a process of pilot testing with two classes prior to full implementation. A more detailed description of the learning design can be found in Bennett (2002).

The Research Study

An in-depth investigation of learners' experiences of the subject was conducted using a qualitative case study approach, which was appropriate for capturing the complexity inherent in the real-life context, and focussing on the perspective of the participants (Glesne & Peshkin, 1992; Stake, 1995; Yin, 1994). A rich data set was collected, comprising student assignment work, discussion list transcripts, class observation notes, student interviews, instructor comments and the researcher's reflections. The composition of the student teams participating in the study and a brief description of their projects is provided in Table 2. Pseudonyms have been used to maintain anonymity.

Outcomes for Learners

The case analysis activity undertaken at the beginning of the subject was designed to prepare students for the collaborative project work. By reading and writing about the real-life cases provided, the students would build on their existing knowledge of multimedia design and development, and reflect on their own prior experiences.

Table 2. Participants and their projects

Participants	Project
Group A Kath, Lynn, Margaret & Steve	A CD-ROM training package about stock management and promotion for franchisees of a national dairy food company.
Group B Anna, Ian, Sheryl & Barbara	A CD-ROM training package for heavy vehicle drivers on the safe transport of dangerous goods, developed for an international manufacturing and resources company.
Group C Joanne, Liz, Rod & Simon	An educational CD-ROM package to support secondary school visual arts students, developed for the local art gallery.

Comments made by the students in their individual analysis assignments revealed that the cases raised their awareness about teamwork issues. For example, establishing good communication and working in separate locations were two common challenges to team work projects identified by the students:

The role of teamwork is important in the development of any multimedia product. This was particularly evident in the development of Exploring the Nardoo. Coming to grips with the crucial issues at the time involved much discussion. The division of tasks that followed on from these meetings required an effective team. The move made by the designers into a common space, produced an effective team, as it allowed for continuous communication between members. [Steve]

The cases were also effective in putting some of the subject readings into context, with many of the students making links between issues in the cases and concepts they had encountered in the literature:

According to Phillips (1998) the most important thing is not to assume anything, as experience shows that when problems have occurred in projects, it is often that a team member has assumed that they knew what was required. This was highlighted in StageStruck. Although this situation was alluded to in Nardoo, each of the members realised that they had to work for the good of the team. [Lynn]

Students also reflected on their previous experiences of working in project teams, and compared these to the cases:

Although never having worked in such a large team as this, I can see parallels between the StageStruck process and my own experiences as a designer. As part of a small training team just starting out in the development of multimedia, the issue of external versus in-house skill is a familiar one. In our situation we lacked the necessary skills in certain areas and needed to look outside the organisation. We did this with mixed results. [Rod]

Analysis of the individual assignments revealed diversity in the perspectives, interpretations and interests of the individual students. This was apparent from the range of design, process and management issues the students identified as relevant from the cases, their discussions of the complexity and interplay between issues and their comments on the consequences of these for the project teams. In their analyses the students summarised and interpreted the detail provided in the cases, offering their own conclusions about the case events. Learners also identified key lessons they considered important and some were able to derive general principles from these, for example:

It is important to effectively communicate with other team members and to keep them up-to-date. Failure to do this could result in the delay of completing your project. Precious time would be wasted and deadlines not met when members don't have a full concept of project. It would be a costly experience and a waste of resources. [Joanne]

At the small group discussion stage, students shared their ideas and considered how issues raised by the case projects might be relevant to their own team's project. Teamwork issues featured prominently, and this discussion led some teams to develop strategies they would apply to their projects, for example:

Our recent experience with articles and in lectures and class influenced our ideas about management of the project... Our discussion of roles, project management issues and our consideration of the operation of the StageStruck project, and the decision to adopt a weekly reporting format are examples of this. [Group B case]

When the team-based discussions were finished, the class reconvened and each group shared their conclusions about the issues they had identified as important. In this forum teams had to explain the issues within the context of their projects, and this served to illustrate some of the similarities and differences across the groups. Learners were again exposed to alternative perspectives and this provided an opportunity to further consolidate their understanding of some of the issues, and to broaden the discussion to consider them more generally.

In the project phase, teams had the opportunity to put some of their ideas from the cases into practice. This was evident in the protocols teams developed for communicating and working together. However, an increased awareness of the potential problems and the development of proactive strategies were not sufficient for the project teams to avoid difficulties altogether. At this stage the cases often helped students understand the significance of unanticipated issues:

Another challenge reported in the case studies was management of resources. Initially I did not feel we would have this issue, as we were dealing with a much smaller development and therefore fewer resources. I was therefore surprised to find that we experienced the same issue as the StageStruck team encountered — in having a large resource management task. [Sheryl]

The reflective phase again provided opportunities for learners to make links with the cases, and to reconsider some of the issues in light of their own project experiences. In evaluating and critiquing their own projects they commented on similarities and differences, using the cases as a point of reference to "the real world." This served to illustrate some of the limitations of the "authentic" project experience, but also to demonstrate some its realism, for example:

Because of StageStruck's '2 team' approach (Sydney and Wollongong) they faced the challenge of keeping both groups heading in the same direction — something they admit did not always happen. On a much smaller scale and to a minor extent, there were instances in our group where individuals had missed a meeting or had not picked up an important point and were working on what they thought was the requirement only to find that were off the track. [Rod]

The results of the study show that the individual and collaborative case analysis activities were effective in orienting learners to the context of project task and providing a common ground for discussion. This supported learners in their exploration of the project problems and helped teams to negotiate protocols for collaboration. Furthermore, the case provided a credible point of comparison between the student team projects and real-life practice, which helped learners make sense of their experiences.

Conclusion

This chapter describes a learning design based on the use of richly detailed cases to support collaborative project activities. The learning design used Jonassen's (1999) model of a constructivist learning environment as its foundation, and incorporated a sequence of individual and group activities that provided insights into multimedia design and development through the perspectives of practitioners from the field and through personal experience. The learning outcomes achieved by students show that this enabled learners to develop an understanding of the specifics of the cases through their own interpretations and their discussions with other students. They were also able to develop a broader appreciation of the issues through their own project experiences by using the cases as a point of reference to real-world practice. While this chapter discusses the implementation of a particular learning design with a particular group of students, aspects of the approach could be applied to many other situations in which authentic activities are used to introduce students to the world of practice in a discipline.

Acknowledgments

The research described here was conducted as part of the author's doctoral study and she would like to acknowledge the support of her supervisors Professors Barry Harper and John Hedberg, and the funding provided by an Australian Postgraduate Award.

References

Barab, S.A., & Duffy, T. (2000). From practice fields to communities of practice. In D. H. Jonassen & S. M. Land (Eds.), *Theoretical foundations of learning environments* (pp. 25-55). Mahwah, NJ: Lawrence Erlbaum.

Barrows, H. (1994). *Practice-based learning: Problem-based learning applied to medical education.* Springfield, IL: Southern Illinois University School of Medicine.

Bennett, S. (2002). *Learning about design in context: An investigation of learners' interpretations and use of real-life cases design to supported authentic activities within a constructivist learning environment.* Unpublished doctoral thesis, University of Wollongong.

Berryman, S. E. (1993). Learning for the workplace. In L. Darling-Hammond (Ed.), *Review of research in education* (pp. 343-401). Washington, DC: American Educational Research Association.

Blum, B. (1995). *Interactive media: Essentials for success.* Emeryville, CA: Ziff-Davis Press.

Carlson, H. L., Quintero, E., & Karp, J. (1998). Interdisciplinary in-service at the university: A participatory model for professional development. *Teaching in Higher Education, 3*(1), 63-78.

Christensen, C.R. (1987). *Teaching and the case method.* Boston: Harvard Business School.

Dewey, J. (1938). *Experience and education.* New York: Macmillan.

Duffy, T.M., & Cunningham, D.J. (1996). Constructivism: Implications for the design and delivery of instruction. In D. H. Jonassen (Ed.), *Handbook of research for educational communications and technology.* New York: Macmillan Library Reference.

Ertmer, P.A., & Dillon, D.R. (1998). "Shooting in the dark" versus "Breaking it down": Understanding students' approaches to case-based instruction. *Qualitative Studies in Education, 11*(4), 605-622.

Ertmer, P.A., & Quinn, J. (1999). *The ID casebook: Case studies in instructional design.* Upper Saddle River, NJ: Prentice Hall.

Ertmer, P.A., & Russell, J D. (1995). Using case studies to enhance instructional design education. *Educational Technology, 35*(4), 23-31.

Glesne, C., & Peshkin, A. (1992). *Becoming qualitative researchers: An introduction.* New York: Longman.

Grabinger, S. (1996). Rich environments for active learning. In D. H. Jonassen (Ed.), *Handbook of research for educational communications and technology* (pp. 665-692). New York: Macmillan Library Reference.

Goel, V., & Pirolli, P. (1988). *Motivating the notion of generic design with information processing theory: The design problem space.* Berkeley, CA: California University, School of Education.

Harper, B., Hedberg, J. G., & Wright, R. (2000). Who benefits from virtuality? *Computers and Education, 34*(3-4), 163-176.

Hazard, H. (1992). *Teaching, learning and the case method* (MINT, No 7, INT). Copenhagen, Denmark: Copenhagen Business School.

Honebein, P. C., Duffy, T. M., & Fishman, B. J. (1993) Constructivism and the design of learning environments: Context and authentic activities for learning. In T. M. Duffy, J. Lowyck & D. H. Jonassen (Eds.), *Designing environments for constructive learning* (pp. 87-108). Berlin: Springer-Verlag.

Jonassen, D. H. (1997). Instructional design models for well-structured and ill-structured problem-solving learning outcomes. *Educational Technology Research and Development, 45*(1), 65-94.

Jonassen, D. (1999). Designing constructivist learning environments. In C. M. Reigeluth (Ed.), *Instructional theories and models* (2nd ed.) (pp. 215-239). Mahwah, NJ: Lawrence Erlbaum.

Jonassen, D., Mayes, T., & McAleese, A. (1993). A manifesto for a constructivist approach to uses of technology in higher education. In T. M. Duffy, J.

Lowyck & D. H. Jonassen (Eds.), *Designing environments for constructive learning* (pp. 231-247). Berlin: Springer-Verlag.

Julian, M.F., Kinzie, M.B., & Larsen, V.A. (2000). Compelling case experiences: Performance, practice and application for emerging instructional designers. *Performance Improvement Quarterly, 13*(3), 164-201.

Knirk, F.G. (1991). Case materials: Research and practice. *Performance Improvement Quarterly, 4*(1), 73-81.

Le Maistre, K., & Weston, C. (1996). The priorities established among data sources when instructional designers revise written materials. *Educational Technology Research and Development, 44*(1), 61-70.

Levin, B. (1995). Using the case method in teacher education: The role of discussion and experience in teacher's thinking about cases. *Teacher Education and Training, 11*, 63-79.

Lynn, L.E. (1999). *Teaching and learning with cases: A guidebook.* Chappaqua, NY: Chatham House.

Merriam, S.B. (1998). *Qualitative research and case study applications in education.* San Francisco: Jossey-Bass.

Milheim, W.D. (1996). Utilizing case studies for teaching effective instructional design principles. *International Journal of Instructional Media, 23*(1), 23-30.

Miller, B., & Kantrov, I. (1998). *A guide to facilitating cases in education.* Portsmouth, NH: Heinemann.

Morine-Dershimer, G. (1996). What's in a case — and what comes out? In J. A. Colbert, P. Desberg & K. Trimble (Eds.), *The case for education: Contemporary approaches for using case methods* (pp. 99-123). Boston: Allyn and Bacon.

Phillips, R. (Ed.). (1998). *Interactive multimedia design.* London: Kogan Page.

Rowland, G., Fixl, A., & Yung, K. (1992). Educating the reflective designer. *Educational Technology, 32*(12), 36-44.

Savery, J.R., & Duffy, T.M. (1995). Problem based learning: An instructional model and its constructivist framework. *Education Technology, 35*(5), 31-58.

Schön, D.A. (1987). *Educating the reflective practitioner.* San Francisco: Jossey-Bass.

Shulman, J.H. (1996). Tender feelings, hidden thoughts: Confronting bias, innocence, and racism through case discussions. In J. A. Colbert, P. Desberg, & K. Trimble (Eds.), *The case for education: Contemporary approaches for using case methods* (pp. 137-158). Boston: Allyn and Bacon.

Spiro, R., & Jehng, J. (1990). Cognitive flexibility and hypertext: Theory and technology for the nonlinear and multidimensional transversal of complex subject matter. In D. Nix & R. Spiro (Eds.), *Cognition, education and multimedia: Exploring ideas in high technology* (pp. 163-205). Hillsdale, NJ: Lawrence Erlbaum.

Stake, R.E. (1995). *The art of case study research.* Thousand Oaks, CA: Sage.

Stolovitch, H.D., & Keeps, E. (1991). Selecting and writing case studies for improving human performance. *Performance Improvement Quarterly, 4*(1), 43-54.

Whitehead, A.N. (1992). *The aims of education and other essays.* New York: Macmillan.

Visscher-Voerman, I., Gustafson, K., & Plomp, T. (1999). Educational design and development: An overview of paradigms. In J. van den Akker, R. M. Branch, K. Gustafson, N. Nieveen & T. Plomp (Eds.), *Design approaches and tools in education and training* (pp. 15-28). Dordrecht, The Netherlands: Kluwer Academic Publishers.

Yin, R.K. (1994). *Case study research: Design and methods.* Thousand Oaks, CA: Sage.

Chapter XI

Online
Classroom Simulation:
Using a Virtual Classroom
to Support Pre-Service
Teacher Thinking

Brian Ferry, University of Wollongong, Australia

Lisa Kervin, University of Wollongong, Australia

Sarah Puglisi, University of Wollongong, Australia

Brian Cambourne, University of Wollongong, Australia

Jan Turbill, University of Wollongong, Australia

David Jonassen, University of Missouri, USA

John Hedberg, Macquarie University, Australia

Abstract

Research consistently shows that traditional preservice teacher preparation programs are not adequately preparing beginning teachers for the reality of classrooms. The purpose of this chapter is to describe the development and implementation of an online classroom simulation designed to develop pre-service teachers' decision-making skills within the context of young children's literacy education. The classroom simulation allows the user to take on the role of the teacher of a virtual kindergarten classroom (ages five to six years). During the simulation the user makes decisions about the organisation of teaching and learning experiences, classroom management, and responses to individual students. The user is able to monitor and track the progress of three targeted students throughout the course of the simulation. An embedded tool, what we refer to as the "thinking space," has been developed to enable the user to plan and justify new decisions and reflect upon the consequences of previous decisions.

Introduction

For several decades researchers have consistently acknowledged that traditional pre-service teacher preparation programs do not adequately prepare beginning teachers for the reality of modern classrooms (Cusworth & Whiting, 1994; Blackwell, Futrell, & Imig, 2003; Reynolds, 1995). Various small-scale innovations have been suggested, however, one key factor that emerges from the research is the quality of classroom experience during practicum (Ramsay, 2000). Often this factor is more closely controlled in small-scale innovations where supervising teachers and classroom experiences are more carefully selected. The challenge for teacher educators is to reproduce such a quality experience on a larger scale.

The purpose of this chapter is threefold. We describe the development of an online classroom simulation and how we think this can add value to the practicum experience; the specific design features of the prototype version of the software; and our research into our initial trial of this software with pre-service teachers.

The classroom simulation prototype allows the user to take on the role of the teacher of a virtual kindergarten classroom. During the simulation the user is required to make decisions about organising the lesson, classroom management, and responses to individual students. The user is able to monitor and track the progress of three targeted students throughout the course of the simulation. An embedded tool, referred to as the "thinking space," has been used to encourage the user to plan and justify new decisions, reflect upon the consequences of previous decisions and above all, have the opportunity to "think like a teacher."

Development of an Online Simulation to Support Teacher Education

Reviews of teacher education within an Australian context indicate that traditional preparation programs are often not adequately preparing our graduate students for the teaching profession, specifically the reality of classrooms. In fact, between the period of 2000 and 2002 there were three important state and federally funded reviews, all of which highlighted some vital considerations for teacher educators (Department of Education, Science and Training, 2002; Ramsay, 2000; Vinson, 2001). Some of the areas of consideration identified in these reports included: student discipline, motivating students, dealing with individual learning needs, organisation of class work, assessing student work, and relationships with parents and the induction of pre-service teachers into the teaching workforce. When interviewed, final year pre-service teachers claim that they leave the university feeling inadequately prepared for professional practice and often uncertain about what will confront them when they arrive at schools (Armour & Booth, 1999; Cambourne, Kiggins, & Ferry, 2003). Schools that employ recent graduates support such claims and further assert that most recent graduates are often unaware of how classroom cultures operate and find it difficult to transfer what they've studied at the university into effective classroom practice (Ministerial Advisory Council on the Quality of Teaching, 1998).

Hoban (2002) claimed that teacher education courses often represent a fragmented view of learning. He argued that this has enormous potential to hinder the development of pre-service teachers into flexible, progressive practitioners. It is understood that many recent graduates find it difficult to deal with life in the classroom, as they are often unable to retrieve essential knowledge when they need it most (Danielson, 1996; Entwhistle, Entwhistle, & Tait, 1993; Kervin & Turbill, 2003; Stronge, 2002). Our reviews of the literature consistently identify the transfer of knowledge about curriculum and pedagogy to the classroom as areas of concern (Brown, Doecke, & Loughran, 1997; Fieman-Nemser, 2001; Lang, 1999).

Ramsay's (2000) review of teacher education in New South Wales strongly recommended that pre-service teachers receive quality classroom-based experience supervised by an accredited teacher mentor. However, the provision of more extensive classroom-based experience does not guarantee quality experience. Darling-Hammond (1999) and Ramsay (2000) both conceded that school-based practical experience often consists of a series of isolated, decontextualised lessons prepared and implemented according to the requirements of the supervising teacher; and at worst can be an unsupported and disillusioning experience.

Experienced researchers such as Groundwater-Smith, Deer, Sharp and March (1996) and Cambourne et al. (2003) have claimed that pre-service teacher learning is enhanced when pre-service teachers regularly participate in the complex decision-making processes that teachers typically make in classroom settings. In an ideal world pre-service teachers would have unlimited access to quality classroom episodes that progressively develop their classroom practice. However, the cost of the practicum experience, school needs, school availability and university course requirements place limits on access.

Lack of regular access to quality classroom experiences (Ramsay, 2000) frustrates both teacher educators and pre-service teachers. It is recognised that the initial years of a teacher education program are critical for pre-service teachers to develop fundamental understandings about their future work of teachers. Other ways of providing personal experience with classroom-based teaching episodes are needed. We believe that one approach is to make use of online classroom-based simulations.

Gredler (2004, p. 573) defines simulations as having the potential to represent "social reality" as the user is able to "take a bona fide role, address the issues, threats, or problems arising in the simulation, and experience the effects of one's decisions." Furthermore, simulations can support the user's learning as they incorporate feedback and advice, through devices such as an online mentor teacher, and the opportunity to pause or repeat a lesson and explore alternative decisions. In a real classroom once a lesson is taught the exact context cannot be re-created, but a simulation can do this. Whilst we acknowledge that a simulation is only a representation of real life, there are features that can enhance the real-life experience. For example, simulations can provide authentic and relevant scenarios making use of pressure situations that tap users' emotions and requires them to act (Aldrich, 2004).

Simulations can allow the user to see the consequences of the complex decisions teachers make in managing learning environments. We believe that this medium can support the pre-service teacher as a learner to enter "into an intellectual partnership with the computer" (Jonassen, 1996, p. 4). In particular, a simulation has the potential to engage the user in making decisions about student behaviour, classroom organisation and learning decisions and the impact of these decisions upon individual and collective student learning outcomes. Furthermore, users are able to get close to the teacher's and the student's experience within the learning environment and this allows users to understand how teachers and students feel their way, cognitively and emotionally through a learning task (Brookfield, 1995). In fact, simulations can "bridge the gap between the classroom and the real world by providing experience with complex, evolving problems" (Gredler, 2004, p. 573).

The pedagogical focus of the simulation described in this chapter is on the teaching of literacy skills in lower primary schools. These skills are considered one of the keys to success in schooling (Cambourne, 2000; Comber et al., 2001) and from our experiences, are often too abstract for pre-service teachers to understand without being meaningfully linked to actual classroom examples. Teachers of children in the early years of primary schooling need to provide appropriate sequences of learning experiences that develop reading and writing skills (Purcell-Gates, 1995) with explicit teaching in language and literacy (Martello, 2002, p. 48). It is also important that beginning teachers understand the impact of classroom discourse on student learning (Gee, 2000). The simulation is designed to improve pre-service teacher understanding of how students acquire and develop literacy skills in lower primary school classes. It combines the four main categories of teacher learning: technical (skill emphasis); inquiry-based (process emphasis); collaboration; and reflection. It makes use of research data on how exemplar teachers facilitate learning and behaviour management within primary classroom settings, in particular during the teaching of reading, writing and spelling (Freebody & Luke, 1990). As such, the simulation also works as a tool to "…reveal student misconceptions and understandings" (Gredler, 2004, p. 573) about the issues presented which can then facilitate and be the catalyst for subsequent learning.

Simulations as learning environments have a long history of use in education and training (Grabinger, 1996). However, there is only "…sketch anecdotal evidence or personal impressions" reported on such use (Gredler, 2004, p. 576). We acknowledge that over the past decade simulations have become increasingly popular for creating realistic digital environments that closely replicate the world and the workplace. Research and development in virtual reality and simulation engines have led to the release of some popular simulation games, such as the Sim series that includes SimEarth, SimCity and the Sims (Mangis, 2002). By manipulating these simulated environments users learn how to manage complex tasks situated in virtual environments. Some critics such as Tripp (1993, p. 75) assert that computer-based simulations based on a situated learning model are of limited educational value because "true expertise is learned by being exposed to experts." However, Jonassen (2000) argued that computer-based simulations can be powerful vehicles for learning by applying the critical characteristics of the traditional apprenticeship and his research with business simulations supports this assertion.

Studies into the complex learning situations presented in video games and other simulations by researchers such as Gee (2000), Gredler (2004), Jonassen, (1997) and Reigeluth and Schwartz (1989) have identified various overlapping learning principles that share four common features. First, they involved socially shared intellectual work that is organised to achieve a task. Second, they contain elements of the traditional apprenticeship process (described by Lave &

Wenger, 1991) that encourage student observation and comment, make explicit much of the know-how acquired, and permit the participation of the relatively unskilled players. Third, they are organised around strategies needed to acquire a particular body of knowledge. Fourth, the process of playing a simulation or video game is focused on the individual, but makes use of a learning group to support decisions and provide reflection. These features emphasise inquiry, skill development, collaboration and reflection (Tan, Turgeon, & Jonassen, 2001).

Limited research has been conducted on simulations in teacher education. However, recent educational software advances have demonstrated that simulations are powerful tools for analysing, designing and operating complex systems. Such a simulation has the capabilities to enable users to test hypotheses around teaching practice in a safe environment and provide a method for evaluating these decisions. The simulation should also be capable of communicating some of the learning events that occur in classrooms. Harper, Hedberg, Corderoy and Wright (2000) claim that it is feasible to create communication tools that allow users to view the effects of their decisions from multiple perspectives. The structure of our simulation incorporates feedback and advice through a device called a "thinking space." It also provides the opportunity to repeat a lesson and explore alternative decisions. Usually this is not feasible, nor practical in traditional modes of classroom experience for pre-service teachers.

Significance of This Research

This project addresses a gap in the research on educational simulations and specifically focuses on their potential to develop learners' understanding of complex situations. The key feature of an educational simulation is that it makes use of a model to represent a process, event or phenomena that has some learning significance. Most simulations are based on models that are static in the sense that they have been pre-programmed to respond to inputs from users. The learning environment developed for this research uses computer-mediated communication tools to create an illusion of a simulation that is dynamic and evolving, reflecting the true nature of classrooms. It was recognised that online communication and thinking tools could support real world decision-making as the learners participated in classroom scenarios in which events evolved and required a series of complex teacher interventions. As the pre-service teacher gains in both experience and confidence, the levels of complexity can be increased.

The simulation is designed to allow users to fully participate or to be an observer from the boundary engaging in what Lave and Wegner (1991) call "legitimate peripheral participation." This process allows the neophyte to progressively piece together the culture of the group and to understand what it means to be a classroom teacher. Over time the user will move from the role of observer to a fully functioning agent in the simulation. Thus, the simulation represents an authentic context that reflects the way that the knowledge of a teacher is used in real life (Brown, Collins & Duguid, 1989).

Herrington and Oliver (2000) propose that many researchers and teachers accept that well designed multimedia environments provide viable alternatives to the real-life setting provided they do not sacrifice the authentic context. Their review of the literature identified nine design elements of situated learning environments: the provision of authentic contexts that reflect the way that knowledge is used in real life; authentic activities; access to expert performance or advice; multiple roles and perspectives; support for the collaborative construction of knowledge; reflection so that abstractions and generalisations can be formed; tools that enable tacit knowledge to be clearly articulated; scaffoldings and coaching by the teacher at critical times; and authentic assessment of learning within the tasks.

This study builds on the research of Herrington and Oliver (2000), and Herrington, Oliver and Reeves (2003), by investigating how the design elements they identified in an online simulation could be operationalised. It extends their work by incorporating the research on simulations and video games.

Design of the Simulation

Gredler (2004, p. 579) identifies two key questions for designers of simulations:

1.   Does the simulation meet the criteria for the type of exercise?
2.   What is the purpose of the simulation?

The simulation follows a diagnostic design as the user is asked to take the professional role of the teacher and make decisions based on problems and situations encountered by the teacher. The user is presented with a kindergarten class (five- to six-year-olds) consisting of 26 students. The initial screen (Figure 1) presents both the situation and the purpose of the user's interaction in his or her role as the virtual teacher.

Figure 1. Introductory screen (screen design by Sprout Media: www.sproutmedia.com.au)

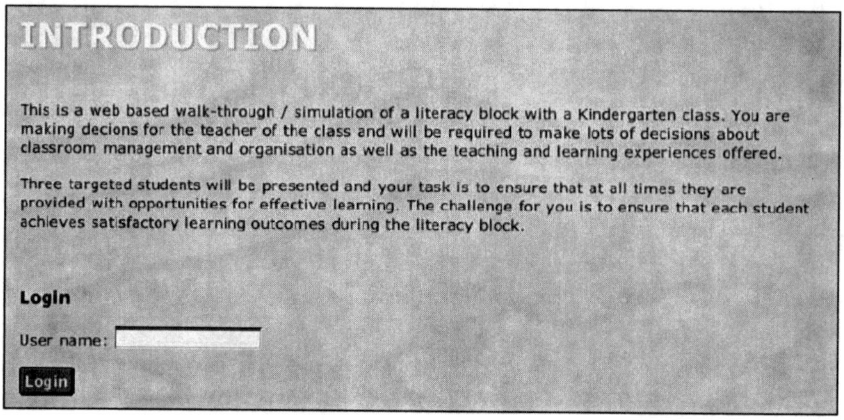

INTRODUCTION

This is a web based walk-through / simulation of a literacy block with a Kindergarten class. You are making decions for the teacher of the class and will be required to make lots of decisions about classroom management and organisation as well as the teaching and learning experiences offered.

Three targeted students will be presented and your task is to ensure that at all times they are provided with opportunities for effective learning. The challenge for you is to ensure that each student achieves satisfactory learning outcomes during the literacy block.

Login

User name: [   ]

[Login]

The Cycles

Recognising the problem-solving nature of classroom life, the user is then required to make a series of decisions about the management of the classroom, of students and of random events that typically occur during a lesson. At other times they will be required to make decisions about the sequence of teaching, for example: do they begin a lesson with a sequencing episode, or a modelled reading episode, or a modelled writing episode, or a retelling of a familiar story episode? Each of these decisions has the potential to impact on subsequent decisions in each of these described areas.

As the users make decisions about the management of the classroom and how they will organise their teaching and learning experiences, the simulation allows access to a branching cycle, representative of a slice of time within the whole teaching period. Each cycle that the users engage with, presents them with decisions related to that specific cycle. Care has been taken to ensure that a number of alternate cycles can lead to similar student outcomes. This reinforces the notion that there can be several suitable approaches to specific student learning needs.

The cycles incorporated within this simulation focus on the concept of the days of the week within literacy-based learning and teaching experiences — we believe this is a typical learning experience in a kindergarten classroom. The cycles within the simulation have been organised as listed in Box A.

Box A.

Management Decisions	Teaching and Learning Decisions
The organization of the classroom	Sequencing episode
The start of the day	Modelled reading episode
The late arrival of a student	Modelled writing episode
Random decisions	Retell of a familiar story episode

Targeted Students

Three targeted students have been represented in the simulation, based on our own classroom teaching experiences and research. A general description of the three targeted students follows.

Bibi is a refugee child from Afghanistan. She has been in Australia for two months, one month of which was spent in a detention centre. She has limited English and listens intently to the teacher. Bibi has a friend, Mary, who has also been built into the simulation story. The user is faced with a number of decisions relating to this relationship.

Harley is medicated for Attention Deficit Hyperactivity Disorder (ADHD). He finds the classroom situation difficult and he is frequently not engaged during classroom lessons. If he is not medicated he tends to distract and annoy other children. The teacher is aware that Harley is being bullied by Gavin and as such the situation is being monitored.

Figure 2 shows how the information about Gavin is presented in the form of teacher notes to the user. The notes are based on the type of notes that teachers typically keep. It is designed to add authenticity to the simulation.

Gavin has significant behavioural problems and as such a classroom teaching assistant has been employed for 20 hours per week to support Gavin in the classroom. The teacher has negotiated a behaviour contract with Gavin and his parents (although his parents are not supportive of this). The user has access to this contract throughout the simulation. Gavin often finds classroom tasks difficult.

A key feature of the simulation is the ability to track the learning of the three targeted students. Throughout each cycle there are opportunities for the user to pause the simulation and view the impact of the users teaching and classroom management decisions on each of the targeted students. These are viewed when

Figure 2. Teacher notes (screen design by Sprout Media www.sproutmedia.com.au)

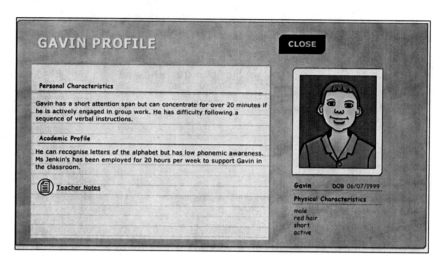

users select the student update button (individual buttons for each of the three targeted students have been developed). The updates have been organised according to the New South Wales (NSW) model of pedagogy (DET, 2003) and as such provide feedback on "Intellectual Quality," "Quality Learning Environment" and "Significance." The DET (2003, p. 5) describes each of these dimensions.

Intellectual Quality refers to pedagogy focused on producing deep understanding of important, substantiative concepts, skills and ideas ... Quality Learning Environment refers to pedagogy that creates classrooms where students and teachers work productively in an environment clearly focused on learning ... Significance refers to pedagogy that helps make learning more meaningful and important to students.

At these points a sliding scale is available for the user to plot the expected performance of the targeted students as identified in the model of pedagogy. Written feedback is presented according to these criteria so users can compare their predictions to that of a panel of experts. Once the user has made their predictions they are able to select a button entitled "see what the experts think." At this time, they will be presented with the plotting of an "expert" for that student at that time. In addition, artefacts may be available to further illustrate student performance. Figure 3 shows an example of the teacher's thinking about the sequencing episode and predictions about how Gavin will respond to this. The

Figure 3. Sample of student update within sequencing cycle according to NSW Pedagogy Model (screen design by Sprout Media www.sproutmedia.com.au)

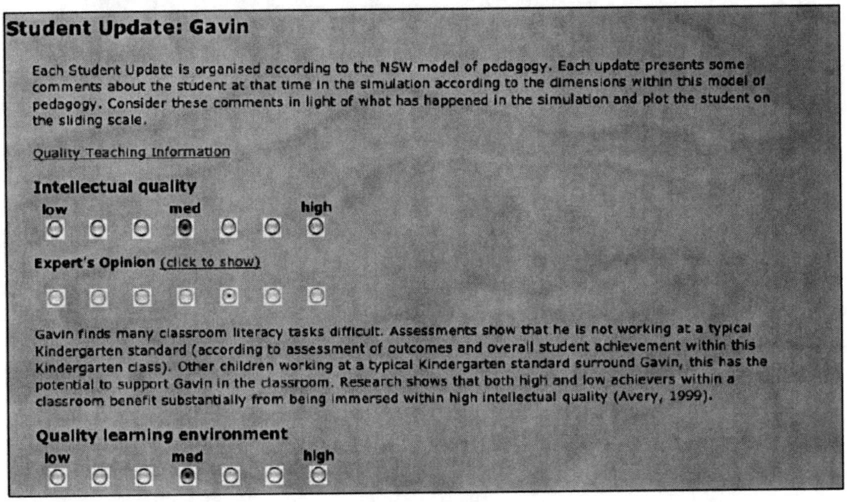

user is able to employ sliding scales to plot their expectations of student outcomes in relation to each criterion. They can then compare their expectations with those of experts.

Embedded Tools

A "thinking space" is located at decisive points throughout the simulation, with the aim of encouraging users to articulate and justify the decisions they have made. These spaces also provide opportunities for the user to reflect upon the impact of previous decisions on the targeted students. It is our intended aim in these spaces to engage the user in Jonassen's understanding of critical thinking, that is, "generalizable, higher-order thinking, such as logic, analyzing, planning, and inferring" (Jonassen, 1996, p. 24).

The thinking space presents three key questions to prompt thoughtful decision making. These key questions are supported by a help screen that offers additional ideas to consider. The users type reflections and thoughts into the blank space and can save their notes. Users are able to retrieve and review their previous decisions and thoughts throughout the duration of the simulation. An example of a "thinking space" is captured in Figure 4.

Figure 4. Thinking space (screen design by Sprout Media www.sproutmedia.com.au)

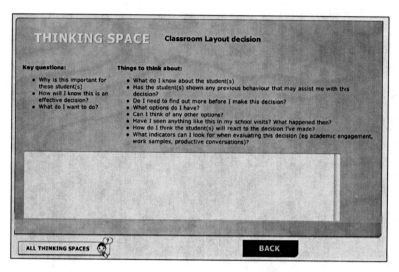

Figure 5: Support material (screen design by Sprout Media www.sproutmedia.com.au)

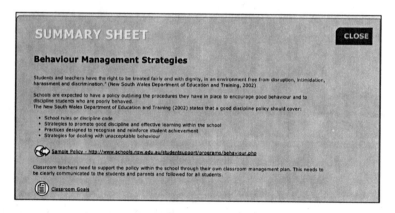

Support Materials

Support materials were integrated into the simulation prototype to support pre-service teacher learning and decision making. This included links to Web sites, textbook references and information summary sheets compiled and annotated by the research team. Textbook links are related to first-year core textbooks in the primary teacher education program in the Faculty of Education, University of Wollongong. An example is shown in Figure 5.

The Initial Trial of the Simulation with Pre-Service Teachers

The initial trial of the prototype simulation was conducted with a group of 24 pre-service teachers enrolled in the first year of a primary (elementary) teacher education course. The participant ages ranged from 18 to 43 years and 19 were females. Nineteen were under 25 years of age.

During the introductory session, the group was broken in to two sub-groups of 12, and each sub-group spent 90 minutes familiarising themselves with the simulation. In these sessions, three observers took field notes. The users were videotaped and audio recorders were placed on computer work-stations to capture dialogue between the users. After this introductory session, each member of the trial cohort was provided with access to the simulation on CD. Another 90-minute session was held with participants the following week, where once again they engaged with the simulation. Twenty-one of the users gave permission for the researchers to download and analyse the comments that they entered into their personal thinking spaces throughout the simulation. A purposive sample of four users was then interviewed. The interviews were audio-recorded, transcribed and analysed.

Findings

Our analysis of the collected data suggested that whilst the users engaged with the simulation to varying degrees, there appeared to be three key levels of engagement: the simulated environment, simulation processes and pedagogy. These levels and their interaction are represented in Figure 6.

The Simulation Environment

The findings of the trial suggested that certain characteristics of the simulated environment were significant in contributing to the development of the pedagogy of these pre-service teachers. These characteristics included the safety of the simulated environment, the support materials and the embedded thinking tools.

Safe Learning Environment

The data collected indicated that the safety of the simulated environment provided these participants with a sense of freedom to make decisions without

Figure 6. Model of the findings

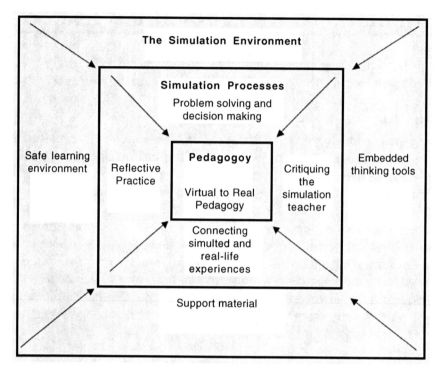

serious consequences. Working within a safe, self-contained setting (McMahon, 2000) appeared to support these pre-service teachers to develop their decision making and problem solving skills. Within the simulated environment, this cohort of beginning teachers demonstrated that they were able to test different strategies, reflect on consequences and then return to the start of the simulation and try an alternative path (Brown, 1999).

When questioned about the value of a learning environment free of serious consequences, case study participants responded favourably to this characteristic. One participant identified the benefit of testing decisions on simulated children that closely resembled students encountered during classroom-based experiences, and to then be able to observe the consequences before testing such decisions on "real" children in practicum situations. Another participant stated that it was advantageous to be able to implement strategies and observe how children responded without impacting on real children. Another referred to the simulation as providing the opportunity to develop her skills without using real children as "guinea pigs." These findings support the literature by Zhu and Roberts (2003) who state that an advantage of using simulation technology is the opportunity for users to practice making "virtual" decisions, which would otherwise have serious consequences. Just as simulated patients are becoming increasingly popular in providing medical students with practice in a "safe" environment (Stewart, 2003; Doyle, 2002), the simulated students within this "virtual" classroom appeared to allow pre-service teachers to test their skills.

While the importance of classroom-based experiences in the development of the pedagogy of pre-service teachers is recognised, it seems reasonable to suggest that the safety of a simulated environment has the potential to assist in supporting beginning teachers' emerging pedagogy. Pre-service teachers are able to practice and gain experience in the intricacies of teaching in the simulated environment while avoiding any real consequences.

Support Material

The findings of this study indicate that an important feature of the simulated environment is the support material available to the user. This material appeared to provide participants with avenues to develop their professional knowledge, through information sheets, Web links and textbook references. The enthusiasm these users displayed towards the support material indicates that this may be an effective way to support pre-service teachers with sourcing and interpreting professional information.

One participant identified the advantage of textbook references in assisting him to make connections between the theory of teaching he was expected to engage with and where it fits in classroom reality. Another participant referred to the flexibility afforded to pre-service teachers in the simulated environment, as the Web links allow beginning teachers access to relevant information that they could retrieve if and when they wanted it. The support material available within the simulation is embedded in the simulated environment, and the findings of this trial indicate that this material was perceived to be a highly valuable characteristic of the setting.

Embedded Thinking Tools

Analysis of the data in this study revealed that the embedded thinking tools are an important characteristic of the simulated environment. These tools appeared to support participants in articulating and expressing their "virtual" experiences. The thinking tools act as a journal, which according to Lee (2004) is a valuable device in pre-service teacher education in fostering connections between theory and practice.

The findings of this trial indicated that the embedded thinking tools supported pre-service teachers to make links between their understandings acquired in their university studies with their classroom-based and simulated experiences. The pre-service teachers engaged in several processes while using the embedded thinking tools, including justifying decisions and beliefs, reflective practice and critique of the simulated teacher. According to Lee (2004), pre-service teachers need to be "pushed" to think and reflect on the issues that arise in the classroom. The findings of this trial indicated that the embedded thinking tools encouraged this thinking and reflecting.

Simulation Processes

While working within the simulated classroom environment, participants appeared to engage in several processes that assisted them to develop their pedagogy. As illustrated in Figure 5, these processes were embedded within the simulated environment, and included opportunities for reflective practice, critiquing the simulation teacher, problem solving and decision-making.

Reflective Practice

Analysis of data indicated that the participants engaged in reflective practice while working in the simulated environment. The literature acknowledges that an important element of effective models of pre-service teacher education includes fostering reflective practice. DEST (2002) found that while practicum experiences are important, pre-service teachers need to be provided with further opportunity to reflect on teaching practice.

The reflection that the participants engaged in while using the simulation appeared to focus on issues such as: beliefs, teaching strategies, behaviour management, personal limitations and areas for improvement. While interacting with the support material, one participant stated that this gave her direction and motivation to seek out and utilise professional learning information. It is reasonable to suggest that the pre-service teachers were supported in their development of emerging pedagogy by the opportunity to reflect on their professional knowledge and strategies, building on both their real and simulated classroom experiences. This is supported by Groundwater-Smith et al. (2003), who assert that improvements in teaching practice can only occur when teachers look beyond what they do in the classroom and reflect on why they are doing it.

As shown in Figure 6, analysis of collected data showed that the simulated environment supported the participants' engagement with the simulation processes. This supports the views of Brown (1999) and Gibson and Halverson

(2004) who assert that a simulated environment has the potential to allow learners to test actions, consider teaching practice and reflect on the consequences of decisions. Likewise, Venlehn et al. (1994, cited in Brown, 1999) assert that simulations have the potential to encourage pre-service teachers to articulate, reflect on and evaluate their own theories of learning and teaching. The following transcript captures a discussion between two of the participants (pseudonyms used) as they engaged with the simulation:

Therese: *As a teacher, I should be able to get through a day with no preparation really.*

Sally: *Well, I thought because she gets worried a lot...*

Therese: *Mmm.*

Sally: *I thought maybe we could just, you know, finish it, and go and do...so she's a bit more comfortable.*

Therese: *She's sitting there in the morning... She's sitting there in the morning and she's worried about, oh will Harley be naughty,*

Sally: *Yeah.*

Therese: *Will Bibi cry?*

Sally: *Yeah.*

Therese: *It's like, why aren't you thinking, how am I going to keep Harley on track and motivated?*

Sally: *That's what I was thinking.*

Therese: *And, um you know, what tactics am I going to use?*

Sally: *Yeah.*

Therese: *And what about ...I have 27 students you know, how am I going to give them a good day?*

Sally: *I'm thinking 12 years experience, you'd think you'd have some examples of those, that behaviour anyway, even if you haven't experienced it from teacher's college and stuff like that. So I thought...*

Therese: *So you'd be thinking more along the lines of... This is what I'm going to...well it's not very positive is it?*

Sally: *No.*

At this stage of the simulation, the users were presented with a teacher with 12 years of experience preparing for the class, articulating concerns about some of the children within the class. What is interesting about this transcript is the articulation of the beliefs that these two participants held about what understandings teachers should have. The findings of this trial indicated that many of the participants did engage with opportunities to articulate, reflect on and evaluate their own theories of learning and teaching.

Connecting Simulated and Real-Life Experiences

Figure 6 depicts a process of making connections between simulated and real-life experiences. As discussed previously, the connections that were made appeared to centre on teaching and learning experiences, behaviour management and an awareness of individual students.

DEST (2002) found in their research that 25% of respondents affirmed the need for better links between the theory and practice of teaching. The findings from the trial of this simulation indicated that these pre-service teachers were engaged in this process of making connections. One participant described how using the simulation assisted her to "put things into perspective." She also made reference to the simulations ability to encourage her to think more deeply about the decisions that are made on a daily basis as a teacher. Another participant, when deciding which teaching strategy to use, chose the modelled reading option. Upon reflection, this participant expressed his belief that this strategy was successful and explained that "we have that [modelled reading] at our school in my class" and concluded that this was probably the reason for his choice. The simulation technology appears to assist the user in making such connections between classroom-based and virtual experiences.

Critiquing the Simulation Teacher

The practice of critiquing the simulation teacher is depicted as a simulation process in Figure 6. Most participants in this trial critiqued the simulation teacher at some point, whether through conversations with peers, interviews or most commonly in thinking space entries. Throughout the simulation the user has the option to ignore aspects of student behaviour. One participant commented on this in their thinking space entry by writing:

It is irresponsible of the teacher to say, you can call out, as she has just spent the last half hour establishing the class routine. Hands UP before answering. By saying 'you can call out', she is undoing her hard work and the students will not know, unless she tells them every time she wants hands up when to call out and when to wait to respond.

In this entry, the participant identified the inconsistent directions and rules he observed and explicitly critiqued the teacher's statements and how these may confuse students within that classroom.

The data suggested that some participants focussed on evaluating the actions of the simulated teacher, while other participants engaged with the simulation as problem solvers, by suggesting alternative strategies. The critiquing of the simulation teacher appeared to assist participants in developing their emerging pedagogy as they justified and reflected upon their decisions. Thus it is fair to suggest that by analysing and interpreting the actions of the simulation teacher, the pre-service teachers in this study were able to develop their professional understandings.

Problem Solving and Decision Making

Problem solving and decision making are processes which teachers employ on a daily basis in the school environment. Figure 6 indicates that these pre-service teachers engaged in these processes while working within the "virtual" classroom, thereby supporting the development of their emerging pedagogy. What is particularly interesting is that there was some evidence that these processes were transferred to classroom situations external to the "virtual" classroom. One participant sent the researchers an e-mail several weeks after the trial sessions of the simulation stating, "I had a teaching experience at school last week that was unexpectedly impacted upon through my experiences and insights gained during use of the teacher simulation exercises." She went on to say the simulation assisted her in dealing with a behaviour management issue in this classroom, as she searched for a solution:

I racked my brain and something interesting popped up! I remembered Class SIMS and how the teacher used questions to keep a troublesome child focused on the lesson, on task and participating...That's what I'll do!

This participant implemented this strategy from the simulation and concluded, "It worked brilliantly."

The findings from this trial indicated that the participants felt that they were less constrained and could take on a more active "teaching role" in the simulated classroom compared to the traditional practicum classroom. Many of the participants articulated that this setting allowed them to practice their decision making skills without the constraints brought about by the presence of a supervising teacher. It appears that the pre-service teachers had more ownership of decisions in the simulated environment and this seemed to assist them in the development of their pedagogy (Ali & Franklin, 2002).

Model of the Development of Pedagogy

The centre of the model presented in Figure 6 is concerned with the development of pedagogy. While working within the simulation environment and engaging in previously discussed processes, the participants in this trial appeared to be developing their pedagogical understandings. Figure 7 depicts in more detail how these participants moved from the "virtual" to "real" pedagogy.

In moving from the "virtual" to the "real," the participants seemed to be able to develop their pedagogical understandings within the simulated setting with an assumed intention of then using these skills in real classrooms. The findings from this trial indicated that the development of pedagogical understandings involved many areas of knowledge and skills. These areas included: developing the skills

Figure 7. Model of the development of pedagogy

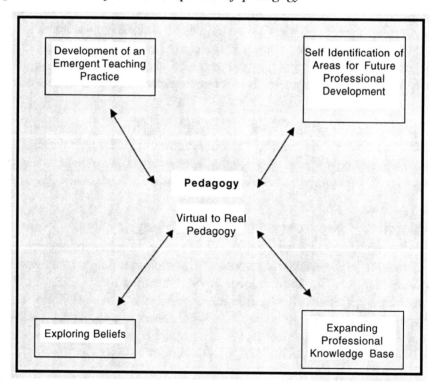

of teaching, expanding professional knowledge base, exploring beliefs and self-identification of areas for future professional development. Each of these areas will be discussed further.

Development of an Emergent Teaching Practice

Data collected from this trial indicated that the simulation appeared to contribute to the development of the pedagogy of these pre-service teachers as it provided them with opportunities to practice and develop their understanding of teaching practice. These intricacies of teaching included reflective practice, decision-making and problem solving skills. These pre-service teachers were encouraged to reflect on their teaching practices and decisions in the simulation, primarily in the form of thinking space entries. The participants were given the responsibility to make decisions for the teacher, which empowered them in the simulated setting without the influence of a supervising teacher and with the knowledge that any consequences would be contained within the "virtual" environment. Presented with a series of decisions to make, the pre-service teachers were able to use their problem solving skills in the immediate simulated setting.

Expanding Professional Knowledge Base

Data collected in this trial indicated that the support material was useful in the expansion of the participants' knowledge. One participant claimed that the support material element of the simulation had the potential to expand her knowledge base "exponentially." These participants while working in the simulated environment formed new ideas. As the participants interacted with the elements of the virtual classroom they appeared to gain ideas from their actions and observations. After analysing the data it seems appropriate to conclude that these participants were supported in the development of their pedagogical understandings as they engaged with the simulation.

Exploring Beliefs

The findings from this trial indicated that the simulation assisted pre-service teachers to explore their beliefs. Collected data showed that many of the participants felt that the time they had already spent in schools as both students and on teaching practicums had provided them with enough experience to construct some beliefs and ideas about the teaching profession.

One participant stated in an interview: "We've been in schools I think for six weeks...so you've formed those ideas about things." For this participant and others, the simulation was a tool used to explore their existing beliefs. However, it was also used to reconsider pre-conceived ideas, as one participant said "[the simulation] does make you think about the ideas that you did form earlier...so you rethink." It appears that the simulation challenged pre-service teachers to review and reflect on their existing and developing beliefs about the pedagogy of teaching.

Self Identification of Areas for Future Professional Development

This trial revealed that the simulation appeared to prompt the pre-service teachers to identify their personal limitations and areas for future professional development, supporting Morrow's (2003) view that teacher educators have a responsibility to foster knowledge about the importance of professional development in their students. Some participants identified areas of their teaching that required attention, as well as the impact their learning style has on their own tertiary education. It appears that the simulation supported the pedagogical development of these pre-service teachers, as they gained experiences in the self-identification of professional needs.

Concluding Remarks and Future Directions

Our first experience with the initial cohort showed that the simulation design has the potential to engage pre-service teachers in deep thinking about the virtual classroom environment. In particular, we noticed that many users were able to link their own school-based experiences to those presented within the simulation, and some were able to link the theory presented in their pre-service teacher education training to classroom practice.

We are interested in following up the current research by exploring mechanisms to further engage users in thinking processes to extend and enhance their links between the theory and classroom practice. In addition we have identified the need for other cohorts from different pre-service teacher education programs, and at different stages within these, to engage with the simulation. We acknowledge that the current study was limited to 24 students enrolled within a specialised program. This in turn limited the range and quality of data that we were able to gather at this time.

However, the initial use showed that all users were deeply engaged with the simulation for a sustained period of time. Our data indicates that during the two 90-minute sessions, all users were on task and actively interacting with the simulation for almost all of the time. Similarly, evidence of deep thinking was apparent in their responses in the thinking spaces and in their interactions with researchers. We are optimistic about the potential of this design for a range of authentic contexts that are similar to that presented in this research.

References

Aldrich, C. (2004). *Simulations and the future of learning*. San Francisco: Pfeiffer.

Ali, A., & Franklin, T. (2002). Technology and pedagogy: Changing roles of pedagogy in a project-based constructivist environment. In *Proceedings of E-Learning World Conference on E-Learning in Corporate, Government, Healthcare and Higher Education* (pp. 120-125). Montreal, Canada: Association for the Advancement of Computing in Education.

Armour, L., & Booth, E. (1999). *Analysis of a questionnaire to primary educators at schools accepting students for the six week extended practicum.* Report by Faculty of Education: University of Wollongong.

Blackwell, P. J., Futrell, M. H., & Imig, D. G. (2003). Burnt water paradoxes of schools of education. *Phi Delta Kappan, 85*(5), 356-361.

Brookfield, S. (1995). *Becoming a critically reflective teacher*. San Francisco: Josey-Bass.

Brown, A.H. (1999). Simulated classrooms and artificial students: The potential effects of new technologies on teacher education. *Journal of Research on Computing in Education, 32*(2), 307-318.

Brown, J.S., Collins, A., & Duguid P. (1989). Situated cognition and the culture of learning. *Educational Researcher, 18*(10), 32-42.

Brown, J., Doecke, B., & Loughran, J. (1997). Understanding beginning to teach: Learning about the transition from tertiary education to a professional career. Paper presented at Australian Association for Research in Education Conference, Brisbane, Australia. Retrieved November 2004, from *http://www.aare.edu.au/97pap/lougj039.htm*

Cambourne, B. L. (2000). Conditions for literacy learning: Observing literacy learning in elementary classrooms: Nine years of classroom anthropology. *The Reading Teacher, 53*(6), 512-517.

Cambourne, B., Kiggins, J., & Ferry, B. (2003). Replacing traditional lectures, tutorials and exams with a knowledge building community (KBC): A constructivist, problem-based approach to preservice primary teacher education. *English Teaching: Practice and Critique, 2*(3), 7-21. Retrieved June 2004, from *http://www.tmc.waikato.ac.nz/english/ETPC/article/pdf/2003v2n3art1.pdf*

Comber, B., Badger, L., Barnett, J., Nixon, H., Prince, S., & Pitt, J. (2001). *Socio-economically disadvantaged students and the development of literacies in school: A longitudinal study.* South Australia Department of Education, Training and Employment and University of Adelaide.

Cusworth, R., & Whiting, P. (1994). Beginning teachers' attitudes to preservice training. Paper presented at *Australian Association for Research in Education Conference*, Newcastle.

Danielson, C. (1996). *Enhancing professional practice: A framework for teaching.* Alexandria, VA: Association for Supervision and Curriculum Development.

Darling-Hammond, L. (1999). *Teacher education: Rethinking practice and policy. Unicorn, 25*(1), 31-48.

Department of Education, Science and Training. (2002). *An ethics of care: Effective programmes for beginning teachers.* Sydney: Commonwealth of Australia.

Department of Education and Training. (2003). *Quality teaching in NSW public schools: An annotated bibliography.* Sydney, Professional Support and Curriculum Directorate.

Doyle, D.J. (2002). Simulation in medical education: Focus on anesthesiology. *Medical Education Online, 7*(16), 1-15.

Entwhistle, N., Entwhistle A., & Tait, H. (1993*).* Academic understanding and the contexts to enhance it: A perspective from research on student learning. In T.M. Duffy, J. Lowyck & D.H. Jonassen (Eds.), *Design environments for constructive learning* (pp. 331-357). Heidelberg: Springer-Verlag.

Fieman-Nemser, S. (2001). From preparation to practice: Designing a continuum to strengthen and sustain teaching. *Teachers College Record, 103*(6), 1013-1055.

Freebody, P., & Luke, A. (1990). Literacies programs: Debates and demands in cultural context. *Prospect, 5*(3), 7-16.

Gee, J. P. (2000). New people in new worlds: Networks, the new capitalism and schools. In B. Cope & M. Kalantzis (Eds.), *Multiliteracies: Literacy learning and the design of social futures.* Melbourne, Victoria: Macmillan.

Gibson, D., & Halverson, B. (2004). Simulation as a framework for preservice assessment. *Society for Information Technology and Teacher Education International Conference 2004,* (1), 3322-3325.

Grabinger, R. S. (1996). Rich environments for active learning. In D. H. Jonassen (Ed.), *Handbook of research for communications and educational technology* (pp. 665-692). New York: MacMillan.

Gredler, M.E. (2004). Games and simulations and their relationships to learning. In D.H. Jonassen (Ed.), *Handbook of research on education communications and technology* (2nd ed.) (pp. 571-581). NJ: Lawrence Erlbaum.

Groundwater-Smith, S., Deer, C. E, Sharp, H., & March, P (1996). The practicum as workplace learning: A multi-modal approach in teacher education. *Australian Journal of Teacher Education, 22*(2), 21-30.

Harper, B., Hedberg, J., Corderoy, R., & Wright, R. (2000). Employing cognitive tools within interactive multimedia applications. In S. Lajoie (Ed.), *Computers as cognitive tools* (Vol. 2) (pp. 227-245). Mahwah, NJ: Lawrence Erlbaum.

Herrington, J., & Oliver, R. (2000). An instructional design framework for authentic learning environments. *Educational Technology, Research and Development, 48*(3), 23-37.

Herrington, J., Oliver, R., & Reeves, T. C. (2003). Patterns of engagement in authentic online learning environments. *Australian Journal of Educational Technology, 19*(1), 59-71.

Hoban, G. F. (2002). *Teacher learning for educational change.* Philadelphia: Open University.

Jonassen, D. H. (1996). *Computers in the classroom: Mindtools for critical thinking.* Edgewood Cliffs, NJ: Prentice-Hall.

Jonassen, D.H. (1997). Instructional design model for well-structured and ill-structured problem-solving learning outcomes. *Educational Technology Research and Development, 45*(1), 65-95.

Jonassen, D.H. (2000). Toward a design theory of problem solving. *Educational Technology Research & Development, 48*(4), 63-85.

Kervin, L., & Turbill, J. (2003). Teaching as a craft: Making links between preservice training and classroom practice. *English Teaching: Practice and Critique, 2*(3), 22-34.

Lang, C. (1999). When does it get any easier?: Beginning teachers' experiences during their first year of teaching. Paper presented at *Australian Associa-*

tion for Research in Education/New Zealand Association for Research in Education Conference, Melbourne. Retrieved December 2003, from http://www.aare.edu.au/99pap/lan99269.htm

Lave, J., & Wenger, E. (1991). *Situated learning: Legitimate peripheral participation.* Cambridge: Cambridge University.

Lee, C. (2000). A paradigm shift in the technology era in higher education. In *Proceedings of the World Conference on Educational Multimedia, Hypermedia and Telecommunications 2000* (pp. 575-580).

Ministerial Advisory Council on the Quality of Teaching. (1998). Teacher preparation for student management: Responses and directions. *Report by Ministerial Advisory Council on the Quality of Teaching, October, 1998.* Sydney: NSW Department of Education and Training.

Mangis, C.A. (2002, May). Will Wright on the secret of Sims. *PC Magazine.*

Martello, J. (2002). Many roads through many modes: becoming literate in early childhood. In L. Makin & C. J. Diaz (Eds.), *Literacies in early childhood* (pp. 35-52). Sydney: Maclennn + Petty.

McMahon, M. (2000). Developing web-based learning strategies: A comparison between the Web and traditional learning environments. In *Proceedings of the World Conference on Educational Multimedia, Hypermedia and Telecommunications 2000* (pp. 693-701).

Morrow, L.M. (2003). Make professional development a priority. *Reading Today, 21*(1), 6.

Purcell-Gates, V. (1995). *Other people's words: The cycle of low literacy.* Cambridge, MA: Harvard University.

Ramsay, G. (2000). *Quality matters revitalising teaching: Critical times, critical choices. Report of the Review of Teacher Education in NSW.* Sydney: NSW Department of Education & Training.

Reigeluth, C. M., & Schwartz, E. (1989). An instructional theory for the design of computer-based simulations. *Journal of Computer-Based Instruction, 16*(1), 1-10.

Reynolds, A. (1993). The knowledge base for beginning teachers: Education professionals' expectations versus research findings on learning to teach. *The Elementary School Journal, 95*(3), 199-221.

Stewart, D. (2003). Medical training in the UK. *Archives of Disease in Childhood, 88*(8), 655-659.

Stronge, J. H. (2002). *Qualities of effective teachers.* Alexandria, VA: Association for Supervision and Curriculum Development.

Tan, S.C., Turgeon, A.J., & Jonassen, D.H. (2001). Computer-supported collaborative argumentation: An innovative approach to group problem solving. *Journal of Natural Resources and Life Sciences Education, 30,* 54-61.

Tripp, S.D. (1993). Theories and traditions and situated learning. *Educational Technology, 33*(3), 71-77.

Vinson, T. (2001). *Inquiry into the provision of public education in NSW.* Annandale: Pluto Press Australia.

Zhu, L., & Roberts, C. (2003). A Web-based simulation built on constructivist learning. In *Proceedings of the World Conference on E-learning in Corp., Govt., Health, & Higher Ed. 2003* (pp. 1272-1277).

Chapter XII

Speaking Snake:
Authentic Learning and the Study of Literature

John Fitzsimmons, Central Queensland University, Australia

Abstract

In the second Harry Potter novel, Harry discovers by accident that he is a Parselmouth, that he can speak "snake," not crudely, like Dr. Dolittle, who speaks apparently perfect English to animals that somehow understand him, but actual "snake." This chapter explores the basic proposition that those who read and teach literature have been speaking authentic learning all their lives, perhaps a little crudely — more Dr. Dolittle than Harry Potter — but speaking it nonetheless. This exploration will take the form of three related lines of reasoning. First, it will be argued that literature is and has always been a form of authentic learning to the extent of being an exemplary model. This assertion will be supported using an example from the Harry Potter series. Second, it will be argued that an engagement with the "real-life" themes of literature requires a conversation between the world of the text and that of its readers, thereby fulfilling one of the major requirements of authentic learning — situating content in context. It is not possible in this chapter to rehearse the discipline-specific and extensive critical and theoretical debates that might support this assertion, so an autobiographical example from the distinguished critic Gerald Graff will be used to evoke these debates instead. Third, it will be argued that methods of assessment in literary subjects might usefully adopt some of the principles of authentic learning to enhance the relation between assessment outcomes and the world of employment. The chapter concludes that some of the nervousness experienced by humanities academics when contemplating a more focused relation between their disciplines and the principles of authentic learning is misplaced.

Literature as Authentic Learning

Literature, or more specifically the novel, is and has always been a form of authentic learning. For example, Harry Potter, the eponymous hero of the novels about Hogwarts School for Witchcraft and Wizardry, engages in his most serious learning, not where we might expect, in the classroom, though knowing spells and stuff is crucial for the plot, but in the quests he and his friends enter in labyrinthine spaces between classrooms that are out from under the watchful eyes of the adults assigned to teach and protect them. Typically, Harry is confronted with a crisis that only he can resolve, which he does by using his special powers and with the help of his friends, Ron Weasley and Hermione Granger. In this, Harry lives in an "authentic learning" environment with a problem-based learning dimension.

In *Harry Potter and the Chamber of Secrets* (Rowling, 1998), the second in the series, Harry and his friends discover that someone has opened the Chamber of Secrets — a hidden chamber of evil, built by one of Hogwart's founders, the sly Salazar Slytherin, who believed that students of non-pure wizard blood should not be allowed to study at the School. Only the true heir of Slytherin can open the Chamber, from which a snakelike beast will emerge to purge the school of wizards and witches who come from non-magic heritage. The beast sets about terrifying students and teachers, not to mention petrifying, literally, a succession of unfortunates. As a Parselmouth, Harry's power to speak "snake" is both a gift and a curse. It is a gift because as he wanders about the school trying to solve the mystery — who opened the Chamber and what can be done about the beast — the very walls themselves seem to speak "snake" to him, providing him with all sorts of clues. It is a curse because Salazar Slytherin was himself a Parselmouth, a coincidence which places Harry under suspicion as his possible heir.

Harry is unperturbed by any of this, as befits the hero, and eventually solves the riddle — Tom Riddle, that is, an earlier version of the dreaded dark lord, Voldemort, who, through a magic diary left behind from his own Hogwart's days, possesses Ron Weasley's unfortunate younger sister Ginny and makes her do his bidding. The climax of the story has Harry facing off against the dark lord and his beast, over the prostrate body of Ginny, who is about to be sacrificed so that Voldemort can regain the physical form he lost after he tried to vanquish Harry when he was a baby. The themes of the Potter stories are every bit as confronting as everyday life and include Gothic horrors, betrayal and narrow-mindedness, counterbalanced by bravery, allegiance, cooperation and acceptance.

This brief summary does not do the story justice, but it does show that the Harry Potter stories rely on formulas that have made all kinds of children's fiction popular: the hero is a child and the story child-centred. Adults are relegated to the role of helpers or villains (and are often unreliable), and the hero relies on his or her friends and on access to all kinds of information to resolve the crisis (for example, Hermione spends considerable time in the library gathering information). Whatever else might be going on in Harry's stories, and there is a great deal, it is fairly clear that the school's Headmaster, Professor Dumbledore, seems to believe in principles of constructivist learning utilising authentic learning environments. Dumbledore is the greatest wizard in the world, according to the students, and he clearly has the power to vanquish all evil including, one suspects, the dreaded Lord Voldemort. And yet he allows Harry and his friends to deal with those "real-life" problems consequent on encounters with this evil in an authentic environment. They will, after all, grow up and, having mastered their own powers, face evil themselves, including their own dark sides, in their daily lives.

Literature generally models authentic learning with a problem-based learning inflection. In brief, authentic learning is typically defined as active learning, involving "real-life" situations that include ill-formulated and ill-structured problems that comprise complex tasks to be investigated over a sustained period of time. These "real-life" problems have context, depth, complexity and duration. They involve cooperative situations and shared consequences, and they are worth solving, and provide benefits when solved. Authentic learning activities provide the opportunity to examine the task from different perspectives, promote reflection to enable abstractions to be formed, promote articulation to enable implicit knowledge to be made explicit, and provide coaching and scaffolding by faculty at critical times (Lefrere, 1997; Herrington, Sparrow, & Herrington, 2000; Herrington & Oliver, 2000; Pennell, Durham, Ozog, & Spark, 1997). The Harry Potter stories all exhibit these major characteristics.

Milan Kundera indirectly supports the idea that literature, or more specifically the novel, is a way of knowing that models authentic learning and knowing in his discussion on the "art" of the novel. Kundera (1986) notes that, in 1935, the philosopher Edmund Husserl gave some lectures in Vienna and Prague on the "crisis of the European humanities," where he argued, against expectations that he would discuss the coming war and nationalism, that the European spiritual identity and the philosophy that underpinned it had, for the first time, perceived the world as a question to be answered, not for practical reasons, but because "the passion to know had seized mankind." This passion had, since Galileo and Descartes, reduced the world to an object of mathematical and technical investigation, and propelled humanity into tunnels of specialised disciplines, with the crushing effect that the concrete world of life, "*die Lebenswelt,*" had slipped beyond its horizon. The more humanity advanced in knowledge, the less it could see either the world as a whole or its own self, and as a result, humanity plunged further into what Heidegger, Husserl's pupil, called "the forgetting of being." Kundera comments that for Husserl:

Man [sic] has now become a mere thing to the forces [of technology, of politics, of history] that bypass him, surpass him, possess him ... To those forces, man's concrete being, his 'world of life' has neither value nor interest: it is eclipsed, forgotten from the start. (pp. 2-4)

Kundera's response to Husserl's critique of the European spirit is to suggest that if Descartes was the founder of the modern era with his *cogito ergo sum* — the idea that the thinking, rational self is the basis of everything — then Cervantes, with his novel *Don Quixote*, published around the same time, must be regarded as the co-founder because he inaugurated the novel as a way of knowing that is distinct from and yet complements Descartes' rationalist, scientific paradigm. Kundera believes that while scientists and philosophers were busy dividing the world into disciplines and sating their passion to know, novelists were discovering the untended dimensions of existence and scrutinising humanity's "concrete life," its *die Lebenswelt*, to protect it against any forgetting of being and to hold it under a "permanent light." What novelists since Cervantes had faced was not a single absolute truth of the kind embodied in religious dogma where God is the supreme Judge of all, but a "welter of contradictory truths (truths embodied in *imaginary selves* called characters)" where the only certainty is the "wisdom of uncertainty" (pp. 5-7). Consequently, the novel not only helps humanity to grapple with the "monster of [its] own soul," but the novel also assists humanity in grappling with this soul's nemesis, history, which is "impersonal, uncontrollable, incalculable, incomprehensible — and inescapable" (p. 11). Put simply, Kundera argues that the novel is a way of knowing outside the technical and mathematical excesses of the Cartesian self, and he subscribes to Hermann Broch's view that "the sole *raison d'etre* of a novel is to discover what only the novel can discover" (cited in Kundera, 1986, p. 5). If the novel is a way of knowing that rivals the kind of scientism inaugurated by Descartes, a distinction needs to be made between what happens within the novel — Harry Potter's activities — and how readers might respond to the act of reading novels.

Literature:
Situating Content in Context

An engagement with the "real-life" themes of literature requires a conversation between the world of the text and that of its readers, thereby fulfilling one of the major requirements of authentic learning. Gerald Graff tells a story that supports Kundera's account of the significance of the novel, but from a very different perspective, one that addresses the question of how readers respond to the novel, and gives us an example of the relation between content and context. Graff (1994) tells us that when he was growing up, he disliked and feared books and that his "vivid recollections" of college are of "assigned classics" he failed to finish because he saw little in them that resembled his own experience (p. 37). He explains this in part by suggesting that it was unclear to him what he was supposed to say about literary works, and why. He experienced a sea-change in his view of literature when he got involved in a debate about the ending of *The Adventures of Huckleberry Finn*. Ernest Hemingway had argued that the real ending of the story is where Jim is stolen by the boys: "The rest is cheating" (cited in Graff p. 38). Hemingway believed that the remainder of the story, where Jim is subjected to Tom Sawyer's slapstick humour, and then it is revealed that Jim has already been freed by his benevolent owner, deprives the story of its motivation. This deprivation reverberates back through the story and renders its critique of racism redundant. It also suggests that the underlying premise of the story — the risk to Jim and Huck and their actions to avoid it — has been no risk at all. Other eminent critics, such as T.S. Eliot and Lionel Trilling, disagreed with Hemingway, and Graff got caught up in the debate.

Graff reports that he reread the novel with an excitement he had "never felt before" because he now had some "issues to watch out for" (p. 38). He had found a voice, one that engaged with the critics and allowed him to enter the debate. This approach, he suggests, goes against the conventional wisdom relating to a love of literature — the idea, popular in the fifties and sixties, that students ought to be left alone to engage with the great works on their own, with the teacher and the critics being left in the background to avoid any premature corruption by criticism's sectarian debates (pp. 39-40). Graff concludes that "our ability to read well depends more than we think on our ability to talk well about what we read" (p. 40), a view that leads inevitably to the conclusion that to teach a text means teaching an interpretation of it, and this means, as much as anything, teaching students how to talk about literature, a skill which depends not only on their individual abilities, but also on their relation to "a critical community of readers" (p. 42). Put simply, "making an effective argument depends on having a sense of what other people are saying, of what the state of discussion is" (p. 43). As a way of knowing, then, the novel is, according to Kundera, without peer. But this way of knowing, for Graff, requires being situated in the debates that the novel engenders.

Although Graff and Kundera arrive at their conclusions separately, they both recognise that the fundamental nature of the study of literature concerns the problem of life itself—the self, being, memory and forgetfulness, how the world is or ought to be organised — and that situating this essence as an ill-structured problem within a transparent scaffold of authentic contexts not only gives life to the study of literature, but also engages students in compelling debates that connect with their own personal experiences. As such, literature is the perfect place for authentic learning as it brings together readers and characters, who are both immersed in a self-directed encounter with a focus on an ill-structured but authentic life experience where they pose questions about what they do not understand, working from their own prior knowledge. For teachers of literature, the problem is how to bring the two sets of authentic learning practices together — how to engage the young Gerald Graff in a conversation that includes the world of the text (the concrete world of life, its "*die Lebenswelt*") and that of its readers, using an authentic learning environment that includes issues associated with their own reading practices. The discipline-specific and extensive critical and theoretical debates that deal with the relation between text and context go beyond the scope of this chapter.

Assessment and Employment Outcomes: A Model in Practice

Methods of assessment in literary subjects might usefully adopt some of the principles of authentic learning to enhance the relation between assessment outcomes and the world of employment.

A constructivist (problem-based learning) approach was introduced into an advanced level Bachelor of Arts course, North American Fiction and Film, at Central Queensland University. The course is designed to provide students with the skills to describe and analyse selected American writings of the nineteenth and twentieth centuries within a framework of issues such as ideology, gender, race and the politics of literature, and to examine the way various discourses and narratives are used in the construction of America as a community and the attempts that have been made to negotiate these constructions.

The approach adopted for the course supports Winn's (1997) model of student learning: it will be consistent enough to allow new information to be interpreted, but flexible enough to adapt to new interpretations. It will also be sufficiently abstract to apply to a large number of cases, and to allow students to draw inferences even though all the information is not available. It will allow speculation about the world and enable students to construct and test new hypotheses that then serve as new sources of information. It will allow students to describe what they understand to other people, and guide students to relevant sources of information. Such a model requires a fashioning of knowledge that is active so that students can connect information with existing mental models and alter them to accommodate the information. Moreover, the social nature of knowledge construction must be considered and opportunities provided for students to interact with other students, teachers, or other members of the community.

More specifically, students are expected to focus their work through an "authentic" assessment task, one that mirrors the kind of thing they might be expected to do post-graduation in a variety of occupations. In this case, they were expected to participate in the preparation and publication of an edition of an electronic journal called NAFF-Online (2001). Students are required to perform as members of the editorial board of this journal, with myself acting as editor. Only the best papers are published.

Students are required to produce a Book Review Article, a "How to Write a Book Review Article Guide," and an essay/article. In addition, students are required to present an "academic" conference paper based on one of their written papers to a one-day "academic" conference, during which they are also expected to peer review at least three of the papers presented by their "colleagues." Students typically prepare PowerPoint slides and handouts, and use video clips as part of their presentation. They also network extensively during the conference day. The overall rationale used is that the task should be authentic (the online journal), ill-defined (students are expected to research both the tasks associated with the production of the online journal and the writing of material for a particular issue), and problem-based (the students act as members of an editorial board whose task is to see material through from conception to publication, solving problems along the way).

Classes are run as seminars, and are task- rather than text-focused. The writing of the Book Review Article is broken down into three tasks: a book review, a literature review, and the joining of these two into a book review article. Students are given the task of writing a book review first, which they then present to the class through a series of writer's workshops. Here, students are broken into groups, each of which reads a particular book review and gives constructive feedback to the author. This is followed by class discussion regarding that particular text which includes insights into the major focus of the course — the clash of the individual and the community in North American fiction — as well as theoretical concerns regarding fiction (narrative point of view and so on). A similar exercise is conducted with the literature review. Final Book Review Articles are then submitted to editorial panels, which have the job of editing, requesting revisions and re-drafts. Time is set aside in each seminar for discussion of the "How to Write a Book Review Article Guide," and students are expected to produce these in groups. The task is normally extended over ten weeks so that progressive experience can be included and the guides updated throughout the course. The rationale for the guide is that it would be published from a compilation of the group's efforts on the grounds that student readers of the online journal may find it useful.

The essay/article can be written using the same process as the Book Review Article (students are encouraged to do this as the process of "deep learning" in relation to the main objectives of the course comes from serious and extended engagement with the literature itself). Resources for the course are accessible online (including material ranging from the course outline to library resources). In addition to the online journal, all communication outside of class, including the circulation of and commentaries on drafts and "How to" guides, is conducted using a discussion list.

Thus far, the results have been bi-modal. Students who exhibit adult learning characteristics (largely to do with independent learning skills) have found the task-oriented course to their liking, and their work has improved dramatically. Their Book Review Articles exhibit depth of analysis and a standard of writing beyond their previous work in other courses, and they feel more confident in the medium of the essay and better able to deal with problems associated with literature. Students who rely on child-like models of learning have had a much harder time assimilating the material and producing outputs through the various stages of the writing process. These students, characteristically, have never before attempted to produce a literature review of any substance, and many lack the kind of library/information skills assumed of advanced-level degree students.

Conclusion

Literature is and has always been a form of authentic learning to the extent of being an exemplary model. Engaging students in the critical debates that surround the "real-life" themes of literature requires a conversation between the world of the text and that of its readers, of situating content in context. Whilst the connection between authentic learning and literature may not be obvious in our post-literate age, it can be made more visible by enhancing the relation between assessment outcomes and the world of employment. Further work needs to be done within other humanities disciplines to explore similar kinds of parallels.

Humanities academics may experience a little nervousness when contemplating a more focused relation between their disciplines and the principles of authentic learning. However, like Molière's Monsieur Jourdain (*The Bourgeois Gentleman*), who was surprised to discover that he had been speaking prose all his life, academics need to acknowledge that the language they are speaking is already imbued with these principles and to recognise ways in which the "text" of authentic learning can be situated in the context of discipline-specific practice. It may be a case of Dr. Doolittle learning to be Harry Potter, but if you want to be a Parselmouth, you have to know how to speak snake.

References

Graff, G. (1994). Disliking books at an early age. In D.H. Richter (Ed.), *Falling into theory: Conflicting views on reading literature* (pp. 36-43). Boston: Bedford Books of St Martin's Press.

Herrington, J., & Oliver, R. (2000). An instructional design framework for authentic learning environments. *Educational Technology Research & Development, 48*(3), 23-48.

Herrington, J., Sparrow, H., & Herrington, A. (2000). Instructional design guidelines for authentic activity in online learning units. *Proceedings of World Conference on Educational Multimedia, Hypermedia and Telecommunications 2000* (pp. 435-440). Charlottesville, VA: AACE.

Kundera, M. (1986). *The art of the novel.* London: Faber and Faber.

Lefrere, P. (1997). *Teaching in hyperspace: The potential of the web: A professional development workshop for educators.* International University Consortium and Institute for Distance Education. Retrieved July 2004, from *http://www.umuc.edu/ide/potentialweb97/lefrere.html*

NAFF-Online (2001). Retrieved August 2004, from *http://www.ahs.cqu.edu.au/humanities/litstud/LITR19053/jnl/online_jnl.html*

Pennell, R., Durham, M., Ozog, M., & Spark, A. (1997). Writing in context: Situated learning on the web. In R. Kevill, R. Oliver & R. Phillips (Eds.),

What Works and Why: Proceedings of the 14th Annual Conference of the Australian Society for Computers in Learning in Tertiary Education (pp. 463-469). Perth, WA: Curtin University.

Rowling, J.K. (1998). *Harry Potter and the Chamber of Secrets*. London: Bloomsbury.

Winn, W. (1997). *Learning in hyperspace: The potential of the web: A professional development workshop for educators.* International University Consortium and Institute for Distance Education. Retrieved July 2004, from *http://www.umuc.edu/ide/potentialweb97/winn.html*

Chapter XIII

Using IT to Augment Authentic Learning Environments

Sandra Jones, RMIT University, Australia

Abstract

This chapter discusses how information technology (IT) can be used to augment the authenticity of the learning experience in student-centred learning environments. It argues that technology provides the opportunity to embed students in learning activity by bridging the gap between the "real world" and the classroom. The particular learning environment used to illustrate this is a restaurant complex with a number of outlets that was designed by the author to provide a common work environment. Using the Distributed Learning System (DLS) to which all students have access, the author was able to increase the authenticity of the "case" by first, having students access information (as employees and/or lessees') about the commercial conditions facing the company, and its policies and practices). Second, "employees" were able to communicate through discussion boards. Third, students were able to access resources through hyperlinks to external Web sites. The author concludes that there is need for a mixture of face-to-face and virtual learning opportunities in order to add real-world authenticity to experiential learning opportunities.

Introduction

Universities are confronted by enormous challenges as the sophisticated knowledge economy develops. Allee (1999) states that in order to develop a knowledge culture there is need for a fundamental change in human thinking. Brown (1999) takes a similar expansive view of the change required, and states that there is need for change that involves multiple, intertwining forces of content, context, and community. He states that the real formula for success in a knowledge economy is continuous learning to see and do things differently. To meet these challenges, employees need to not only have advanced skill, systems understanding, and intuition, but also need to be self-motivated and creative.

The need for graduates with broad capabilities provides challenges for universities that, as is argued elsewhere, have not traditionally taught these skills (Davenport & Prusak, 1998). What is needed is a new, more student-centred, co-operative learning environment in which teachers create "a context of learning which encourages students actively to engage in subject matter" (Ramsden, 1992, p. 114). This context requires teachers to become "guides, coaches, motivators and facilitators," and students to become active "doers" — presenting, analysing, solving and constructing ways to develop the knowledge provided by the teacher into skills required to function effectively. Laurillard (1994) describes this as an educational environment in which students move from acquirers of knowledge, to collaborators in the educational process.

Others have argued that as well as changing the nature of the teacher-student relationship, for learning to occur conceptual knowledge needs to be placed in its cultural context. Brown, Collins and Duguid (1989) advocate design of "authentic" learning environments in which "activities of a domain are framed by its culture. Their meaning and purpose are socially constructed through negotiations among past and present members ... are most simply defined as the ordinary practices of the culture" (p. 4).

This authenticity is difficult to create in a classroom environment where the context is inevitably transmuted into "classroom tasks and part of the school culture" (Brown, Collins, & Duguid, 1989, p. 4). Rather, they argue that learning should be part of a "cognitive apprenticeship" in which tasks are embedded in familiar activity and particular tasks through which students generate their own solution paths to develop problem solving. This has led to calls for work-integrated learning and action-based learning as the means to develop authentic learning environments. Schön (1985, 1987) argues that students should be encouraged to analyse and reflect upon their own work experiences. Quasi-experiential, real-world experience presented by practitioners speaking of their own experiences, case-studies of real-world events, videos, photographs, and slides, are also advocated as means to provide students with "authentic" learning environments (Bailey & McAtee, 1998; Jones, 1999, 2000, 2001a).

The advent of computers has led to discussion on how interactive communication technology can be used to further assist the development of student-centred, authentic learning environments. Reeves, Herrington and Oliver (2002, p. 565) argue that Web-based courses of study can add to the authenticity of a face-to-face learning environment. However, they also recognise that designing and creating Web courses to support authentic activities is not easily accomplished. This supports the contention of Jones and Richardson (2002) that advanced technology should be used to augment rather than replace face-to-face educational environments by providing opportunities for students to become "communities of learners."

This chapter seeks, by presenting a case study of an authentic situated learning environment that was augmented by online activities for students, to demonstrate that such environments can be created in a classroom without distorting the real-world culture. To assist the analysis, the ten characteristics of authentic situated learning tasks identified by Reeves, Herrington and Oliver (2002) are used as an analytical framework.

Case Study:
A Situated Learning Environment
for Improving Negotiations

The learning environment in which this case study is set is a course in negotiation skills to post-graduate managers, human resource managers and employment relations practitioners. This first section presents the face-to-face learning environment in which the students were introduced to the situated learning environment (SLE), with the following section explaining how the SLE was augmented by a "virtual" learning environment.

Before describing the environment, it is necessary to introduce the students. This course is offered to post-graduate practitioners who find that the transition to student status presents a number of challenges. On the one hand, they are returning to study from an educational model that was, in the main, governed by a teacher-centred pedagogy in which the teacher provided information. On the other hand, they are keen to share their practitioner experiences, but tend to resist challenges that take them out of their comfort zone, especially when these tasks question their values. They welcome the opportunity to describe their experiences, and hear "experts" describe their experiences, but are less comfortable with learning through engaging in self- or group reflection, tending to counter requests to engage in reflection from a "customer" perspective that demands a more teacher-centred input. This is made more difficult by the limited time they have to devote to their studies. For international students these challenges are intensified by the need to immerse themselves in a new culture. For these students, authentic experiential exercises require an understanding of the local culture, local business, and the local dialect (often not found in the English dictionary). This makes it difficult for them to become immersed in the activity (Kemlo, Jones, & Bigelow, 2002).

Using technology to engage post-graduate students in experiential activities can exacerbate the challenges. Computer-based experiential simulations, although they may assist group activities, often require student time outside the normal face-to-face learning environment. Web-based communication and sharing of reflections, although welcomed by students to assist their own reflections, can add to student angst about the "correctness" of their reflections, especially if the teacher does not adequately explain the purpose, process, and assessment criteria for reflection (Kemlo & Jones, 2002).

Engaging postgraduate students in authentic learning environments that are similar to, but different from, their actual work environment has the advantage of providing a safe learning environment in which their participation and reflection does not compromise their actual work environment. With this in mind, a work environment, or SLE, was designed based on a restaurant complex. The assumption was made that all students, local and international, would have either worked, or been a customer, in a restaurant and this would add experiential authenticity to the work environment. Into this environment, a number of issues requiring a negotiated solution were designed, together with roles for the students to play.

Given that the course was on negotiation skills, it was important that it was designed to develop these skills. Several classes were held initially, and periodically throughout the course, to discuss principles and practices of negotiation, but the principal emphasis was on reflection, and analysis of, experiential activities.

The authenticity of the workplace was further increased by adding a virtual situated learning environment, with students accessing company information as a company Web site located on the DLS. Students were also provided with ongoing information updates through the announcement facility, a virtual discussion board, and hyperlinks to external Web sites. The next section describes these in more detail.

Delicate Dining Restaurant Complex

The organisation that was created provide the setting for negotiation activities was the *Delicate Dining* restaurant complex owned by one person, but with outlets leased to lessee/managers in a number of urban city locations (the number depending on the number of students in the class). The restaurant complex has a marketing concept that includes a common restaurant layout, service and menu. Students are allocated to each outlet as either a lessee/manager of one of the outlets, or as an employee in one of the outlets (waitress, bar staff, chef, kitchen staff or *Maitre de*). Mid-way through the course students reverse roles so that they can consider the experience of negotiations from both a management and employee perspective. Although this could be assumed to upset the authenticity of the experiential activity, this has not been the experience. Indeed students readily assume the change in roles based on their knowledge of the organisation.

A number of negotiation situations associated with working in restaurants have been designed, chiefly concerned with negotiations of wages and working conditions, health and safety, and equity issues. The negotiations are given real-world relevance by the design of the work environment, the allocation of roles, and the issues required to be negotiated. The negotiations require students to define the tasks and sub-tasks needed to complete the activity, with the actual negotiation process being ill-defined, and requiring student input. The tasks to be investigated are complex and require student participation over a sustained period of time. This is achieved by providing students with very broad information associated with their role, and supplementing this with information about the company structure, financial situation, pressures facing the company, current employment conditions, and the culture of each outlet. Data sheets from the union to its members, minutes of management meetings, and communication broadsheets from the owner are provided periodically over the semester.

The activity also provides the opportunity for students to examine the tasks from different perspectives, using a variety of resources, by requiring students to source information from a broad range of industry, government and union bodies. Negotiations provide the opportunity to collaborate as students gradually recognise the superior negotiation skills they develop if they share resources, knowledge and ideas. The negotiations enable integration and application across different subject areas and can lead beyond domain specific outcomes by updating the issues that require a negotiated outcome to reflect the current business environment.

Student reflection, aimed at developing an understanding of their personal beliefs and values, is built into the activity through the assessment requirements. Assessment is designed to seamlessly integrate with the activity. For example, students are asked to reflect upon the activity and to write a number of short reflection papers that deal with not only what skills they observed being used, but also the personal beliefs and values the exercise exposed. The reflection also requires students to consider what alternate solutions there may have been and the degree of diversity that may occur in the outcome often depending on the diversity of input.

In summary, the negotiations in which students engage as virtual employees in the SLE presents them with an experiential opportunity to participate in, and learn from, a real-world negotiation through a polished product valued in its own right, rather than as preparation for something else. Student feedback on the activity has been positive, particularly in relation to the real-world relevance of the exercise, and the ability it provides for postgraduate students to examine the tasks from different perspectives. Teacher observation of the activity confirms the positive nature of the exercise. Students readily adopt the character of the role they play, despite the fact that the role is fairly ill-defined (e.g., "You are a full-time student working part-time in a restaurant in x locality"). Student-written reflection of the activity clearly identifies how their beliefs and values are questioned and/or confirmed, and how they develop a more collaborative approach. Moreover, increased research skills are evidenced by resources called upon to support their knowledge. Finally, and most importantly, students are able to demonstrate the ability to relate their learning to their own work environment.

Delicate Dining:
The Virtual Environment

The addition of a company Web site which students access through the DLS University, not only provided greater real-world relevance but also has the potential to integrate and apply the exercise across different subject areas. For example, discussion is currently being held with lecturers in Accounting and Health Sciences about how the *Delicate Dining* Web site can be used as the basis for an activity that can link students with different expertise. Students in an Occupational Health and Safety course can role-play as Health Inspectors, and Accounting students can identify the costs of changing employment conditions. Discussion is also being held currently with teachers of students in undergraduate degrees with the idea that these students could be brought into the exercise as "new recruits" to the workplace, with the postgraduate students role-playing the managers.

Opportunities to immerse students in the real-world culture of the activity, and to sustain the activity over time, is provided by enabling students to hyperlink to other resources, such as relevant government authorities, other companies, and broader literature. This provides students, particularly part-time students, with the ability to collect background information in a flexible way. Increased communication between the parties over the 13 weeks of the course was also enabled through the DLS. This meant that the restaurant "Owner" could communicate on an ongoing basis with the "Lessees," the "Lessees" with their "employees," and the "union officials" with their "members."

The ability for students to meet and discuss "virtually" provided the opportunity for students to explore competing solutions and diversity of outcome, and examination of tasks from different perspectives. This in turn provided opportunity for student collaboration enabling communication between students to explore alternatives rather than simply relying on the lecturer.

Finally, the opportunity to seamlessly integrate the activity with the assessment and to encourage students to reflect upon their own beliefs and values was encouraged by gaining permission from those students who had presented more advanced reflection papers to publish these papers online, thus providing opportunities for other students in the course to consider how they could develop their reflective writing skills.

Assessment of the Delicate Dining Learning Environment

In assessing the virtual learning environment as an authentic learning environment, it is interesting to observe that different participants place different emphasis on different issues. First, from the developers' perspective, it was important to establish a collaborative team of academics, technical design experts, and instructional design experts, to ensure the Web site had the look and feel (or graphics and navigation) of an actual Web site and thus add to the real-world nature of the exercise. Collaboration was also required to ensure the activity remained "live." The academic had to be trained in the DLS tools that enabled regular distribution of material to students. The facility for student discussion had to be established and maintained with student access ensured. Given the part-time, post-graduate nature of the student body, such technical expertise was also required to enable students to satisfy company "firewall" problems (Jones, 2002).

From the teachers' perspective, having students access the information via the Web site increased the authenticity of the exercise, as did the ability to provide regular updates to students-as-employees of the company. However, new technical skills had to be learned, a new approach to instructional design had to be considered, and a more collaborative approach to course design had to be accepted (Jones, 2001b). Furthermore, the need for regular updates of information, regular announcements to students, and regular checks on student communication, was time consuming. However, the benefit in terms of student involvement in the activity was testimony to its effectiveness as part of an authentic learning environment. Students' written reflections demonstrated an improved ability to examine tasks from different perspectives, to use a variety of resources, to reflect upon their beliefs and values, and to present a variety of solutions and diversity of outcomes. Despite the value of the online augmentation of the activity, however, the face-to-face negotiation remained invaluable to the authenticity of the learning.

From the student perspective, despite an initial resistance given the time and skills required to access the DLS, over time there was an increased acceptance of the value of the online component. In their feedback assessment, student comments included:

The communication facility enabled exposure to different viewpoints and an ability to discuss issues in more detail.

The DLS was valuable as we as students don't as a rule get to read what other students write (Student Feedback, Course Evaluations).

However, student feedback also confirmed the importance of a face-to-face learning environment:

Works in relationship with face-to-face classes, wouldn't like to do it without personal contact.

Use it as an option, as a tool, not a compulsory process (Student Feedback, Course Evaluations).

Further comments made by students about the advantages of sharing examples of well-constructed reflection papers included the following:

Absolutely effective, those samples stimulate my thinking.

Really effective, made everything much clearer (Student Feedback, Course Evaluations).

Conclusion

In summary, this chapter has discussed the additional learning outcomes that can result from using an experiential authentic learning experience. The value added by technology is the ability to augment the authenticity of the learning experience by enabling information to be communicated on a timely basis, by facilitating students' access to resources outside the teacher-provided material, and by providing opportunities for student reflection and discussion. However, the discussion also warned against exclusive reliance on a virtual environment, and argued the advantage of using a virtual environment to augment rather than replace the face-to-face learning opportunity.

References

Allee, V. (1999). *The knowledge evolution.* Newtown, MA: Butterworth-Heinemann.

Bailey J., & McAtee, M. (Eds.). (1999). *'The Workers' Embassy Scrapbook':* *Papers in Labour History,* No. 20. Perth, WA: The Australian Society for the Study of Labour History, Perth Branch.

Brown, J.S. (1999). Foreword. In R. Ruggles & D. Holthouse (Eds.), *The knowledge advantage.* Dover: Capstone.

Brown, J.S., Collins, A., & Duguid, P. (1989). Situated cognition and the culture of learning. *Educational Researcher, 18*(1), 32-42.

Davenport, T., & Prusak, L. (1998). *Working knowledge.* Boston: Harvard Business.

Jones, S. (1999). Avoiding the spider, how to use technology to achieve collaborative education. *Cornerstones of Higher Education* (Vol. 22). Jamison, ACT: HERDSA.

Jones, S. (2002). Designing flexibility through collaboration, *Mimeo RMIT Teaching and Learning Flexibility Forum,* June.

Jones, S. (2001a). Partner or predator in teaching employment relations. *The International Employment Relations Review, 7*(1).

Jones S. (2001b). Collaboration — A threat to academic autonomy? In G. Kennedy, M. Keppell, C. McNaught, & T. Petrovic (Eds.), *Meeting at the Crossroads. Proceedings of the 18ᵗʰ Annual Conference of the Australian Society for Computers in Learning in Tertiary Education.* Melbourne: Biomedical Multimedia Unit, The University of Melbourne.

Jones, S. (2000, Autumn). Politics, power and persuasion: Documenting a drama for students - The 1998 Waterfront dispute. *Australian Screen Education,* 22, 80-88.

Jones, S., & Creese E. (2001). E-education: Creating partnerships for learning, *Ultibase.* Retrieved December 10, 2002, from *http://ultibase.rmit.edu.au/ Articles/online*

Jones, S., & Richardson, J. (2002). Designing an IT-augmented student-centred learning environment. In A. Goody, J. Herrington & M. Northcote (Eds.), *Quality conversations: Research and Development in Higher Education, Volume 25.* Jamison, ACT: HERDSA.

Kemlo, L., & Jones, S. (2002, November). Reflective assessment — Have I made myself understood? *QUT, Evaluations and Assessment Conference: Closing the Loop,* Brisbane.

Kemlo, L., Jones, S., & Bigelow, H. (2002, November). Creating a partnership learning environment for international and local students. *QUT 2002 Effective Teaching and Learning Conference: Valuing Students, Valuing Staff,* Brisbane.

Laurillard, D. (1994). Multimedia and the changing experience of the learner. *Proceedings: Asia Pacific Information Technology in Training and Education Conference and Exhibition,* June 28-July 2, Brisbane (pp. 19-25).

Ramsden, P. (1992), *Learning to teach in higher education.* London: Routledge,

Reeves, T. C., Herrington, J., & Oliver, R. (2002). Authentic activities and online learning. In A. Goody, J. Herrington & M. Northcote (Eds.), *Quality conversations: Research and development in higher education* (Vol. 25) (pp. 562-567). Jamison, ACT: HERDSA.

Schön, D. (1985). *The design studio.* London: RIBA.

Schön, D. (1987). *Educating the reflective practitioner.* San Francisco: Jossey-Bass.

Chapter XIV

An Authentic Approach to Facilitating Transfer of Teachers' Pedagogical Knowledge

Anthony Herrington, University of Wollongong, Australia

Jan Herrington, University of Wollongong, Australia

Evan Glazer, Roanoke Valley Governor's School, USA

Abstract

The pedagogical knowledge learned by pre-service teachers often fails to transfer to teaching practice. Instead, new teachers revert to instructional strategies they observed as children. This chapter describes design research conducted over four years, where pre-service teachers were immersed in an authentic learning environment using multimedia to learn mathematics assessment strategies. The first study was conducted with pre-service teachers in the second year of their degree, and then the second study followed up with the same people in their second year as practising teachers. The first study revealed several constraints for the participants on professional practice, including limited time and the influence of the supervising teacher. Later, as practising teachers, they faced cultural and practical constraints within the school environment that prevented them from fully operationalising the pedagogical principles they learned as pre-service teachers.

Transfer of Learning

Transfer — or the lack of it — continues to be a critical issue in education. Educators (as described by Whitehead, 1932) have been challenged to develop strategies to ensure that learning does not remain "inert" at those times it is needed to solve real problems. Elliot Eisner summed up the problem well:

The really important dependent variables in education are not located in classrooms. Nor are they located in schools. The really important variables are located outside schools...It's what students do with what they learn when they can do what they want to do that is the real measure of educational achievement. (Eisner, 2001, p. 370)

While the transfer of learning is important in the school context, the issue has continuing relevance for university educators as well. In particular, the outcomes for teacher education courses must go beyond knowledge of the theoretical notions encountered in philosophies, psychologies and sociologies of education, to reflect how these theories apply in practice in the classroom. Unfortunately, the evidence to show that theory transfers to practice in teacher education courses is not strong. In mathematics education courses, for example, modern constructivist theories of learning have been promoted in recent years. However, the practices of novice teachers in schools continues to reflect traditional approaches to teaching, based on their own school experiences as students (Brown & Borko, 1992; Raymond, 1997). These traditional practices reflect beliefs about teaching and learning, built up over many years of schooling, that are deeply ingrained and difficult to change (Ball, 1990).

Another reason for the inability of teacher education courses to transfer theory to practice is too little engagement with genuine situations and too much emphasis on theoretical perspectives (Resnick, 1987). The challenge for teacher educators is to make meaningful connections between theory and practice, where practice is often reflective of traditional approaches to teaching and learning. School practicums, for example, should provide real world experience where theory can be observed in practice (Ensor, 2001). For many pre-service teachers, however, their school practicum experience is often a reaffirmation of the traditional approaches that are already ingrained from their own schooling (Comiti & Ball, 1996). Breaking the cycle is critically important for teacher educators, and for the school students who will inevitably benefit from a rejuvenated and informed approach.

So, how can pre-service teachers experience practices that reflect current theories of education? And more importantly, how can they experience practices that challenge their pre-existing beliefs and practices, and enable them to transfer their learning to the classroom?

This chapter describes an authentic learning environment that used multimedia to engage pre-service teachers in solving complex problems — the kinds of problems encountered by teachers in their day-to-day teaching. It was hypothesised that teachers using this multimedia would modify their existing beliefs about assessment practices and adopt recent assessment practices when they taught in classrooms, both during their school practicum and in their initial school postings as beginning teachers.

The design of the authentic multimedia environment was based on the theory of *situated learning* (Brown, Collins & Duguid, 1989; Collins, Brown & Newman, 1989; Lave & Wenger, 1991). Situated learning places learning in the context in which it will later be applied. One of the principal effects claimed for the theory is that it facilitates transfer of learning to new situations. Park and Hannafin (1993) cite the improvement of transfer as *the* distinguishing feature of situated learning as a theory in their analysis of new learning theories in relation to the design of interactive multimedia.

Multimedia Program on Assessment

Nine critical characteristics of situated learning environments have been defined to inform the instructional design of new learning environments (described in detail in Herrington & Oliver, 2000): provide an authentic context and task; provide access to expert performances; provide multiple roles and perspectives; support the collaborative construction of knowledge; provide coaching and scaffolding; promote reflection, and articulation to enable tacit knowledge to be made explicit; and provide for integrated assessment of learning.

A multimedia program entitled *Investigating Assessment Strategies in Mathematics Classrooms* was developed in light of these characteristics to enable teachers and pre-service teachers of mathematics to explore issues of assess-

ment (Herrington, Sparrow, Herrington, & Oliver, 1997). Twenty-three assessment strategies suitable for K-12 classrooms were identified and grouped in the
following categories: *Questioning, Interviewing, Testing, Problem-solving,
Reporting* and *Self-assessment,* and presented in a multimedia format. Five
complex, authentic activities were designed consisting of memos and other
documents, to enable students to explore the resource within the parameters and
constraints of a realistic task. For example, in one task, students respond to a
letter to the school from a parent requesting that her child be assessed without
formal tests due to the stress this caused in the family. In response to this
dilemma, the students need to prepare an alternative assessment approach for
the whole mathematics department. To do this, they can access the wealth of
resources provided in the multimedia program (listed below), and to further add
to the authenticity, they must deliver their report in a "staff meeting." The
interface of the program (see Figure 1) simulates the front part of a classroom
with the resources represented by appropriate metaphors (such as video
cassettes, filing cabinet drawers, folders on the desk) giving direct access to the
following:

- Video clips of teachers using various assessment techniques
- Video clips of teachers' comments on the strategies
- Video clips of children's comments on the strategies to present their own
  thoughts
- Interviews with experts in the field to provide theoretical perspectives
- Reflections by third-year pre-service teachers to provide practical advice
- Text descriptions of each assessment category
- Teachers' resources and children's work samples
- An electronic notebook to enable students to copy text and to write their
  own ideas
- Problems and investigations to enable the students to complete authentic
  tasks

Using a design research approach (Brown, 1992; Collins, 1992; Reeves, 2000),
two studies were conducted over a five-year period to investigate the transfer
effect of the multimedia program on the extent of use of alternative assessment
strategies. The first study investigated these effects in pre-service teachers'
teaching practicum, and four years later, the second study examined the effects
when the same students were in their second year of teaching.

Figure 1. Annotated interface of the multimedia program

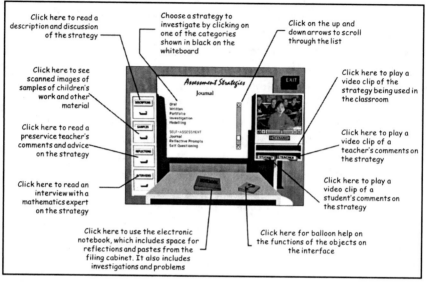

Transfer to School Practicum

In the first study, pre-service teachers explored a variety of assessment strategies appropriate to K-12 mathematics classrooms using the multimedia assessment program. The students spent three weeks of the semester examining strategies within the context of a complex and sustained authentic activity, where in small collaborative groups, they prepared and presented a report on a new assessment plan for mathematics in a school. In order to do this, they were asked to consult with experts, look at what was happening in classrooms, talk to teachers, talk to students and so on — all of which could be done "virtually" from the CD-ROM.

Three pairs of students were interviewed and observed as they used the multimedia program. An analysis of their conversation revealed that students used a substantial amount of higher-order thinking as they worked with the assessment program (reported in Herrington & Oliver, 1999). A study of the transfer of a variety of assessment strategies to classroom practice was conducted with the students as they completed two weeks of professional practice in schools approximately five weeks after the completion of their work on the assessment program (reported in Herrington, Herrington, & Sparrow, 2000). All the students were required to teach mathematics classes in this teaching practice, and it was expected that they would have the opportunity to implement some of the assessment strategies they had investigated in the multimedia program. Students and their supervising teachers in the schools were interviewed and the comments were transcribed and analysed. Transfer was thought to have occurred if firstly, students using the interactive multimedia program on assessment had demonstrated a good understanding of the diversity of assessment approaches in the mathematics classroom and were able to articulate this understanding; and secondly, if they employed a variety of the assessment techniques shown in the program, as opposed to the predominant use of pencil-and-paper tests (Cognition & Technology Group at Vanderbilt, 1993).

Analysis of the data showed that all the students could speak knowledgably and confidently about assessment, and all the students used a variety of techniques to assess children's understanding. All pre-service teachers were influenced strongly by the supervising teacher in the schools, many of whom had planned assessment strategies in advance of the students' arrival. However, pre-service teachers still incorporated some informal assessment techniques — such as checklists, anecdotal records and open interviews — without the contribution or agreement of the supervising teacher. Five of the six students attributed their use of alternative assessment techniques directly to the interactive multimedia program. These findings were qualified by two mitigating factors: the brevity of a two-week professional practice and the substantial influence of the supervising teacher. In the words of one student: "I'm not the qualified teacher. I'm in their situation, in their room, conforming to their rules. So I can't just suddenly say: Hey, let's do some oral assessment."

Many of the students in the first study were inhibited in the choice of assessment strategies by the influence and authority of their supervising teachers, in a way that may not have been an issue if the students were practising teachers with their own classes. In order to investigate this issue further, a follow-up study of those same students who had gained employment as teachers was carried out when the students were in the second year of teaching, four years after the first study.

Transfer to School Practice

Four students from the original study had gained employment as teachers, and all were in their second year of teaching. Three students (two female, one male) were teaching mathematics in private schools in the metropolitan area of Perth, Western Australia, and one (female) was teaching in a remote outback government school in the north of the state.

In addition to providing informal information about their teaching approaches, participants were interviewed at their schools, for approximately 90 to 120 minutes each, using an interview schedule described by Denzin (1989) as *Non-scheduled standardised interview*. Students were questioned about: their beliefs about assessment; their knowledge and use of assessment strategies in mathematics; the influence of factors such as school policy, colleagues, and national guidelines, on their assessment practices; and the influence of their teacher training on their current practices. Interviews and notes were transcribed and analysed using a qualitative data analysis program.

The longitudinal nature of the study, incorporating interviews with the same people over a four-year period of immense growth and change, provided a unique opportunity to observe the development of these teachers. Our initial impression of the pre-service teachers was that they were enthusiastic, idealistic and positioning themselves as agents of change in classrooms where they believed they could do better than the teachers they had observed. But as teachers, they seemed to have lost much of their enthusiasm, and were struggling to deal with a range of factors that appeared to have compromised their ideals. For example, Zoe (pseudonyms used) commenting on her practicum supervising teacher's use of assessment strategies in 1996, appeared to have a range of alternative strategies in mind which failed to be used in her teaching practice in 2000:

Interview with Zoe (1996) as a pre-service teacher:

[The multimedia program on assessment] opened my eyes a lot more ... and also watching my teacher and really disagreeing with a lot of the assessment strategies he'd use. He only used pencil and paper assessment strategies. Of course I didn't say anything, but I'd sit there thinking 'Oh remember what we learnt'.

Interview with Zoe (2000) as a practising teacher:

Testing. That's the main approach. With years 8, 9 and 10 mainly topic testing, and then at the end of their year we do an exam to get them ready for Year 11 and 12 ... If you put it on a piece of paper, you know if they can interpret it. I don't think that sort of testing is fantastic for every student [because] some kids can't read very well ... It's hard for them, so it's got its weaknesses, but I can't think of another really appropriate assessment task.

Similarly, the enthusiasm Evie had in 1996 to try a range of assessment strategies in her own classes, by 2000 had been overwhelmed by significant social and cultural problems:

Interview with Evie (1996) as a pre-service teacher:

There were only limited types of assessment that I could use [on teaching practicum], but hopefully in the future I'll be able to use a wider range of the ones that were on the multimedia. Hopefully I'll be able to ... start journals and things like that.

Interview with Evie (2000) as a practising teacher:

I'd like to vary a lot of things, such as I'd like to do a lot more collaborative work with the kids, group work. And probably even presentation type stuff, where kids can actually demonstrate or explain their findings, whether it be an investigation or even project work ... I just find that all these fantastic ideas that I come up with, they usually seem to backfire when I use them in the classroom. I don't see myself as being a really boring teacher, I just think the kids — I'm not blaming it on the kids — but they just lack any self-motivation. And it's not just me, it's across the curricula. All the learning areas are having the same problems with the same kids. You can just tell when you don't have kids coming to school. I think the problem is they don't see the importance of education ... there is a high rate of kids dropping out, and girls falling pregnant at a young age which is really sad.

While the first study revealed constraints for the participants as pre-service teachers on professional practice (limited time and the influence of the supervising teacher), as teachers they were also faced with cultural and practical constraints. Constraints include the requirements of the mathematics department in the school, National Curriculum guidelines, issues of practical classroom management, personal issues (such as the amount of time that can be devoted to planning), and convictions about the suitability of certain types of assessment for certain students. Ensor (2001) found that beginning mathematics teachers in South Africa experienced similar constraints. As such, the teachers' pedagogical beliefs do not always translate to classroom practice.

These findings do not suggest the teachers' approaches to assessment will remain static. When prompted with various assessment strategies, all teachers indicated that they would be willing to try these techniques in the future. One teacher indicated that she would try journals as an assessment strategy when she could develop strategies to help students write them. Further research with the same teachers in 2-3 years' time might reveal more self-assured and confident classroom managers, by then willing and capable of using a variety of assessment strategies in appropriate ways in their mathematics classrooms.

A Way Forward

It is clear from this study that these teachers face challenges in their implementation of new assessment techniques learned during their pre-service teaching experiences. One confounding variable in this situation is teaching experience. Teachers may start to overcome constraints in their teaching once they establish themselves in schools and gain confidence. Unfortunately, the statistics on teacher retention suggests that this strategy might be self-defeating. In the USA, a national study by Ingersoll (2001) indicated that 39% of beginning teachers leave the profession in their first five years of teaching. A similar statistic of 30% was found in a UK national study (Adams, 2003). While no national studies have occurred in Australia, it is estimated that up to 25% of beginning teachers leave the profession in their first five years (DEST, 2003).

In an effort to overcome stagnation, pre-service educators and administrators need to develop strategies to help beginning teachers transfer innovative ideas into practice. The need for effective induction programs appears to hold merit, particularly where they involve mentoring programs. Such programs have generally evolved from individual school initiatives to district, state and national systemic approaches. Their success, however, appears to depend to a large extent on the individual school culture and the support provided by the principal (DEST, 2002). For those beginning teachers who enter schools where such support does not exist, then other strategies need to be available, such as participation in collegial groups outside of the school walls.

In recent years, a number of online sites have become available to provide support and professional development for beginning teachers (e.g., Ontario Teachers' Federation's *Survive and Thrive Virtual Conference for Beginning Teachers;* Indiana University's *Novice Teacher Support Project*). Typically these Web sites provide resources linked to the appropriate educational system, and importantly provide a system of mentoring and support that enables novice teachers to seek advice from content and issues experts. These sites may also provide connections to other beginning teachers where a virtual *community of practice* (Wenger, 1998; Wenger, McDermott & Snyder, 2002) develops. In such a way, the problems faced by beginning teachers can often be resolved in a collaborative and authentic way. These sites hold much promise, although effective strategies for design, implementation, and sustainability of these online communities has not been clearly defined. In addition, further research is needed to explore the impact these online communities have on teacher retention and transfer of pedagogical knowledge and practice (Herrington, Herrington, Lockyer, & Brown, 2004).

Conclusion

The notion of transfer implies a situation where people have the choice to apply the knowledge they have learnt. Unapplied knowledge suggests the learning environment may be inadequate for transfer, and modifications may be necessary in order to promote transfer. As Bransford, Brown and Cocking (2000) indicated, transfer involves a number of factors: a threshold of initial learning must be achieved; thoughtful and meaningful learning must occur; knowledge needs to be learnt in a variety of contexts; transfer involves knowing *how* as well as *when* to use knowledge; transfer effects subsequent learning; and, all learning involves transfer (p. 235). Even if all of these conditions are met, evidence of transfer may exist within teachers' changed beliefs but not in practice, simply because of external constraints. Removing those constraints, or providing novice teachers with professional experiences to deal more effectively with them, might enable the vision of modern theories of education to transfer to practice early in a teacher's career, rather than later.

To paraphrase Eisner's earlier quote: it's what novice teachers do with what they learn *when they can do what they want to do* that is the real measure of teacher education. Establishing communities of practice where beginning teachers are supported by their peers and experienced teachers, may well provide an "authentic community" in which beginning teachers feel secure to transfer the pedagogical knowledge encountered in their teacher education courses.

References

Adams, C. (2003). *Address to the North of England Education Conference.* Retrieved June 2004, from *http://www.gtce.org.uk/news/newsDetail.asp?NewsId=480*

Ball, D. (1990). The mathematical understandings that prospective teachers bring to teacher education. *The Elementary School Journal, 10*(2), 17-24.

Brown, A.L. (1992). Design experiments: Theoretical and methodological challenges in creating complex interventions in classroom settings. *The Journal of the Learning Sciences, 2*(2), 141-178.

Brown, C.A., & Borko, H. (1992). Becoming a mathematics teacher. In D.A. Grouws (Ed.), *Handbook of research on mathematics teaching and learning* (pp. 209-239). New York: Macmillan.

Brown, J.S., Collins, A., & Duguid, P. (1989). Situated cognition and the culture of learning. *Educational Researcher, 18*(1), 32-42.

Cognition and Technology Group at Vanderbilt. (1993). Anchored instruction and situated cognition revisited. *Educational Technology, 33*(3), 52-70.

Collins, A. (1992). Towards a design science of education. In E. Scanlon & T. O'Shea (Eds.), *New directions in educational technology* (pp. 15-22). Berlin: Springer-Verlag.

Collins, A., Brown, J.S., & Newman, S.E. (1989). Cognitive apprenticeship: Teaching the crafts of reading, writing, and mathematics. In L.B. Resnick (Ed.), *Knowing, learning and instruction: Essays in honour of Robert Glaser* (pp. 453-494). Hillsdale, NJ: LEA.

Comiti, C., & Ball, D. (1996). Preparing teachers to teach mathematics: A comparative perspective. In A.J. Bishop, K. Clements, C. Keitel, J. Kilpatrick & C. Laborde (Eds.), *International handbook of mathematics education* (pp. 1123-1153). Dordrecht: Kluwer.

Denzin, N.K. (1989). *The research act: A theoretical introduction to sociological methods* (3rd ed.). Englewood Cliffs, NJ: Prentice Hall.

Department of Education Science and Training. (2002). *An ethic of care: Effective programmes for beginning teachers.* Canberra, AGPS.

Department of Education Science and Training. (2003). *Australia's teachers: Australia's future: Advancing innovation, science, technology and mathematics.* Canberra: AGPS.

Ensor, P. (2001). From preservice mathematics teacher education to beginning teaching: A study in recontextualizing. *Journal for Research in Mathematics Education, 32*(3), 296-320.

Herrington, A., Herrington, J., Lockyer, L., & Brown, I. (2004). Beginning teacher network: The design of an online community of practice for beginning teachers in Australia. In L. Cantoni & C. McLoughlin, (Eds.), *Proceedings of EdMedia 2004: World Conference on Educational Multimedia, Hypermedia & Telecommunications* (pp. 3251-3257). Norfolk, VA: AACE.

Herrington, A.J., Sparrow, R.L., Herrington, J., & Oliver, R.G. (1997). *Investigating assessment strategies in mathematics classrooms* [Book and CD-ROM]. Perth: MASTEC, Edith Cowan University.

Herrington, J., & Oliver, R. (1999). Using situated learning and multimedia to investigate higher-order thinking. *Journal of Interactive Learning Research, 10*(1), 3-24.

Herrington, J., & Oliver, R. (2000). An instructional design framework for authentic learning environments. *Educational Technology Research and Development, 48*(3), 23-48.

Herrington, J., Herrington, A., & Sparrow, L. (2000). Assessment strategies: Using multimedia to promote transfer to classroom practice. In J. Bana & A. Chapman (Eds.), *Mathematics Education Beyond 2000: Proceedings of the 23rd Annual Conference of the Mathematics Education Research Group of Australasia* (pp. 307-315). Perth: MERGA.

Ingersoll, R.M. (2001). *Teacher turnover, teacher shortages, and the organization of schools.* Washington: University of Washington, Center for the Study of Teaching and Policy.

Lave, J., & Wenger, E. (1991). *Situated learning: Legitimate peripheral participation.* Cambridge: Cambridge University.

Novice teacher support network. Retrieved September 17, 2004, from http://ntsp.ed.uiuc.edu/

Park, I., & Hannafin, M. J. (1993). Empirically-based guidelines for the design of interactive multimedia. *Educational Technology Research and Development, 41*(3), 63-85.

Reeves, T. C. (2000). Socially responsible educational research. *Educational Technology, 40*(6), 19-28.

Resnick, L. (1987). Learning in school and out. *Educational Researcher, 16*(9), 13-20.

Survive and thrive virtual conference for beginning teachers. Retrieved September 17, 2004, from *http://www.survivethrive.on.ca/*

Wenger, E. (1998). *Communities of practice: Learning, meaning and identity.* Cambridge: Cambridge University.

Wenger, E., McDermott, R., & Snyder, W. M. (2002). *Cultivating communities of practice: A guide to managing knowledge.* Boston: Harvard Business School.

Whitehead, A. N. (1932). *The aims of education and other essays.* London: Ernest Benn.

Chapter XV

Applying Situated Learning Theory to the Creation of Learning Environments to Enhance Socialisation and Self-Regulation

Catherine McLoughlin, Australian Catholic University, Australia

Joe Luca, Edith Cowan University, Australia

Abstract

Although much effort is devoted to investigating the use of technology to teach course content, an emerging area of some importance in online teaching is how to enhance the student experience of learning and communicating online. Associated with this is the creation of social and supportive environments for learning when there is little face-to-face contact between distance learners and their teachers. An examination of the literature on authentic learning suggests that there are a variety of frameworks and approaches on how to foster positive learning experiences through online delivery. While there are many frameworks that emphasise the cognitive aspects of learning, it is clear that the socio-affective aspects are of equal importance in creating a positive learning experience for students. Two approaches that balance cognitive and social aspects of learning are: the creation of online knowledge building community, and Social Presence Theory which emphasises interpersonal and social strategies that reduce psychological and physical distance between teachers and students. By synthesising findings from these two areas of research, this chapter provides a framework and a set of strategies that can be used to create an authentic learning climate, and illustrates a range of tasks that create positive social, learning experiences.

The Student Experience Online

Evaluations of technology innovations have shown that the weakest part has been the implementation of the technology, and the failure to consider environmental and contextual factors that impinge on the learner and the teacher (Alexander & McKenzie, 1998). Social and contextual support for learning is essential, as online learners often have little direct contact with tutors and other students. Constructivist theory provides guidelines and principles indicating that successful learning occurs when it is contextualised, social, conversational, collaborative and reflective, yet translating these principles into effective pedagogy and support for learning remains the greatest challenge. There are several empirical studies attesting to negative learner experiences online, and to feelings of anonymity and isolation. Wegerif's (1999) study of an online group of learners found that individual success related to the degree to which participants were able to cross a threshold from feeling like outsiders to becoming insiders. Social factors such as the degree of support, connectedness and peer feedback have been found to be powerful determinants of success and satisfaction in online courses of study (Barab, Thomas & Merrill, 2001). Constraints that operate in online computer conferencing environments are often what Sherry (2000) refers to as "finding a voice and having something to say." Affirmation that students need to feel the human touch in online learning has long been recognised by adult and distance learning theorists (Rowntree, 1992; Kearsley, 2000). Social, contextual and affective dimensions of the learning experience remain powerful determinants of successful learning, according to research in social psychology. Common themes that distance educators embrace are the need to make the learning experience personalised, affective, interactive and positive (Hiltz, 1998).

What Learning Experiences
Do Students Value?

Investigations of student perceptions of online learning have provided evidence that students value the increased peer interaction, control, convenience, flexibility and sharing of personal experience (Coomey & Stephenson, 2001; Collis & Moonen, 2001). In-depth studies of student learning and interaction online have shown that students value the following aspects of online interaction (e.g., Laurillard, 2002; Salmon, 2000):

- Active participation and sharing of ideas;
- The provision of responsive and constructive feedback; and
- An affective climate for learning focused messaging.

These aspects of student support are depicted in Figure 1.

Despite the many acclamations that online experience is positive and valuable, there remain valid calls from educators and researchers to improve and investigate online learning, and provide the authentic learning experience with a view to creating more effective learning environments (Barab, Makinster, Moore & Cunningham, 2001; Herrington & Oliver, 2002). Eastmond (1995) maintains that learning tasks and human factors are central to successful teaching and learning online, while Coomey and Stephenson (2001) suggest that paying attention to pedagogy and overcoming negative aspects of the student experience are also important. This means addressing issues of engagement, motivation, the need for connectedness and personalised feedback. Overall, the most salient issues to emerge from the literature on online learning are the need to increase feedback, reciprocity and support for interpersonal and social interaction (Gunawardena, 1995; Chickering & Erhmann, 1996).

Figure 1. Student expectations of the learning environment

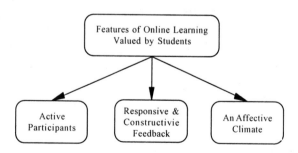

Supporting Sociability

Throughout the literature there are common factors that emerge in discussions of students learning online. Tait (2000) proposes a threefold functional model of student support that includes cognitive, affective and systemic elements. The cognitive dimension covers provision of appropriate learning resources, the affective includes the provision of a supportive student-centered environment to enhance self-esteem and the systemic aspect entails the provision of administrative process that are effective, transparent and student-friendly. The literature refers to many kinds of support needed by individuals to assist them to perform tasks and interact online. Most frameworks are supported by theories of socio-cultural learning and refer to the pedagogical roles of the teacher as coaching, scaffolding and guidance (Hannafin & Land, 1997). Barab et al. (2001) refer to the term sociability as the social policies and structures that facilitate and support a shared purpose and a sense of belonging in an online community.

Bonk (2000) responds to the call for increased learner support by suggesting that there are four overlapping roles for the online instructor. These are: administrative, pedagogical, social and technological. Rourke, Anderson, Garrison and Archer (1999) propose a community-of-inquiry model where learning occurs through the interaction of three core components: *cognitive presence, teaching presence* and *social presence*. Laurillard's (2002) iterative model of conversational dialogue leading to learning is an example of a communication model that can involve learners socially and cognitively. All three theorists recognise the primacy of the social dimension.

Research also indicates that there are intersecting concerns that need to be addressed in assisting the learner: *affective, regulative* and *cognitive* (Vermunt, 1999) (Figure 2). If we conceptualise these concerns from a socio-cultural perspective, all three dimensions of supporting learning can be viewed as essential. For example, teaching online requires attention to the cognitive dimension and this might be achieved by creating tasks and problems sufficiently complex so as to stretch students' current level of understanding: having them present cases, arguments and conflicting views so as to encourage articulation and justification of ideas. Tutors can provide the affective dimension by giving students personal responsibility for learning, by enabling them to achieve success and by emphasising the importance of setting personal goals that can be realised. The regulative or metacognitive dimension of learning may be supported by allowing students to monitor their own and others' progress, by fostering reflection through learning logs or diaries and by incorporating self-assessment.

Other indications of the need for socialisation support are signalled in the literature through social presence and knowledge building communities. These are discussed next.

Figure 2. Three supportive roles for online tutors based on Vermunt (1999)

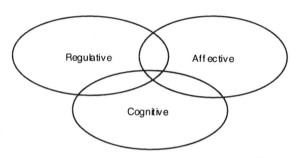

Social Presence Theory

Presence can be defined as the degree to which a medium allows the user to feel socially present in a technology-mediated situation (Short, Williams & Christie, 1976). This means the degree to which the person is perceived as "real" and able to convey messages through facial expression, voice, posture and attitude. Gunawardena and Zittle (1997) found that both the medium and the communicator can convey aspects of presence. Further, Steuer (1992) found that perception of presence was more powerful than actual physical surroundings, and that telepresence referred to participants' feeling of belonging to a virtual world. Emerging from this is the issue of how to create a feeling of social presence in a text-based medium such as computer conferencing (Leh, 2001).

Early uses of computer-mediated communication (CMC) involved the coordination of tasks among dispersed populations, not necessarily in educational settings (Hiltz, 1994). The lack of social contact cues was regarded as a positive attribute in settings where the exchange of information could be achieved without the hindrance of hierarchical status. In addition, many early uses of CMC did not last long enough for participants to develop socio-emotional communication, and it was regarded as positive that computer conferencing enabled participants to shift focus from the affective to the functional aspects of communication and remain task-focused. More recent studies conducted on social presence and learning effectiveness found that students often see the presence of others such as peers, tutors and mentors as an essential part of the learning experience (Fazey & Fazey, 2001), and that student satisfaction with the tutor and course are linked with their perception of social presence (Richardson & Swan, 2001).

In summary, the literature on social presence in computer-mediated communication provides contradictory perspectives, and yet effective utilisation of online technologies in educational settings is evident (Swan, 2001). If there is any agreement in the literature on social presence theory it is this: attributes of environment design, how technology is used, and the pedagogies adopted by teachers influence student perceptions of social presence, and therefore instructional design becomes an important consideration. This places the onus squarely on teachers and designers of learning environments. It is also clear from studies of social presence that both interactive and affective experiences can be used effectively to support student learning, and when combined with effective pedagogy, can focus students on both skills development and the process of online learning (Murphy & Cifuentes, 2001).

Supporting Process-Based Learning Through Authentic Activity

The second major area of research exploring social support in online environments derives from social constructivist and situated learning theories. Social presence theory places the onus on the teacher to provide social support and demonstrate positive immediacy behaviours, whereas the concept of an online community is regarded as a function of both teachers and learners. Balancing this view of socialisation support with that suggested by constructivists means that educators must relinquish control and students must assume more responsibility. According to Jonassen, Mayes and Aleese (1993), the challenge is to provide supportive rather than intervening learning environments. Instead of learners being focused on acquiring established knowledge, the emphasis needs to change to learners making contributions to collective knowledge, and teaching as supporting knowledge building communities (Scardamalia & Bereiter, 1996). According to this framework students and teachers have responsibility in supporting knowledge building. Three key elements that characterise this approach follow:

1. Students create knowledge "products" that are made available to the learning community and used as the foundation of more advanced products.

2. Knowledge creation is collaborative and products created by individuals or groups become stepping stones for others. Learning is dynamic, social and adaptive rather than static, personal and inflexible. Assessment processes need to reflect these dimensions.

3. Every student shares responsibility for planning, organising, questioning and summarising.

In this environment, the teacher becomes a co-learner and sometimes a model for students. While knowledge advancement is the core activity of a knowledge building community, it requires authentic activity and productive interaction. According to Herrington and Oliver (2000), "Authentic context is the cornerstone of the situated learning model, the fundamental premise upon which the theory rests" (p. 23). Essential factors include the creation of a climate and a commitment to advancing knowledge through peer interaction and feedback while the broader community ensures that students view ideas from the perspective of multiple expertise.

Cognitive approaches to Web-based instruction do not sufficiently acknowledge the social and contextual dimensions of learning and tend to highlight the cognitive processes involved in learning such as information organisation and access, and acquiring declarative knowledge (Sugrue, 2000). Authentic learning theory recognises that the socio-affective attributes of learning need to be supported in online learning environments, as these are features that characterise competent, achieving learners. For example, the social-psychological aspects of behaviour such as motivation, decision-making, and self-regulation need to be acquired and developed in all learners, and recognised as personally meaningful (Fazey & Fazey, 2001; Shaffer & Resnick, 1999). The following recommendations on supporting learning as authentic social experience are derived from a synthesis of the literature on authentic learning, situated cognition and frameworks for knowledge building communities (Barab et al., 2001; Herrington & Oliver, 2000).

Design Recommendations for Provision of Socialisation Support in Online Environments

The elements described below are derived from theories of situated cognition and are instantiations of Herrington and Oliver's (2000) framework for authentic learning. The difference in focus is that while activity drives the learning environment, the social aspects are given priority. These strategies include metacognitive aspects of planning, monitoring and evaluation, that is, regulative as well as affective aspects.

Strategy 1: Design for social activity and interactive learning

In order to ensure a motivating learning context, learning activities should not only seek to foster cognitive outcomes but also develop group and individual social skills and processes. Cooperative learning activities such as group investigations, team- and project-based learning enable the integration of interpersonal, social and cognitive aspects of learning online. Providing effective models and examples of group interaction protocols online, or by direct modelling in computer conferencing, provides scaffolding for the social aspects of learning (Herrington, Oliver & Reeves, 2002).

Strategy 2: Foster intentionality and goal-setting in learning

Scardamalia and Bereiter (1993), in their work on creating knowledge building communities, state that the capacity to acquire expertise and high-level reasoning is determined by intentionality. Intentional learning is defined as cognitive processes that have learning as a goal rather than an incidental outcome. This kind of intentionality can be fostered be giving students more agency in learning, and by allowing expression of personal and collective goals for learning. Students need to perceive themselves competent in self-managing their learning and coming to terms with new knowledge, while being given the opportunity to reflect on new skills. Among distance learners, self-perceptions of scholastic competence are essential to motivation (Tait, 2000). It is important to provide resources to students that allow them to acquire interdisciplinary competence across fields of study.

Strategy 3: Employ role differentiation to foster multiple perspectives

Online environments provide scope for students to assume multiple participatory roles, enabling varying levels and forms of responsibility for contributing, questioning, mentoring and demonstrating expertise. Role differentiation puts learners in alternating roles of novice, researcher and expert. Reciprocal teaching enables learners to develop process skills, self-regulation and confidence (Bonk & Cunningham, 1998).

Strategy 4: Ensure that learning becomes a constructive social experience

The provision of regular, timely and personalised feedback is important in counterbalancing the impersonal effects of online learning. Well-timed constructive feedback increases students' perception of positive social presence (Gunawardena, 1995). Another strategy for feedback in online forums is to focus on group problems of understanding and to clarify misconceptions to the group as a whole. Students can also be encouraged to provide responses to teacher and peer feedback openly, and engage in dialogue and articulation so that tacit knowledge becomes explicit.

Strategy 5: Foster metalearning

Students new to online learning often need an orientation to learning in this new mode and an opportunity to talk about and reflect on their experiences. Often student satisfaction with online learning is a product of their use and comfort with the technology. In creating a supportive environment for online study, with attention to self-appraisal, reflective practice and peer review, students learn metacognitive skills and the capacity to judge their own performance and that of others (Lin, Hmelo, Kinzer & Secules, 1999).

Strategy 6: Enable student autonomy and a sense of ownership

Ownership for learning is linked to self-regulation as it sees learners as socially, metacognitively and motivationally proactive in their own learning (Zimmerman, 1995). Equally, to participate in the knowledge building community, learners need to take primary responsibility for setting learning goals, accomplishing tasks and self-evaluating their own performances. Teachers need to foster self-regulatory behaviours and self-directed learning, by offering tasks that require both collaborative and independent work.

Strategy 7: Balance both personal and interpersonal orientations in creating a motivating climate for learning

While learners need to orient themselves to the content domain and course outcomes, they also need to be given scope to discuss the perceived relevance of the course and articulate reasons for taking the course. This can be achieved through conferencing and discussion. The relational element of learning is a product of our desire for affiliation, association and connection (Walther, 1992). Establishing relationships with students online is therefore a priority, while ensuring that students know that sources of help are available. The following examples, depicting an authentic online environment, exemplify these principles.

A Case Study

Final year students enrolled in the Interactive Multimedia course at Edith Cowan University are required to develop skills and expertise in project managing the development of multimedia products. These skills are taught through a Project Management Methodology unit where students practice creating Web sites using project management models, performing needs analysis, developing design specifications, and conducting formative and summative evaluation. The unit consists of 13 three-hour class sessions and runs over a full semester, or 13 weeks. Each session consists of a one-hour lecture followed by a two-hour, team-based activity. Social and communicative skills and collaboration are continually promoted and reinforced throughout the unit with teams of four or five students working together to build the Web site. Learning outcomes include:

- Working in teams to develop a team-based, Web-based product
- Creating and developing suitable project management models
- Documenting and reporting on quality assurance procedures, communication strategies, timesheet estimates, overall costs, proposal, legal, design, etc., which are representative of industry expectations
- Evaluating the quality and effectiveness of the product
- Communicating and collaborating in a team-based environment to solve problems, resolve conflict and make appropriate decisions

As shown in Figure 3, learning activities are designed to promote self-regulation, team skills, social and peer accountability as well as reflection and metalearning though peer and self-assessment. Using these seven instructional strategies outlined above, the design process focuses on developing learning activities to support the required outcomes. This process firstly required decisions to be made about the form of assessment and what proportion would be allocated to team and individual activities.

As shown in Figure 4, the main interface of the Web site was designed for functionality and context and contains icons such as an in-tray for weekly tasks, a journal for weekly self- and peer assessment, a contract to gain commitment at the beginning of the semester, a pin-up board which shows weekly requirements, a video player with streaming video of industry representatives, a filing cabinet which contains support materials, a conference centre where students post weekly solutions to problems (as well as assessing three other teams'

Figure 3. Learning activities and reflective tasks

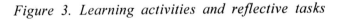
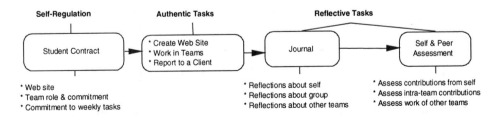

Figure 4. Main user interface

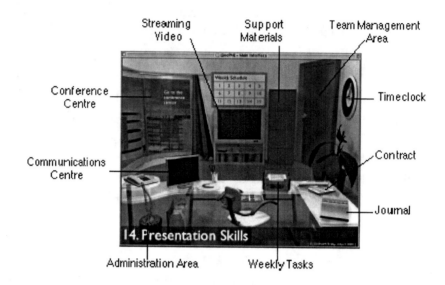

solutions), and a computer screen which allows forum discussions and views of other students' work. The whole environment supports the seven principles outlined above as well as supporting social learning, interactivity and reciprocity.

Example of Strategy 1: Design for social activity and interactive learning

An example of social learning activity based on self and peer assessment uses the Conference Centre in which all student teams complete weekly tasks based on key concepts related to the unit outcomes. Students are given both print and online resources to help develop solutions for these tasks. Solutions have to be submitted to the conference centre at a specific time, as after this the system is locked to prevent late postings. Student teams are then asked to peer review other team submissions. Tutors also provide feedback to solutions and post grades and feedback to the conference centre, as well as the best three solutions for the week. This approach to learning is highly social and engaging, while allowing student opportunities for peer interaction and review.

Example of Strategy 2: Foster intentionality and goal setting

To help foster intentionality, students are encouraged to complete a student contract at the beginning of the semester, signed by themselves and team

Figure 5. Sample learning contract

	@ [JoePM] - Team Member Contracts		
		Estimate total time commitment (over 15 weeks)	Major Deliverable's (up to 3 points)
Ass 1	Weekly Activities	26	read and contribute to the weekly tasks and submissions
Ass 2	Project Proposal	32	Executive summary, major objectives, scope, content overview
	Design Specifications	10	To oversee the specifications to ensure everything has been addressed
	PM Procedures	16	Reflect on how I have met the commitments that I proposed in the beginning and how it turned out
Ass 3	Production	10	Again to oversee that quality issues have been met and overall requirements have been addressed
	Final Report	32	All information to be collated and put into presentation format ready for submission. Ensure all areas have been addressed.
	PM Procedures	16	A final reflection of how I performed within the group, and how I thought this unit went, what I could have done differently and how we worked as a team.
Total:		**142**	

members. The contract outlines students' responsibilities needed for developing the Web site and weekly tasks. Students are expected to choose a project topic, defined their team role, choose topics for their portfolio, and plan the amount of time they intend to commit to achieve these tasks (Figure 5). This is completed in Week 3, with a meeting of all team members so that there is agreement on roles, tasks and responsibilities. This helps both individuals and teams to set realistic goals and also creates a collaborative environment in which there are clearly agreed and negotiated objectives.

Examples of Strategy 3: Support role differentiation and feedback, and Strategy 4: Support learning as a constructive social experience

Throughout the semester students perform a number of different roles such as redesigning Web pages, supporting peers, giving critical advice, researching and synthesising information. In most cases, students were assessed on their performance and given feedback on these roles through an assessment system that allowed students to consider their own and other team members' contributions through online weekly journals completed at the end of each week. This gave an indication of team members' progress in completing a variety of different tasks to the required quality and within time. The weekly journal allowed students to assess how they perceived others had performed and also gave comments in support of their assessment.

Example of Strategy 5: Foster metalearning

The approach to assessment based on self and peer evaluation, combined with the online facility for the online journal and conference centre, provided scope for the adoption of multiple roles and gave students multiple sources of feedback and opportunities to reflect on their own learning. Once formed, student teams remained together for the whole semester, and relied on each other to develop the Web site and solve weekly problems. The learning environment promoted activities that were highly representative of real-life industry practice. Project proposals, design specifications, budgets, progress reports and legal contracts are all needed in commercial jobs. Students were engaged in developing these reports for clients who had "real" needs within the industry. Within this context, students recognised that clear and effective communication protocols were needed to convey messages between the team and the client, as well as within the team. This included written documentation, speaking skills, listening skills, and presentation skills. For example, Sue (pseudonyms used) discusses the importance of these reports, and was focused on developing a range of quality assurance document templates to help promote effective communication. Also, she felt that these templates would give her an advantage in job interviews, when asked about report writing and communication skills:

The reports we were producing were just like industry ones. We had to scope the project, and then develop a contract the client was happy with, as well as giving him an accurate costing. This had to be presented in a way that was professional and easy to read. In industry, if this isn't done well, you just don't get the job. I can see why employers would want new employees to have these skills, that's why I developed templates that I can show people as part of my portfolio. (interview with Sue)

Almost all the students made comments about the importance of communicating effectively within their teams to save time. For example, Liz considered that communicating effectively with her team was an essential skill needed in the industry:

When we get a job, we'll have to communicate sensibly all the time. We'll always be in a team, and we'll always have to talk to people and write reports. You have to do it properly otherwise you get problems and waste lots of time. (interview with Liz)

These meta-comments expressed by students on the development of effective communication skills were drawn from real-life activities promoted through the learning environment.

Example of Strategy 6: Enable student autonomy and a sense of ownership, and Strategy 7: Balance both personal and interpersonal orientations

In this course, students were given an orientation and advice on how to structure teams, and the importance of effective teamwork. Much time was spent at team meetings considering how the team would develop their product, and within this setting all team members were expected to contribute ideas and solve problems. For example, one student (Jeff) recognised that it was important to actively contribute ideas at team meetings to support the development of the teams' product. He realised that by sitting back at team meetings and not listening carefully, he would miss opportunities to contribute ideas that could help the whole team perform better:

At the beginning of the semester I was happy to sit back and listen to others say all sort of things. I would only really push a point or say something if nobody else had anything to say. After a few weeks I realised that things I didn't say could have really helped the team. If you have ideas, you've got to get in there and let everybody know. (interview with Jeff)

Many other students made comments about helping others whenever possible, with a view of improving the quality of the final product. For example, Chris describes how he helped one of his team members when they were having trouble using animation software that he was skilled with. By helping his peers learn how to use this software, Chris felt that the whole team benefited as the required animation was completed on time, and the team didn't have to waste time rescheduling and discussing alternative action:

I noticed Pat was having problems using Flash to produce the opening sequence. He kept asking dumb questions that showed a basic lack of understanding. So, I took some time to help him get going with it. It was better to help him do it, rather than have team problems that would cause everything to slow down and cause arguments. Another team had major problems with one team member not doing his jobs because he didn't know how to do it. Nobody helped him out, and in the end the whole team suffered for it. (interview with Chris)

As the semester progressed, most students gained a greater appreciation for the value of helping others in their team. They saw or experienced the effects of teams in conflict, as well as the negative effects of team members not completing their tasks on time, and wanted to avoid this whenever possible. Thus, the environment was extremely motivating and engaging for students, replicating real-life issues and concerns. Table 1 shows the features of the learning environment and how they meet the design guidelines depicted by Herrington and Oliver (2000).

Table 1. Situated learning elements in the learning environment

Element of Situated Learning	Implementation	Example from the Learning Environment
An authentic context that reflects the way the knowledge will be used in real life	• Environment reflecting real use • Large number of resources • No attempt to simplify	• Students work in teams and to develop a multimedia product to meet the needs of a "real" client. • The final product hosted on university server for students to use as a CV item
Authentic activities	• Authentic tasks that have real world significance • Ill-defined activities • Student negotiation of tasks	• Students consider what roles to adopt (project manager, content developer, programmer, or graphic designer) • Student negotiation on who they should team up with and which project topic and client they should choose • Negotiating contracts (online) with their peers to determine, roles, duties, standards and time commitment
Access to expert performances and the modeling of processes	• Access to expert thinking and modeling • Access to other learners • Sharing of expertise	• Multiple employer perspectives presented through streaming video of local multimedia developers • Online product and documentation available of past student projects, annotated by tutors and clients
Collaborative construction of knowledge	• Tasks for group work rather than individual effort • Incentive structure for whole group participation	• Fifty percent of the overall assessment is allocated to teamwork • Tutor-led peer assessment focus, with confidential student reporting to tutors to enable moderation of marks based on effort and quality
Reflection to enable abstractions to be formed	• Authentic context and task • Opportunity for learner to compare with experts • Collaborative grouping for tasks	• Weekly confidential self and peer assessment (online) to give students the opportunity to reflect on how well they have performed, as well as their peers. • Students estimate time for given tasks, and continually compare against actual times to develop metrics for costing • Tutor-led peer assessment sessions

Table 1. Situated learning elements in the learning environment (cont.)

Element of Situated Learning	Implementation	Example from the Learning Environment
Articulation to enable tacit knowledge to be made explicit	• A complex task with opportunity to participate • Public presentation of argument	• Bulletin boards enable students to pose questions, and reflect on the responses • Presentation night at end of semester enables students to show final product, as well as metrics developed and issues encountered (both positive and negative)
Coaching and scaffolding at critical times	• Support for learning • Modeling of expert performance	• Teams are tutor-led peer assessment sessions, where the tutor discusses the progress of the team and makes suggestions for improvement, as well as moderating marks (based on effort) • Through the online bulletin boards, students request feedback and advice about the quality of their products. Tutors, ex-students and industry representatives are invited to pass comments about how these may be improved, or fixed
Authentic assessment of learning within the learning tasks	• Opportunity for learners to produce high level outcomes and performances • Complex ill-structured challenges • Multiple indicators of learning	• The assessment task is based on the needs of a real client that may be ill defined. Often these clients are potential employers, so students are aware that a high level performance can provide employment opportunities • The client, the tutor, as well as each team member assess the efforts of each student. Students then reflect on each of these (reflective reports, team meetings and bulletin boards), and consider how they may improve their performance
Multiple roles and perspectives	• Different perspectives on topics form various points of view • Opportunity to express alternative views • Opportunity to take on a range of learning roles	• Students are required to reflect on success and failure, but also to comment on others' comments through the use of the bulletin board. • The bulletin boards provide a medium in which different perspectives are given by students, tutors and clients. Often disagreement occurs, in which students will defend their point of view based on their interpretation of the situation.

Summary

Research now recognises the need to create active learning environments in which learners engage in conversations and inquiry processes that are authentic and relevant to the needs of students. The authentic learning framework adopted in this chapter emphasise the social, interactive and generative nature of learning tasks and forms of engagement. The activities are selected because they are socially engaging rather than purely cognitive, and the underlying pedagogy is community and learner-centered rather than didactic. The whole design concept is based on theories of situated and authentic learning, social psychology and constructivist knowledge-building communities. It is not being suggested that cognitive aspects are less important, but rather that social aspects of learning, interaction and engagement may be overlooked in many teaching contexts.

This chapter challenges purely cognitive approaches to learning and affirms the centrality of situated cognition where content and context are related and knowing and doing are linked to activity. Authentic learning theory provides educators with a holistic perspective and a framework for supporting learners by creating environments that value the social, experiential, participatory and interpersonal dimensions of experience. For educators, the most important lesson learnt from a decade or more of research on online learning is that students need authentic environments that provide support for learning through social interaction, engagement and community building.

References

Alexander, S., & McKenzie, J. (1998). *An evaluation of information technology projects for university learning (CUTSD)*. Canberra: National Capital Printing.

Barab, S. (2001). Designing and building an online community: The struggle to support sociability in the learning inquiry forum. *Educational Technology, Research and Development, 49*(4), 71-96.

Barab, S.A., Makinster, J.G., Moore, J.A., & Cunningham, J.A (2001). Designing and building an online community: The struggle to support sociability in the inquiry learning forum. *Educational Technology Research and Development, 49*(4), 71-96.

Barab, S.A., Thomas, T.K., & Merrill, H. (2001). Online learning: From information dissemination to fostering collaboration. *Journal of Interactive Learning Research, 12*(1), 105-143.

Bonk, C.J. (2000). Advances in pedagogy: Finding the instructor in post secondary online learning. Paper presented at the *American Educational Research Association*, New Orleans, April.

Bonk, C.J., & Cunningham, D.J. (1998). Searching for learner-centered, constructivist and socio-cultural components of collaborative educational learning tools. In C. J. Bonk & K. S. King (Eds.), *Electronic collaborators* (pp. 25-50). Mawah, NJ: Lawrence Erlbaum.

Chickering, A., & Ehrmann, S. C. (1996, October). Implementing the seven principles: Technology as lever. *AAHE Bulletin*, 3-6.

Collis, B., & Moonen, J. (2001). *Flexible learning in digital world*. London: Kogan Page.

Coomey, M., & Stephenson, J. (2001). Online learning: Its all about dialogue, involvement, support and control — according to the research. In J. Stephenson (Ed.), *Teaching and learning online* (pp. 37-52). London: Kogan Page.

Eastmond, D.V. (1995). *Alone but together: Adult distance education through computer conferencing*. Creskill, NJ: Hampton Press.

Fazey, D.M., & Fazey, J.A. (2001). The potential for autonomy in learning: Prceptions of competence, motivation and locus of control in first year undergraduate students. *Studies in Higher Education, 26*(3), 345-361.

Gunawardena, C.N. (1995). Social presence theory and implications for inter-action and collaborative learning and intellectual amplification. *International Journal of Educational Telecommunications, 1*(2/3), 147-166.

Gunawardena, C.N., & Zittle, F.J. (1997). Social presence as a predictor of satisfaction within a computer-mediated conferencing environment. *The American Journal of Distance Education, 11*(13), 8-26.

Hannafin, M.J., & Land, S.M. (1997). Foundations and assumptions of technol-ogy enhanced learning student-centered learning. *Instructional Science, 25*, 167-202.

Herrington, J., & Oliver, R. (2000). An instructional design framework for authentic learning environments. *Educational Technology, Research and Development, 48*(3), 23-48.

Herrington, J., Oliver, R., & Reeves, T. (2002). Patterns of engagement in authentic online learning environments. *Australian Journal of Educational Technology, 19*(1), 59-71.

Hiltz, S. R. (1994). *Learning without limits in the virtual classroom*. Norwood, NJ: Ablex.

Hiltz, S. R. (1998). Collaborative learning in asynchronous learning networks: Building learning communities. Retrieved October 2003, from *http://eies.njit.edu/~hiltz/*

Jonassen, D., Mayes, T., & Aleese, R.M. (1993). A manifesto for a constructivist approach to uses of technology in higher education. In T. Duffy, J. Lowyck, D. Jonassen, & T. M. Welsch (Eds.), *Designing environments for constructive learning* (pp. 231-248). Berlin: Springer Verlag.

Kearsley, G. (2000). *Online education: Learning and teaching in cyberspace*. Belmont, CA: Wadsworth.

Laurillard, D. (2002). *Rethinking university education* (2nd ed.). London: Kogan Page.

Leh, A.S. (2001). Computer-mediated communication and social presence in distance learning. *International Journal of Educational Telecommunications, 7*(2), 109-128.

Lin, X., Hmelo, C., Kinzer, C., & Secules, T.J. (1999). Designing technology to support reflection. *Educational Technology Research and Development, 47*(3), 43-62.

Murphy, K.L., & Cifuentes, L. (2001). Using Web tools, collaborating and learning online. *Distance Education, 22*(2), 285-305.

Newman, F.M., & Archbald, D.A. (1992). The nature of authentic academic achievement. In H. Berlak, F.M. Newman, E. Adams, D.A. Archbald, T. Burgess, J. Raven & T.A. Romberg (Eds.), *Towards a new science of educational testing and achievement*. Albany: State University of New York.

Ramsden, P. (1992). *Learning to teach in higher education*. London: Routledge.

Richardson, J., & Swan, K. (2001). An examination of social presence in online learning: Students' perceived learning and satisfaction. Paper presented at the *American Educational Research Association*, Seattle.

Rourke, L., Anderson, T., Garrison, D. R., & Archer, W. (1999). Assessing social presence in asynchronous, text-based computer conferencing. *Journal of Distance Education, 14*(3), 51-70.

Rowntree, D. (1992). *Exploring open and distance learning*. London: Kogan Page.

Salmon, G. (2000). *E-moderating*. London: Kogan Page.

Scardamalia, M., & Bereiter, C. (1996). Computer support for knowledge building communities. In T. Koschmann (Ed.), *CSCL: Theory and practice of an emerging paradigm* (pp. 249-268). Mahwah, NJ: Lawrence Erlbaum.

Shaffer, D.W., & Resnick, M. (1999). "Thick" authenticity: New media and authentic learning. *Journal of Interactive Learning Research, 10*(2), 195-215.

Sherry, L. (2000). The nature and purpose of online discourse. *International Journal of Educational Telecommunications, 6*(1), 19-51.

Short, J., Williams, E., & Christie, B. (1976). *The social psychology of telecommunications*. Toronto: John Wiley.

Sproull, L., & Kiesler, S. (1986). Reducing social context cues: Electronic mail in organisational communication. *Management Science, 32*, 1492-1513.

Steuer, J. (1992). Defining virtual reality: Dimensions determining telepresence. *Journal of Communication, 42*(4), 73-93.

Sugrue, B. (2000). Computers as cognitive tools. In S.P. Lajoie (Ed.), *Computers as cognitive tools: No more walls* (Vol. 2, pp. 133-162). Mahwah, NJ: Lawrence Erlbaum.

Swan, K. (2001). Virtual interaction: Design factors affecting student satisfaction and perceived learning in asynchronous online courses. *Distance Education, 22*(2), 306-331.

Tait, A. (2000). Planning student support for open and distance learning. *Open Learning, 15*(3), 287-299.

Tu, C.H. (2000). From social learning theory to social presence in an online environment. *Journal of Network and Computer Interactions, 23*(1), 39-58.

Vermunt, J.D., & Verloop, N. (1999). Congruence and friction between learning and teaching. *Learning and Instruction, 32*(3), 257-280.

Walther, J.B. (1992). Interpersonal effects in computer-mediated communication. *Communication Research, 19*(1), 52-90.

Wegerif, R. (1998). The social dimension of asynchronous learning. *JALN, 2*(1), 34-49.

Wiggins, G. (1998). *Educative assessment*. San Francisco: Jossey Bass.

Zimmerman, B. (1995). Self-regulation involves more than metacognition: A social cognitive perspective. *Educational Psychologist, 30*(4), 217-221.

Chapter XVI

Using Online Discussions to Provide an Authentic Learning Experience for Professional Recordkeepers

Karen Anderson, Edith Cowan University, Australia

Abstract

Providing authentic learning in a distance education course that leads to a professional qualification is challenging. However, working in a totally online environment on ill-defined problems provides students with opportunities to seek and evaluate their own learning resources and to collaborate with others in their learning. This chapter provides an example of a performative assessment strategy for students in archives and records management studies, requiring them to find on the Internet, analyse and evaluate examples of policy documents and standards, just as they would in the workplace. Student evaluations of the exercise were unanimously positive. Discussions helped to overcome isolation felt by remote students; depth of knowledge gained was improved and students' reflections developed awareness about learning through the assessment.

Introduction

The strategies discussed in this chapter aim to meet two challenges. One is to provide authentic, situated learning for students who will graduate to become professional archivists and records managers. The other is to overcome the isolation of distance learning by providing opportunities for collaborative learning. Consequently, I have put a great deal of effort into building effective learning communities for distant students to help them develop generic skills such as effective communication and interaction with peers, teamwork and constructive critical engagement with others' work. I also use these strategies to help reduce the sense of isolation often suffered by distance education students and thus reduce attrition. I have been guided by the work of Salmon (Salmon, 2000) and Palloff and Pratt (1999, 2001) in particular.

The subject *Electronic Recordkeeping* is taught online concurrently to undergraduate and postgraduate students. One of the advantages of this teaching strategy is that it mixes two groups who bring different skills and knowledge to their studies. Most students in both groups are mature-aged. However, students in the postgraduate course are often already employed in archives and records services and seeking an appropriate qualification as they work. They usually have at least some practical experience and bring knowledge of the "real world" to class discussions. Undergraduate students, on the other hand, tend to be gaining a qualification pre-service, even if mature-aged. However, because their course is broader, incorporating a major that frequently includes studies in communication and information technology, they often bring better knowledge and skills in technology to the discussions.

All unit materials and resources are provided online and students submit their assignments electronically. Although challenging to some students, the totally online environment provides opportunities to encourage distant students to seek and evaluate their own resources and to collaborate in their learning, both of which were inhibited by paper delivery.

Using Authentic Assessment
to Promote Competence

Designing strategies for assessing students' attainment of professional competencies in courses that aim to produce graduates qualified to practice in a
profession is a complex issue. There is also a move away from assessment by
reproduction of subject content, and towards student-centred learning. A vision
for student-centred learning for archivists and records managers was very
persuasively presented by Thomassen (2001) who suggested that:

*"Student-centred learning requires the educator to design programs that
encourage students to actively take charge of their learning by selecting
resources and applying their studies of the subject in some way. Learning
moves from abstracted, knowledge-based learning to learning that reflects
context and usage of the information in appropriate ways."* (Thomassen, 2001)

The teacher's challenge is to provide an equitable, stimulating experience to
meet the needs of students and then to design stimulating and challenging
assessments that test understanding of the topic. Herrington, Reeves, Oliver, and
Woo (2004) point out that: "Activities, investigations and problems are at the
heart of student involvement in meaningful learning contexts. Teachers provide
activities to enable students to interact with the learning environment, and to
learn, apply and practice newly acquired skills" (p. 6). Further, the activities
should be "ill-defined," requiring students to decide what the problems are in a
given complex situation, then to look for resources and solutions to resolve the
problems identified.

Professional recordkeepers work with the constant challenge of capturing and
preserving evidential records in the ever changing and developing electronic
environment. In the workplace they must stay abreast of these changes,
evaluating solutions and standards and constantly seeking to implement best
practice.

Essay writing has a time-honoured place in professional education, and is
particularly useful for encouraging development of research skills, as well as for
demonstrating an ability to synthesise and structure information and to present
a coherent argument. However, there is a wide range of other skills required in
the workplace that cannot be developed or demonstrated appropriately in an
essay. Engagement in constructive professional debate is one such skill. It is
possible to design assessments based on hypothetical situations and case studies
that reflect authentic practice. Such situations are often used as role-plays or

group debates in the face-to-face classroom. Combined with technology that allows the use of electronic discussion boards to overcome problems with time-zone differences and variations in students' personal commitments, this type of activity is entirely appropriate for distance students.

Use of discussion boards encourages students to progress to Salmon's stage four of knowledge construction (Salmon, 2000, p. 25), in which students interact and respond much more participatively, take responsibility for their own learning and support each other. In effect, the students are building and participating in a virtual community of practice:

Communities of Practice is a phrase coined by researchers who studied the ways in which people naturally work ... together. In essence, communities of practice are groups of people who share similar goals and interests. In pursuit of these goals and interests, they employ common practices, work with the same tools and express themselves in a common language. Through such common activity, they come to hold similar beliefs and value systems. (Community Intelligence Labs, 2001)

Discussion builds understanding. Brown, Collins and Duguid (1989, p. 36) note that:

A concept ... will continually evolve with each new occasion of use, because new situations, negotiations, and activities recast it in a new, more densely textured form. So a concept, like the meaning of a word, is always under construction. This would appear to be true of apparently well-defined, abstract technical concepts. Even these are not wholly definable and defy categorical description; part of their meaning is always inherited from the context of use.

Encouraging students to go beyond their initial research into a topic, through discussion of their own and others' findings should result in deeper, more soundly grounded understanding of the issues involved.

The Problem

The subject matter of *Electronic Recordkeeping* addresses the issue of ensuring the capture and long-term preservation of electronic records through systems analysis and design and through implementation of policy and "best practice" standards for electronic documents and systems. One of the key objectives in the unit requires exploration of the role of recordkeeping standards in ensuring the persistence of electronic memory to ensure organisational accountability. The topic is essential to the management of records and archives in the current and future technological environment. Students in earlier classes of *Electronic Recordkeeping* were required to post the results of their own reading concerning three set problems. However, they were much less likely to comment on each other's work. If they did, conversations between several students rarely ensued. Comments posted to the boards were rarely endorsed or challenged by others.

A Strategy to Improve Learning Through Professional Discussion

Students were divided into groups of six to eight to make online discussion more manageable. Trying to follow a discussion to which the full group of 40 people is contributing would have been confusing and likely to overwhelm students. Students were able to read other groups' postings if they wished, although they were asked to confine their contributions to their own group.

The assignment consisted of three problems or topics for discussion, which make up the whole assignment worth 30% of the semester's marks. One of the problems related to the preservation of *metadata*. Recordkeeping metadata captures and provides structured information about records. The use of appropriate metadata standards for recordkeeping and their importance as a strategy for preserving evidential records is crucial to the long-term preservation of electronic records. Examples of appropriate metadata include information about a record's creation, its context, how long it should be kept, who has right of access to the record and who has used it. Professional archivists must be able to evaluate and implement metadata standards. In a professional situation where standards are emerging, practitioners must be able to participate in informed professional discussion, soundly basing their position on previously published work and discussion papers. Students were asked to research and make an initial posting of not less than 500 words. They were then asked to comment upon other students' postings and engage in discussions that arose. At the end of the discussions they needed to collate and submit their contributions, together with a brief summary of their postings for each problem, and a short reflection on how their thoughts and opinions had developed as a result of the discussions and whether or not the discussion process had assisted their learning in this course. Students were also asked to describe and share a resource that had particularly helped them to gain an understanding of issues concerning metadata standards, a concept that many find difficult when first encountered. Students were required to provide both in-text and end-of-text references in all their postings to the discussion boards to meet both academic and professional standards. Thus this problem is authentic: it is relevant to debate and reflects the decision-making graduates will experience in the workplace.

This approach adopted promotes the generic skills of communication and information literacy by weaving them into the course assessment strategy. The problems are designed to be authentic assessment strategies (Torrance, 1994; Wiggins, 1989), more recently defined by Biggs as *performative* assessment (Biggs, 1999, p. 151): "Preparing students to think, act and decide as they would in the real world in a more informed and effective manner: performatively in other words." Students are required to find, analyse and evaluate policy documents and standards, just as they would in the workplace. In this way, students are encouraged to be active and collaborative in their learning (Kezar, n.d.).

Evaluating the Assessment Outcomes

The effectiveness of the assessment strategy was evaluated by asking students to include in their final submission of the assignment: "a short reflection on how your thoughts and opinions have developed as a result of the discussions and whether or not the discussion process has assisted your learning in this unit." The following are extracts from student reflections in response to this question. The first three quotes (Students V, W and X) demonstrate a developing awareness that it takes a considerable amount of work and social skill to build constructive and meaningful discussions in an environment without face-to-face contact.

Student V:

Electronic communication and dialogue is difficult to establish. It takes building trust to achieve fruitful discussion. I believe Group 3 advanced in the right direction and as a result had the beginnings of a useful learning process. The most useful learnings came from fellow students' initial contributions as it helped to see what others think and clarified problems and issues. The discussions also added to my learning by prolonging my thinking through the issues. (It was very time consuming, though.) As time went on and I progressed through the lecture material the issues raised in the problems also made more sense.

Student W:

For me, the three problems gave rise to a lot of critical thinking on issues in electronic recordkeeping. The problems have assisted my learning for this unit, and I have gained some insights from other postings from students within the group and outside the group as well.

In these discussions, students also benefited from the experience of those who were already working in the profession but enrolled in the course to gain a professional qualification. This helped firstly, those who had no relevant work experience to grasp practical issues that arise in the real world, and secondly, it helped those who were already working in the profession to see beyond the walls of their own organisation, thus benefiting from multiple perspectives.

Student X:

There is no doubt that the Bulletin Board discussions offer the opportunity to exchange ideas and knowledge with other students and take advantage of the different work practices that students have. For instance during the Preservation Metadata discussion I felt the lack of experience with metadata capture and it was very useful to have reflections from students who had worked in public agencies. I found the discussions valuable, informative and sometimes challenging, although also a lot of work. I didn't feel the conversations flowed that naturally, nor that any debates really got underway, but some of the postings from other students were most interesting and helped me understand the topic. Researching the topics has certainly been valuable.

Student Y further benefited by gaining an appreciation of the process of developing professional standards, thus achieving a much deeper understanding of wider issues than the metadata standards that were the principal topic of the discussions.

Student Y:

The discussion concerning metadata preservation was a good one because in asking everyone to choose an article which helped us to understand this concept, everyone had something fresh and informative to offer. My involvement in the discussion mainly concerned the issues of being flexible in our approaches to preserving metadata and also the setting of standards, reflecting the discussion of the group in general. This discussion certainly expanded my ideas on preservation metadata. I actually changed my opinion from feeling that standards should be considered very carefully when dealing with such a new area of recordkeeping but, after reading some interesting responses, seeing the benefit in developing standards as soon as possible. This revelation actually helped me to understand that standards themselves are flexible and the only way to develop them is to experiment. Moreover, a balance can be found between being flexible in order to remain open to all outcomes and also setting standards in order to regulate processes.

The final quote discusses the benefit of stimulating students to research beyond the lecture material in order to make their own meaningful contribution to the discussion as well as their exposure to a wider range of resources than they had been able to find themselves.

Student Z:

I found the problem useful because it delved further into an area only touched on in the lecture notes. As a result of the research I did, I had a better understanding of issues involved with preservation metadata. I also found the articles other students found supplemented my own reading.

Conclusion

The strategy for change in this assessment, to encourage better student participation in the online discussions, worked well. Students have unanimously endorsed the value of these discussions in assisting their learning. Asking students to reflect on their learning is particularly useful to them in developing awareness of what they have learnt and to me in my evaluation of teaching strategies. Asking students to share the results of their reading in this problem was spectacularly successful. Metadata standards and management are difficult concepts for students to understand. Encouraging them to look critically at their reading and share their "successes" in coming to grips with this topic provided a very lively forum. The strategy ensured that individuals were exposed to a wider range of articles on the topic than they would find for themselves and the discussion of the value of metadata standards provoked a livelier discussion than I had expected.

In summary, the improvements to learning through using online discussion boards as an assessment strategy in this unit were several:

1.   The online discussions helped to overcome feelings of isolation experienced by distance students, although numbers of students assigned to each online study group had to be carefully managed to ensure that the amount of reading did not become overwhelming. From the online discussions, students also gained skills in communicating in a professionally authentic and responsible manner.

2.   Through their combined research efforts, students gained a greater depth of knowledge than was available through information provided for them in the lecture notes and recommended reading. They became more aware of the rich and wide range of professional resources available to them through the Internet, thus improving skills for lifelong learning in their chosen profession.

3.   Reflection developed awareness among students that their views and attitudes on the professional topics under discussion had changed and developed as a result of insights gained during the process of research and discussion.

4.   Students learned how professional standards develop, while they were canvassing the specific issues pertaining to current metadata standards.

5.   Students' reactions to this method of assessment were enthusiastic. All respondents indicated that the discussions had been beneficial to them and a number commented that they had found them enjoyable, too.

It was clear from the reaction of students that the approach adopted in this course engaged their interest because of the way that it simulated authentic experiences and problems that they would face in the course of their professional employment. It was both pleasing and rewarding to discover from the students' evaluations of the course that they found it not only stimulating and rewarding but also rather enjoyable.

References

Biggs, (1999). *Teaching for quality learning at university: What the student does.* Buckingham: Society for Research into Higher Education, Open University Press.

Brown, J.S., Collins, A., & Duguid, P. (1989). Situated cognition and the culture of learning. *Educational Researcher, 18*(1), 32-34.

Community Intelligence Labs (2001). Retrieved November 2003, from *http://www.co-i-l.com/coil/knowledge-garden/cop/definitions.shtml*

Edith Cowan University. (2002). *Assessment policy.* Retrieved May 2003, from *http://www.ecu.edu.au/GPPS/policy/ac/ac031.pdf*

Herrington, J., Reeves, T. C., Oliver, R., & Woo, Y. (2004). Designing authentic activities in web-based courses. *Journal of Computing in Higher Education, 16*(1), 3-29.

Kezar, A.J. (n.d.). Higher education trends (1999-2000): Teaching and learning. *ERIC Clearinghouse on Higher Education.* Retrieved May 2003, from *http://eriche.org/trends/teaching.html*

Palloff, R.M., & Pratt, K. (1999). *Building learning communities in cyberspace: Effective strategies for the online classroom.* San Francisco: Jossey-Bass.

Palloff, R.M., & Pratt, K. (2001). *Lessons from the cyberspace classroom: The realities of online teaching.* San Francisco: Jossey-Bass.

Pederson, A., Brogan, M., & Huma, A. (2000). *Documenting society* [CD-ROM]. Perth: Edith Cowan University.

Salmon, G. (2000). *E-moderating: The key to teaching and learning online.* London: Kogan Page.

Thomassen, T. (2001). Modelling and re-modelling archival education and training. Paper presented at *Reading the Vital Signs: Archival Training and Education in the 21st Century: European Conference for Archival Educators and Trainers*, Marburg, 24-25 September. Retrieved November 2003, from *http://www.ica-sae.org/mrconfpaper1.html*

Torrance, H. (1994). *Evaluating authentic assessment:Pproblems and possibilities in new approaches to assessment.* Buckingham: Open University.

Wiggins, G. (1989). Teaching to the (authentic) test. *Educational Leadership, 46,* 44-47.

Chapter XVII

Authentic Cases and Media Triggers for Supporting Problem-Based Learning in Teacher Education

Mike Keppell, The Hong Kong Institute of Education, Hong Kong

Abstract

Within teacher education problem-based learning (PBL) has the potential to enrich teaching and learning across the curriculum. It is suggested that PBL may offer a means of providing authentic scenarios for assisting pre-service teachers before encountering teaching practice. The use of media-based educational triggers and authentic scenarios may form a bridge between their studies and real-world teaching practice. Five media-rich educational triggers are described in early childhood education, physical education, educational technology, project management and inclusive education. Reusable media-based educational triggers may also provide potential resources for other educators within teacher education.

PBL Context

Problem-based learning (PBL) has a long history in the field of medicine, beginning at MacMaster University in 1968. Although its underpinnings can be traced to Gagné, Bruner and Dewey, PBL began with a questioning of the relevance of medical teaching in order to emphasise the patient as opposed to the science. Barrows suggested that "students were passive and exposed to too much information, little of which seemed relevant to the practice of medicine. They were bored and disenchanted when medical education should have been exciting" (Evensen & Hmelo, 2000, p. vii). Problem-based learning has been closely associated with medical education since this time and many medical schools around the world approach their teaching and learning using principles of PBL. In general the approach presents students with a problem and requires them to formulate hypotheses, develop questions, gather and interpret data, and communicate their findings to peers and tutors. It is divided into several phases that involve small group work and independent study (Barrows & Tamblyn, 1980; Schmidt, 1993). It is suggested that PBL fosters independent learning, self-directed learning and lifelong learning. More specifically, Barrows (1986) suggested that there are five primary objectives of PBL in medicine which include: "construction of clinically useful knowledge, development of clinical reasoning strategies, development of effective self-directed learning strategies, increased motivation for learning and becoming effective collaborators" (Evensen & Hmelo, 2000, p. 2). The benefits of PBL have been well documented and PBL has become synonymous with medical education.

Primary Focus of PBL

Koschmann (2002) suggests that PBL focuses on three important areas in constructivist education: *student-centred learning, collaboration* and *authentic teaching materials*. Student-centred learning focuses on allowing students to set their own goals and determine the resources and the activities that are required to achieve their goals. It is an umbrella concept which includes case-based learning, goal-based scenarios, learning by design, project-based learning and problem-based learning (Pederson, 2003). Central to each of these approaches is an implied or explicit question which may focus on a problem, a case, an issue or a project. Often the question is provided to the students and is ill-structured in nature, requiring learners to provide "a solution, an opinion, a decision, a plan of action or product" depending on the question to be addressed (Pederson, 2003, p. 1). In medical problem-based learning a problem is presented requiring students to work toward identifying the key learning issues and then suggesting a plausible diagnosis of a patient.

Collaboration is seen as essential to the process and "at the heart of PBL is the tutorial group" (Hmelo & Evensen, 2000, p. 2). Small groups collaborate with each other guided by a facilitator to discuss the problem. "Before beginning to grapple with the problem as a group, students must get to know each other, establish ground rules, and establish a comfortable climate for collaborative learning" (Hmelo & Evensen, 2000, p. 2). Within this collaborative environment the group extract the key information from the case, generate and evaluate hypotheses, generate learning issues, explain the patient's disease and reflect on what they have learned from the problem (Hmelo & Evensen, 2000).

Authentic learning materials are essential for the PBL process in order to immerse the students within the context. These are also considered to be real-world or authentic learning experiences. They "immerse the learner in the situation requiring him or her to acquire skills or knowledge in order to solve the problem or manipulate the situation" (Jonassen, Mayes & McAleese, 1993, p. 235). For instance, in medical education, media (video, photographs, audio, animations) are sometimes deployed to create educational triggers because it is not always practical to access real patients for undergraduate education. Options include paper-based problems, "trained patient surrogates" (Koschmann, Kelson, Feltovich & Barrows, 1996) and the media-based patient encounters utilised at the University of Melbourne medical school represent an example of this approach (Keppell, Elliott, Kennedy, Elliott, & Harris, 2003). This chapter will focus on the authentic video-triggers created for teacher-education.

Teacher Education

PBL is being widely adopted as a powerful teaching and learning strategy in medicine and law. However relatively little work has focused on its use in teacher-education. In examining these three principles above there appears to be no reason why PBL should not be widely adopted in teacher education. Large student numbers in the classroom (i.e., >35 students) may prevent the adoption of a small group tutorial (5-10 students) with a facilitator which is indicative of medical settings, but a creative teacher should be able to design around these constraints. A creative teacher should be able to utilise PBL principles in a large class setting by using student facilitators. For example, students can act as peer facilitators of small PBL groups clustered within a regular classroom. Teachers can combine brainstorming, authentic materials, questions and small group discussion in the large class setting. In general it appears that there are no insurmountable barriers to the adoption of PBL within the classroom setting.

Similarity of Teacher Education to Medical Education

It may be worthwhile at this point to compare the similarities of professionals in medicine and teaching in relation to PBL as misconceptions may exist which may prevent the adoption of PBL in teacher-education. Firstly, within the PBL process medical students do not have all the knowledge required to solve cases. Within the context of PBL, Schmidt (1993) suggests that the extent of prior knowledge is one of the major determinants of the "nature and amount of new information that can be processed" (p. 424). The importance in focusing on the concept of prior knowledge in the PBL process is that a student soon realises that "prior knowledge of the problem is, in itself, insufficient for them to understand it in depth" (Norman & Schmidt, 1992, p. 557). PBL utilises this inherent dilemma to motivate the learner to seek an understanding of the case and address the deficiency in their knowledge. By using PBL, medical students are exposed to more patient cases which facilitates their learning in their first hospital residency. Similarly, pre-service teacher education students do not have all the knowledge for their first teaching practice in schools. They lack the relevant schemata for teaching practice and thus authentic scenarios may form a bridge between their studies and real-world practice. Without using some form of real-world exposure to cases teacher education students may struggle to ask questions which are relevant. "Pre-service teachers, as long as they are students and not teachers, do not have the cognitive schema or practical knowledge that are acquired from teaching experience to be able to ask appropriate questions and reconstruct their own sense of theory and practice" (Richardson, 1999, p. 121). One of the most difficult areas for pre-service teachers is classroom management and exposing them to classroom management scenarios may develop pre-requisite knowledge to enable them to more effectively cope with teaching practice. Teaching practice is sometimes an enlightening experience for student teachers while most often it is a stressful situation with students eager to test the boundaries and limits of their "new" teacher.

Just as medical students need exposure to real patients, teacher-education students need exposure to authentic cases that may help them to bridge the gap between theory and practice. It is suggested that cases are useful in teacher education as "students…cognitive schema regarding teaching is underdeveloped or inappropriately tied to their experiences as students" (Richardson, 1999, p. 121). In other words, "all pre-service training can be characterised as anticipatory socialisation which inevitably involves giving students answers to questions not yet asked, and not likely to be asked until students are in the thick of actual service" (Richardson, 1999, p. 121). Similarly the purpose of PBL in medical education is to expose students to pseudo-patients before they treat real patients. It may be worthwhile to consider that all content learned by student teachers in the teacher-education setting is still only theory and it is only when they enter practical teaching is it considered to be practice and not theory (Richardson, 1999).

Media-Based Educational Triggers

It is not always practical to access real patients in medical training or access real students in teacher pre-service classes. Media-based educational triggers may have many advantages over paper-based problems as they provide a degree of authenticity for the encounter with the problem. The use of media-based educational triggers allow teachers and student teachers to observe other teachers on video and listen to student interactions. Media-based triggers can replicate some of these authentic encounters and immerse the student within a real-life educational scenario.

In development of medical triggers at the University of Melbourne, an attempt was made to match the nature of the medical condition or context to the appropriate media type (e.g., static image, sequence of static images, video, audio, or Shockwave movie). A trigger, for example, that portrays a medical condition such as myasthenia gravis needs to show the progressive nature of skeletal-muscle fatigue. Consequently, video is the most appropriate media to illustrate this progressive nature. Other triggers needed to demonstrate distinctive sequential changes in a process and were portrayed through a series of digitised photographs using a Shockwave or QuickTime movie. Often, a single digitised photograph conveyed sufficient information to begin the problem-based learning approach (Keppell, Kennedy, Elliott & Harris, 2001).

Similarly it is important to utilise authentic educational triggers to initiate the decision making of pre-service education students. For instance, a one-minute video showing a person climbing stairs and appearing out of breath is a useful trigger to begin discussion of aerobic and anaerobic fitness for the field of physical education. The use of a scenario portraying a client dissatisfied with the development of a Web page for their organisation could initiate discussion of the concepts of needs assessment and analysing user requirements in the field of multimedia production. A video scenario showing the "social isolation" of a wheel-chair bound child in a grade five playground could initiate inclusive educational concepts for both primary and secondary teachers. Similar scenarios for areas such as art, counseling, language learning, music, early childhood education, and mathematics can be developed using media-based triggers.

Why Are Media-Based Triggers Important in the Educational Process?

In PBL the "activation of prior knowledge facilitates the subsequent processing of new information" (Norman & Schmidt, 1992, p. 559). Research on prior knowledge and the need to account for the learner's existing ideas and concepts in teaching and learning has a long history within the education and cognitive science literature. For instance Dewey, (1938) examined experience and education; Ausubel, (1960) examined Subsumption Theory; Mayer, (1979) focused on Assimilation Theory; Rumelhart and Norman (1983) and Gordon and Rennie, (1987) focused on Schema Theory. It appears that there have been few changes since 1979 when Mayer commented that, "it seems that one cannot read a textbook on learning and memory without finding a statement to the effect that learning involves connecting new ideas to old knowledge" (Mayer, 1979, p. 136). Under the guidance of the PBL tutor, an exchange of ideas among students in the PBL session assists in activating their prior knowledge. This exchange needs to occur before students further investigate learning resources, for it creates a "learner readiness" by asking the students to generate hypotheses for the problem. In order to illustrate the usefulness of media-based educational triggers five cases will be outlined below.

Authentic Cases

Although, as stated in Herrington, Oliver, and Reeves (2002), "some argue it is impossible to design truly authentic learning experiences" (p. 60), we attempted to develop learning experiences that would complement and enhance the professional practice of pre-service teachers. The following authentic cases should encourage pre-service teachers to solve complex and ill-structured problems and enhance their ability to reflect on their professional practice. It is hoped that they should be able to monitor their professional thinking and be able to solve new professional problems on an ongoing basis.

In designing the cases it was also essential that the learning design of the five cases was "informed from its inception by some model of learning and instruction" (Koschmann, Kelson, Feltovich, & Barrows, 1996, p. 83). As educators, it is essential that we articulate our learning design for educational interventions from the earliest stages so that we are able to integrate the module into the educational setting and also provide a framework for evaluating the innovation (Koschmann, Kelson, Feltovich, & Barrows, 1996).

We utilised the following principles of authenticity to guide our creation of the five authentic problem-based learning scenarios. Young (1993) suggests six principles. Herrington and Oliver (2000) suggest nine critical characteristics of situated learning. Choi and Hannafin (1995) suggest a conceptual framework that focuses on the role of context, the role of content, the role of facilitation and the role of assessment. These principles are outlined in Table 1.

Learning Design of the Authentic Cases

The explicit rationale for the design of the authentic cases focused on applying key principles of authenticity in the instructional design. As a first step in the process the author wished to focus on five diverse content areas in an attempt to demonstrate the transferability of the approach across the Institute setting. This was undertaken to encourage future adoption of authentic cases and problem-based learning by a number of departments/academics within the Institute. Secondly, the author wished to test the application of authentic design principles within a number of traditional content areas. Encouraging academics to think "outside the box" was another key motivation for the project.

The micro-design of each case involved discussion and collaboration with a number of academics within the Institute. The scripts were written to exploit the affordances of video technology as its strength lies in its ability to portray interpersonal interactions. An attempt was also made to create provocative cases in which the user would react emotionally with the case. For example, one experienced video-producer who evaluated the case stated: "Just one more minor change…" relived some past experiences with unsuccessful projects and commented on the tension displayed by the video-producer and client in the media trigger. In this instance the authentic context enhanced the ability of the user to engage with the case. An attempt was made to make an all-embracing context (Herrington & Oliver, 2000). Often the case design provides no definitive answer and is ill-structured and complex. This principle was explicitly included in the design of each case. For instance there is no correct way to integrate a wheelchair-bound student into physical education. In addition there

Table 1. Principles of authentic problem-based learning

YOUNG (1993)	HERRINGTON & OLIVER (2000)	CHOI AND HANNAFIN (1995)
• Real-life problem-solving • Ill-structured complex goal • Opportunity for the detection of relevant versus irrelevant information • Active/generative engagement in finding and defining problems • Involvement of student's beliefs and values • Opportunity to engage in collaborative interpersonal activities.	Designing for the role of the interactive multimedia program • provide **authentic context** that reflects the way knowledge will be used in real life • provide **authentic activities** • provide access to **expert performances** and modelling of processes • provide **multiple roles and perspectives** Designing for the role of the student • support **collaborative** construction of knowledge • promote **reflection** to enable abstractions to be formed • promote **articulation** to enable tacit knowledge to be made explicit Designing for the implementation of the program • provide **coaching and scaffolding** at critical times • provide for **integrated assessment** of learning within the tasks	Role of Context • general atmosphere • physical setting • background events • authenticity • situational intent • transfer • anchoring knowledge Role of Content • context and content are inextricably connected • content determines authenticity and veracity • knowledge as tool • content diversity and transfer • examples and non-examples • cognitive apprenticeships • anchored instruction Role of Facilitation • modelling • scaffolding • coaching, guiding, advising • collaborating • fading • using cognitive tools and resources Role of Assessment • self-referencing • flexible, transferable knowledge and skill • diversity and flexibility of learner-centred measures • generating and constructing • continuous ongoing process • ecological validity

Table 2. Title and focus of cases

Case	Title	Focus	Resources
One	"What's Wrong With My Baby Boy?"	Early childhood education	Four video-triggers
Two	"Quantum Leap"	Exercise physiology - physical education	Six video-triggers
Three	"Why Can't I Save This File?"	Digital video production	Seven video-triggers
Four	"Just One More Minor Change…"	Project management in educational technology	Seven video-triggers
Five	"Do You Want to Play As Well…?"	Inclusive physical education	Seven video-triggers

are many societal views which affect teachers' decision-making in relation to inclusion of disabled children into regular classes. However the point of the case was to obtain a reaction from pre-service teacher-education students and encourage the student to involve their own beliefs and values with the case. Hopefully they will begin to think about the situation, personally struggle with the issue and reflect on the case in the future. A face-to-face debate on the issue of inclusion also encouraged the students to articulate their beliefs and values about inclusion. Problem-based learning emphasises collaborative learning by encouraging students to discuss the issues in small groups. Through this process each member should obtain multiple perspectives about the issues.

Table 2 provides the title and focus of the five cases. The resources consist of video-based educational triggers which can be accessed via a Web site and streaming media (Keppell, 2004).

Case one demonstrates how the parenting environment can influence the growth and development of a child. Although Chung Chung is only one year old he feels hurt by the neglect of his parents who ask a nursery to be surrogate parents while they work. Kindergarten teachers will need to decipher this information from the case and reflect on how they might best advise parents about this situation. This case has been utilised within the module "Child Growth and Development" in the School of Early Childhood Education. Case two examines physical build and strength in the field of physical education. It examines the age-old issue of students with different physical characteristics and abilities within different sports. Pre-service physical educators should recognise the necessity of designing learning activities to suit all physical builds and aptitudes within their class.

This case was designed for a module on exercise physiology and the paper-based scenario has been utilised in a problem-based learning class. Case three attempts to demystify some of the different file formats used in video production. It also attempts to provide some indication of why different types of video are used in different situations and when for instance streaming media has advantages over other formats. This case will be integrated into the module: Multimedia and Web Authoring in 2005. Case four examines the concept of project management and the tension that occurs between a video producer and a client in terms of their shared understanding of how many changes can be made to the production. Although peripheral to teacher-education, the expectations of clients/customers and communication misunderstandings are common within education. This case will be integrated into the module: Multimedia and Web Authoring in 2005. Case five examines the concept of inclusion of disabled students into the regular physical education class. This case can be utilised in many areas of education and should provoke healthy debate about the issues. The case will be used in a physical education module on inclusion in physical education in 2005.

Case 1:
"What's Wrong With My Baby Boy?"

Context: Chung Chung is a one-year-old boy who lives in a small room of a shared apartment with his parents. Chung Chung's parents migrated to Hong Kong two years ago. Both of them have to work to earn a living, so they send Chung Chung to a nearby nursery (from Monday to Friday, 8a.m. to 6 p.m.). Although they are very busy, they still make Chung Chung look fit and tidy.

This case has been designed to support a face-to-face problem-based learning class in early childhood education. It should assist early childhood educators to evaluate a context and develop a possible intervention plan. Students would watch the video-triggers and then discuss the case in small groups to determine the learning issues. Subsequent videos are viewed to obtain more information about the case. Students also need to complete self-directed learning activities such as reading textbooks and researching the topic to fully understand the case. Nursery teachers can make use of this physical growth and development knowledge to assist parents and families to provide a suitable environment for infants to grow in a healthy environment.

There are four video-triggers which could be used in a sequential manner or as separate triggers for problem-based learning face-to-face discussion. In addition the triggers could initiate discussion about the topic in an online discussion board. The first trigger outlines the context for the case. The second video-trigger outlines the physical and perceptual development of the infant. The third video-trigger outlines the cognitive and language skills development of an infant. The fourth video-trigger outlines the social development of the infant. Kindergarten teachers can make use of physical growth and development knowledge gained from the resources to assist parents and families to provide a suitable environment for infants to grow.

Case 2: "Quantum Leap"

Context: *A PE teacher in a secondary school notices a student in his class is struggling to keep up with the rest of the class during the regular PE class. During another class the PE teacher is pleased to see the student interested in a lecture about strength training.*

This case has been designed to support a face-to-face, problem-based learning class in physical education. This case has been developed to initiate discussion about the topic of strength training and body type and is designed for physical education teachers. The case should assist physical educators to evaluate a student's physical capability and advise them on the best way to train. In addition the case examines how physical education teachers can assist students to choose a sport suitable for their body build. Students would watch the video-triggers and then discuss the case in small groups to determine the learning issues. Subsequent videos are viewed to obtain more information about the case. Students also need to complete self-directed learning activities such as reading textbooks and researching the topic to fully understand the case.

There are six video-triggers which could be used in a sequential manner or as separate triggers. The first trigger outlines the context for the case. The second video-trigger shows Tom limping during PE lesson. He has pain in his arms and legs after using his father's weights at home. The third video-trigger shows Tom discussing his training with his PE teacher. The fourth video-trigger shows Tom undertaking his strength training programme after reviewing the results of his physical tests. The fifth video-trigger outlines the difficulties Tom encounters after a few weeks' training. The sixth video-trigger shows Tom enjoying his new sport of soccer. In addition the triggers could initiate discussion about the topic in an online discussion board.

Case 3: "Why Can't I Save This File?"

Context: *Winnie, Sin, Ngai, and Candice are a group of students taking the subject "General Studies." They are given an assignment about Hong Kong sport, and the outcome of the assignment should be in video format to be viewed on the computer. The lecturer, Tom, did not give them a briefing about the technical issues in video production, and want them to learn from the process.*

This case has been developed to initiate discussion about the topic of digital video in media education. Students would watch the video-triggers and then discuss the case in small groups to determine the learning issues. Subsequent videos are viewed to obtain more information about the case. Students also need to complete self-directed learning activities such as reading textbooks and re-searching the topic to fully understand the case.

There are seven video-triggers that could be used in a sequential manner or as separate triggers for problem-based learning face-to-face discussion. In addition the triggers could initiate discussion about the topic in an online discussion board. The first video-trigger outlines the context for the case. The second video-trigger suggests that there are different video formats in different countries. The third video-trigger examines AVI files and whether it is suitable for a PowerPoint presentation and CD-ROM. The fourth video-trigger examines AVI files and their file size. The fifth video-trigger examines differences between a VCD format and a file format suitable for PowerPoint. The sixth video-trigger examines the use of streaming technology for Web-based video files. The seventh video-trigger examines the use of Windows Movie Maker for making Web-based video files.

Case 4: "Just One More Minor Change..."

Context: A client at a higher education institution wants to produce an introductory video on promoting the physical education facilities at the Institution. A Video Production Company will be working with the client to achieve this goal. We will see several problems that they will encounter in the production process and how they managed these issues.

This case has been developed to initiate discussion about the topic of project management in educational technology. The case has been developed to assist educational technologists to engage students in a project in which a client wants to make multiple changes to the output although these were not identified at the beginning of the project. It represents a means of sensitising students to the reality of project management and would be useful for allowing clients to understand the implications of changes to an educational technology project. Students also need to complete self-directed learning activities such as reading textbooks and researching the topic to fully understand the case.

There are seven video-triggers which could be used in a sequential manner or as separate triggers for problem-based learning face-to-face discussion. In addition the triggers could initiate discussion about the topic in an online discussion board. The first trigger outlines the context for the case. The second video-trigger outlines the first meeting between the client and a video-production company. The third video-trigger outlines the client making a seventh draft to the video script. The fourth video-trigger outlines filming, editing and a meeting in which the client asks for more areas to be included in the video. This means more filming by the production company. The fifth video-trigger shows another meeting in which new people ask for more areas to be included in the video. The sixth trigger shows the inevitable tension between the client and the video-production company as further changes are made to the output. The seventh video-trigger shows the same client working with another video production company. This video-production company clearly outlines the number of changes that can be made to the video.

Case 5:
"Do You Want to Play as Well?"

Context: This scene shows a regular volleyball game in which two teams are playing a long rally. In the foreground you can see Fai who is disabled, in a wheelchair and is being excluded from the game due to his disability. This student has been supportive of the University volleyball team for a number of matches and always attends the inter-university matches without fail.

This case has been developed to initiate discussion about the topic of inclusion of disabled students into the regular physical education class. The problem-based media-based triggers have been developed to assist physical educators to consider how they can adapt team sports such as volleyball to include disabled students. It represents a means of sensitising students to the capabilities of a wheelchair-bound student and how some creative thinking by the physical educator can enrich the learning experience for both able-bodied and disabled students. Students also need to complete self-directed learning activities such as reading textbooks and researching the topic to fully understand the case.

There are seven video-triggers that could be used in a sequential manner or as separate triggers for problem-based learning face-to-face discussion. In addition the triggers could initiate discussion about the topic in an online discussion board. The first video-trigger outlines the context for the case. The second video-trigger shows a regular volleyball game in which a wheelchair bound student can be seen in the background. The third video-trigger shows an empathetic student speaking to the coach about how they could include the wheelchair student in the class. The fourth video-trigger outlines the ways in which the students find different ways of including the wheel-chair student in the volleyball game. The fifth video-trigger shows Fai participating in the activities. The sixth trigger shows a number of successful ways Fai is included in the volleyball game. The seventh trigger asks Fai about his experience in playing volleyball with the class.

Future Directions:
Hong Kong Institute of Education

Within the Hong Kong Institute of Education (HKIEd) there is currently institute-wide interest in problem-based learning and its utilisation for teaching. Future work by the Centre for Integrating Technology in Education will focus on developing a number of problem-based learning media-rich educational triggers for staff to implement PBL. These authentic cases emphasise the immersion of the learner in a real-world problem which is ill-structured in nature and requires collaboration with other students to explore the case. Students should be able to involve their own beliefs and values in the case. The case involving the integration of a disabled student into the regular physical education class should confront the student and assist in developing attitudes and strategies to address a similar situation when the teacher-education student is teaching in the school setting. In addition the learner should be motivated to research the topic in books, journals and on the internet through follow-up activities to the case. A secondary aim of developing these media-rich educational triggers is the development of exemplars for further implementation of problem-based learning within the Institute. It is hoped that we will develop authentic cases in areas as diverse as physical education, music, counseling, art, technology, inclusive education, English and Chinese language, mathematics, early childhood education and science and foster generative activities.

Conclusion

This chapter has examined a rationale for the utilisation of authentic cases for problem-based learning in teacher education. This justification has been focused on immersing pre-service teachers in "issues, problems, and solutions of teaching practice before they have the experience of being first-year teachers, fully responsible for their own classrooms" (Richardson, 2000, p. 122). This process through PBL may allow them to develop the appropriate cognitive schemata so that when they enter the classroom they will understand the meaning of the classroom interactions so that they will be able to make more informed decisions about the best way to teach and improve learning for the students involved. In addition the reusability of media-based educational triggers offers a promising direction. It is suggested that learning objects are "any digital resource that can be reused to support learning" (Wiley, 2002. p. 6). It is useful to think about the media-rich educational triggers in this manner because "instructional designers can build instructional components that can be reused a number of times in different learning contexts" (Wiley, 2002, p. 4).

Acknowledgments

This project was funded by LEARNet. LEARNet is funded by the University Grants Committee and is based at the University of Hong Kong with a management team drawn from all the tertiary institutions in the SAR. http://learnet.hku.hk/ Title of funded project: *Developing reusable 'media-rich educational triggers' for supporting problem-based learning.*

References

Ausubel, D.P. (1960). The use of advance organizers in the learning and retention of meaningful verbal material. *Journal of Educational Psychology, 51(5),* 267-272.

Barrows, H.S., & Tamblyn, R.M. (1980). *Problem-based learning: An approach to medical education.* New York: Springer.

Choi, J-I., & Hannifin, M. (1995). Situated cognition and learning environments: Roles, structures, and implications for design. *Educational Technology, Research and Development, 43*(2), 53-69.

Dewey, J. (1938). *Experience and education.* New York: Collier Macmillan.

Evensen, D.H., & Hmelo, C.E. (Eds.). (2000). *Problem-based learning: A research perspective on learning interactions.* NJ: Lawrence Erlbaum.

Gordon, C.J., & Rennie, B.J. (1987). Restructuring content schemata: An intervention study. *Reading Research and Instruction, 26*(3), 162-188.

Herrington, J., & Oliver, R. (2000). An instructional design framework for authentic learning environments. *Educational Technology Research and Development, 48*(3), 23-48.

Herrington, J., Oliver, R., & Reeves, T. C. (2002). Patterns of engagement in authentic online learning environments. In A. Williamson, C. Gunn, A. Young, & T. Clear (Eds.), *Winds of change in a sea of learning.*

Proceedings of the 19th Annual Conference of the Australasian Society for Computers in Tertiary Education (pp. 279-286). Auckland, New Zealand: UNITEC: Institute of Technology.

Hmelo, C.E., & Evensen, D.H. (2000). Problem-based learning: Gaining insights on learning interactions through multiple methods of inquiry. In D.H. Evensen & C.E. Hmelo (Eds.), *Problem-based learning: A research perspective on learning interactions.* Mahwah, NJ: Lawrence Erlbaum.

Jonassen, D., Mayes, T., & McAleese, R. (1993). A manifesto for a constructivist approach to uses of technology in higher education. In T.M. Duffy, J. Lowyck & D. H. Jonassen (Eds.), *Designing environments for constructive learning* (pp. 231-247). Berlin; Springer-Verlag.

Keppell, M., Elliott, K., Kennedy, Elliott, S., & Harris, P. (2003). Using authentic patient encounters to engage medical students in a problem-based learning curriculum. In S. Naidu (Ed.), *Learning and teaching with technology: Principles and practices* (pp. 85-96). London: Kogan Page.

Keppell, M., Kennedy, G., Elliott, K., & Harris, P. (2001, April). Transforming traditional curricula: Enhancing medical education through multimedia and web-based resources. *Interactive Multimedia Electronic Journal of Computer-Enhanced Learning (IMEJ), 3*(1). Retrieved from *http://imej.wfu.edu/articles/2001/1/index.asp*

Keppell, M.J. (2004). *Reusable media-rich triggers educational triggers for supporting problem-based learning (Version 1.0)* [Computer software]. Centre for Learning, Teaching and Technology, The Hong Kong Institute of Education. Retrieved May 21, 2005, *from http://www.ied.edu.hk/citie/learnetmain.html*

Koschmann, T. (2002). Introduction to special issue on studying collaboration in distributed PBL environments. *Distance Education, 23*(1), 5-9.

Koschmann, T., Kelson, A.C., Feltovich, P.J., & Barrows. H.S. (1996). Computer-supported problem-based learning: A principled approach to the use of computers in collaborative learning. In T. Koschmann (Ed.), *Computer supported collaborative learning: Theory and practice in an emerging paradigm.* Mahwah, NJ: Lawrence Erlbaum.

Mayer, R.E. (1979). Twenty years of research on advance organizers: Assimilation theory is still the best predictor of results. *Instructional Science 8,* 133-167.

Norman, G.R., & H.G. Schmidt (1992). The psychological basis of problem-based learning: A review of the evidence. *Academic Medicine, 67(9),* 557-565.

Pedersen, S. (2003). Teachers' beliefs about issues in the implementation of a student-centered learning environment. *Educational Technology, Research & Development, 51*(2), 57-74.

Richardson, V. (1999). Learning from videocases. In M.A. Lundeberg, B.B. Levin & H.L. Harrington (Eds.), *Who learns what from cases and how? The research base for teaching and learning with cases.* Mahwah, NJ: Lawrence Erlbaum.

Rumelhart, D.E., & D.A. Norman (1983). Representation in memory. *ERIC Documentation Service ED 235 770.*

Schmidt, H.G. (1993). Foundations of problem-based learning: Some explanatory notes. *Medical Education, 27,* 423-432.

Wiley, D.A. (Ed.). (2002). Connecting learning objects to instructional design theory: A definition, a metaphor and a taxonomy. In D.A. Wiley (Ed.), *The instructional use of learning objects* (pp. 3-23). Bloomington, IN: Association for Educational Communications & Technology.

Young, M. (1993). Instructional design for situated learning. *Educational Technology Research and Development, 41,* 43-58.

Section III

Enhancing Widespread Adoption of Authentic Learning Environments

Chapter VIII

Reusable Resources and Authentic Learning Environments

Ron Oliver, Edith Cowan University, Australia

Abstract

There is currently a high degree of energy and enthusiasm in the e-learning world being given to developing strategies and systems that support the reuse of digital learning resources. The activity involves a number of processes including the development of specifications and standards for the design and development of reusable learning resources, the storage and access of these resources, and systems for delivering the resources to students. This chapter explores the potential impact this area will have for teachers developing authentic learning environments, and argues the advantages that teachers employing such learning settings will derive from the developments. The chapter suggests design and development strategies that are needed to ensure that potential advantages are realised.

Introduction

Many of the chapters in this book provide detailed descriptions of learning designs which support authentic learning. In most instances, the descriptions of the learning designs describe settings that are strongly supported by digital and online resources. In recent years, the development of online settings has seen a burgeoning of online resources supporting high quality learning experiences and many moves have been taken to create opportunities for the reuse of these resources (e.g., Littlejohn, 2003). The purpose of this chapter is to explore the advantages and opportunities that this activity will bring to teachers and students involved in authentic learning settings.

There are many advantages to be gained from being able to reuse digital resources in learning settings and much has been written on the topic of reusability as both a design and development strategy for online learning materials and as a general approach to the use of digital resources for teaching and learning (e.g., Downes, 2000). The topic necessarily impacts on the actions of the vast majority of people associated with teaching and learning and includes such stakeholders as:

- Administrative and financial bodies that look to benefit from the potential costs savings associated with reusing and sharing learning resources;
- Policy-makers who are interested in the legal and ethical implications of copyright and intellectual property among the shared objects;
- Instructional designers who need to consider design strategies that facilitate and support sharing and reuse; and
- Developers who need to consider appropriate strategies to ensure interoperability and a capability for use of resources beyond the context for which they are designed (e.g., Downes, 2000; Shepherd, 2000).

Apart from the cost savings that stem from reduced development needs, there is also the advantage of being able to provide learners with access to increased levels of resources. When there are ample reusable resources, teachers can select from among those available to choose the most appropriate and the best quality. Reusable resources facilitate the sharing of materials among and between groups, an activity that can only lead to improved outcomes in terms of providing alternative perspectives and a multiplicity of content sources.

Learning Objects

It is common parlance today to use the term *learning object* when referring to reusable digital learning resources. Many writers, however, find this term distracting and misleading and are very cautious in its use (e.g., Friesen, 2003). The IEEE Learning Technology Standards Committee (LTSC, 2001) describes a learning object as any entity digital or non-digital that can be used for learning education or training. It is an ill-defined term (Wiley, 2000) whose use tends to cause confusion, uncertainty and disagreement among its users (e.g., Rehak & Mason, 2003). Its definition is too broad. There is often uncertainty as to whether a learning object can simply contain information or whether it needs to have some instructional elements. There is uncertainty in the granularity that applies, for example, to questions such as when is a learning object actually two learning objects and what is the minimum size an object might be? (Duncan, 2003). And some authors define different types of learning objects, for example, knowledge objects, tool objects, test objects (e.g., Koper, 2003). But despite this uncertainty, people readily use the term as a catch-all and its usage is frequent and common.

Much of the current work with learning objects is seeking to provide the enabling systems and processes to create an outcome where mainstream teachers creating learning environments will be able to discover and locate online resources that can be seamlessly incorporated into the learning environments they are building. When one examines the types of learning resources that are currently used in educational settings, there are many factors that potentially limit seamless reuse. For example:

- Learning resources come in a huge variety of forms and sizes;
- They are built from a variety of technologies and in a variety of architectures which tend to tie them to particular platforms and operating systems;
- The resources have often been designed for use in a single setting, with hard links and connections that cannot be easily disconnected if the materials are to be used elsewhere; and
- The resources contain references and descriptions from the local setting that would be out of place if the materials were reused.

There has been a huge amount of work undertaken by a number of large organisations and groups to facilitate the reusability and interoperability of digital learning resources (e.g., IMS Global Learning Consortium, ADL, and IEEE). This work appears to be removing many of the barriers that have previously limited reuse of learning resources. The work being done to develop the Sharable Content Object Reference Model (SCORM) is a strong case in point. SCORM

(2001) has been developed by the Advanced Distributed Learning (ADL) initiative and provides a design and development model for learning resources which strongly supports reusability and interoperability.

SCORM (Sharable Content Object Reference Model)

SCORM is a model that describes a standardised way to design and develop reusable learning materials so that learners' pathways and successes in the learning setting can be tracked and monitored. At the same time, SCORM supports an approach that facilitates the reuse and interoperability of compliant resources. The learning materials themselves (learning objects) are managed and coordinated within a compliant learning management system (LMS) such as WebCT or Blackboard. And SCORM also supports ways for the learning materials to be discovered and accessed for re-use. All in all, it proposes a powerful solution to the problems facing those wanting to reuse learning resources.

SCORM supports these capabilities in the way it has been developed. SCORM (the model) describes two main elements: a content aggregation model (CAM) and a run-time environment. The CAM describes the ways in which SCORM materials are organised and packaged so that they can be seamlessly exchanged between different learning systems. The run-time environment provides the means for the learning materials to communicate with the LMS and for the collection of data to track and monitor learners.

Learning Object Metadata

At the same time that ADL has been developing SCORM, there has been a high degree of related work being undertaken to create standardized lists of descriptors (metadata) that can be used to describe and help identify the content of learning objects. There now exists standard sets of learning object metadata (LOM, 2002) which define a range of relevant descriptors to enable the objects to be distinguished and which provide searchable information about an object's form and content including:

- Descriptive information, e.g., author, version, related objects, etc.;
- Technical data, e.g., media type, file size;
- Educational data, e.g., learning objectives, subject area; and
- Management data, e.g., copyright and ownership, costs for reuse.

The advantage of the use of standard metadata forms and processes is that people know the language and vocabulary that needs to be used to locate relevant objects. People know the appropriate number and forms of descriptors that should be applied to objects and similar processes can be used to find objects across a variety of storage systems.

Digital Repositories

Once learning resources have been designed and built, they need to stored in ways that will facilitate their discovery and reuse by others. Specifications for digital repositories are a recent addition to the standards activities. A digital repository is a collection of digital resources that can be accessed through a network requiring no prior knowledge of the collection's structure. Repositories usually hold many forms of digital resource including their metadata descriptors, although the metadata need not necessarily be stored with the various assets. The specifications for digital repositories that are currently being developed by IMS include object querying and locating functions. Recommended standards include the W3C XQuery (2003), W3C SOAP (2000) the simple object access protocol, and ZOOM (2003), the Z39.50 object oriented model.

The development and subsequent application of all these standards appears to hold strong prospects and advantages for teachers planning and developing learning environments. A number of writers, however, express cautions about aspects of this work in relation to the forms of learning upon which it is all premised. Wiley (2003) argues that there are implicit assumptions in the bulk of the work that is colouring the direction the designs and decisions. In particular much of the work is aimed at developing systems that support instructional models where learners learn from computers in independent, machine-controlled systems. The forms of reusable resources that best suit authentic learning settings can be distinctly different to those produced from the above work. When reusability is explored from the context of authentic learning settings, many new possibilities appear to emerge.

Reusable Resources for Authentic Learning Environments

The design of any online learning environment requires the deliberate planning and development of three main elements: learning tasks, learning resources and learning supports (Oliver, 1999). Authentic learning settings involve particular forms of digital resources, and all the constituent elements within authentic learning settings appear to have the potential to be created and developed with reusable components.

Reusable Learning Tasks

In authentic learning settings, authentic tasks are the organisational element around which learning is based. Generally speaking, the specification of learner tasks is used to describe the outputs from the learning process. Tasks are used to describe the products students will deliver and which will demonstrate the learning that has been achieved. The design of tasks as contexts for learning forms the major part of the instructional design process. The choice of task needs to fit with the learning design that is to be used. While the task specifies the outcomes of the learning experience, the learning design provides a framework for the learning process, and provides guidance for the specification of resources and supports needed to deliver that outcome.

Designing learning around tasks requires a high degree of skill and judgment on the part of the teacher. The selection and specification of the task(s) necessitates consideration of:

- The scope of the learning being sought: the task needs to provide the necessary scope for students to engage with the underpinning knowledge, to practice the particular skills involved, and to reflect on their learning across the whole of the planned set of learning objectives.

- The level of learning being sought: the task needs to provide ample opportunity for learners to engage in a learning process able to develop their learning to the particular level being sought, for example, knowledge, comprehension, application, analysis, synthesis or evaluation.

- The specification of a product or artefact: the product is ultimately the tangible outcome of the learning process and usually forms the basis of the assessment and evaluation of learning.

The concept of reusability of learning tasks is more a concept of the reusability of the ideas than discrete objects. The tasks themselves will tend to be highly contextualised to the planned learning setting and for that reason not particularly usable outside this context. But the form of the task and the nature of the product being developed are concepts that can guide others. Tasks are often provided in the form of problems to be solved, investigations to be undertaken, and projects to be completed. Being able to examine and review tasks developed for use in other settings can guide teachers in the task selection process for their own courses. Wiley (2003) argues that these elements should be considered as learning objects themselves.

Reusable Learning Supports

In any learning setting, learners need to be provided with scaffolds and supports that enable them to complete activities and tasks that they cannot as yet do. The idea of scaffolding as a support is that as the learner develops the new skills and expertise the need for the scaffolding diminishes and can be gradually removed. In authentic learning environments where learners are frequently required to undertake tasks outside their zone of comfort and capability, scaffolds and supports are very important.

Learning supports can take many forms including:

- Detailed instruction that decomposes the investigations/problems/ projects (tasks) into smaller elements;
- Suggested learning strategies that can guide learners where they might seek information;
- Collaborative activities designed to enable students to work with other students;
- Discussion forums that enable students to share ideas and understandings with others as part of the learning process;
- File sharing facilities that enable students to share files and resources among themselves;
- Workplace colleagues or mentors who can provide answers to questions and guidance when help is needed;
- Sets of frequently asked questions that can be used as information sources when difficulties arise; and
- Reflective journals and personal learning diaries.

As can be seen from the above list, not all supports are able to be developed as digital resources that support reuse. However, many of the supports can be provided as online tools and resources that can be designed to be reusable. Often these supports will be created by teachers as resources within a Learning Management System (LMS), such as Blackboard or WebCT. In some LMSs, these resources are provided for teachers in customised and reusable forms. Often these learning supports are not those that can be found in digital repositories due to the complex nature of their operation and their technology reliance, which limits them to particular operating systems and platforms.

The learning design employed in a course will often guide the teacher in terms of the forms of learning support needed. Having access to a variety of existing supports that are easily adapted for the local setting can provide considerable advantage and opportunity to a teacher planning an authentic learning setting.

Reusable Learning Resources

When designing authentic learning settings, choosing resources is usually the final step in the design process and a step that is greatly aided by access to existing resources that can be reused. Authentic learning settings provide access to resources that have high levels of relevance and currency, that provide alternative perspectives, and that enable learners to construct their own meaning (e.g., Herrington, Oliver & Reeves, 2002). These resources need to be plentiful and varied and are sometimes are not the forms of resources one normally finds in textbooks and conventional settings. Examples of learning resources that are found in authentic learning setting include:

- Information and reference material;
- Specialist Web sites and Web links;
- Journal and newspaper articles;
- Books;
- Online tutorials and self-paced instructional materials;
- Quizzes and self-tests;
- Training manuals;
- Previous student work samples and products; and
- Workplace documents and proformas.

The resources that are used in authentic learning settings are diverse and varied but within the list are many that are reusable and able to be selected and reused from other settings. Most teachers who design authentic learning environments spend the bulk of their design time preparing learning tasks and supports. Ultimately they have little time to develop their own content and information sources as well and given the depth and breadth of resources required, most teachers seek to reuse already developed resources. The ready availability of high quality, accessible reusable resources would provide strong support to teachers developing authentic learning settings.

Apart from learning objects stored in digital repositories, there are many reusable digital resources freely available today through digital libraries and subject portals. These collections describe organised sets of resources, usually restricted to set discipline and subject areas. The resources are organised within the digital library in some planned fashion and can be accessed through such means as topic lists and keyword searchers.

The content that is contained within digital libraries is usually selected and organised by subject matter experts and drawn from resources worldwide. The collections can include widely varying elements ranging from images, pages, papers, presentations, audio tracks and movies. For example the *Digital Library for Earth Science Education* (DLESE, 2002) supports Earth system science education by providing access to:

- High-quality collections of educational resources;
- Earth data sets and imagery, including the tools and interfaces that enable their effective use in educational settings;
- Support services to help educators and learners effectively create, use, and share educational resources; and
- Communication networks to facilitate interactions and collaborations across all dimensions of Earth system education.

Digital libraries exist for many subject areas and can provide substantial amounts of information for students and teachers. While learning objects can be accessed from keyword searches from repositories, elements in digital libraries usually are accessed through topic lists. In learning settings, resources accessed from digital libraries are usually included as external links, while learning objects typically can be embedded into e-learning materials.

Digital libraries can provide access to very large sets of resources but the resources need to be located though such means as search engines and topic searches. For these reasons, they tend to offer far less in terms of usability and flexibility of use for materials developers.

Learning Designs for Authentic Learning Settings

The term *learning design* is often used to describe the framework that a teacher uses to plan a learning setting. A learning design is a planned and deliberate description of a set of learning activities chosen by a teacher to engage and motivate learners in a course. The design of any online learning environment requires the deliberate planning and development of the three main elements: learning tasks, learning resources and learning supports. Authentic learning settings require that particular forms of learning designs, and the designs and their constituent elements, can all created and developed in ways that support reusability.

Much of the early work in the specification and description of learning objects drew from activities where the implemented settings of the resources involved conventional forms of computer-based learning instruction. In such settings, learners are exposed to learning materials that provide descriptions of learning content and which are supported by tests and assessment tasks that are used to monitor learning (knowledge acquisition). Such learning settings tend to follow very directed learning sequences and involve high degrees of teacher-planned structure.

When the learning design needs to support high quality learning experiences, as is the case with authentic learning settings, a number of complexities arise. Authentic learning involves learning settings that are far more open and diverse. Learning is usually based around tasks rather than content modules, learners work collaboratively rather than individually and learning is assessed in terms of demonstrable capabilities rather than knowledge acquired. Much of the subtlety in the learning environments developed for this form of learning is not easily managed and organised by the forms of learning systems and resources which are the current focus of learning objects activity. But these limitations have been recognised and there are currently many projects exploring possible extensions to existing work and standards. The Educational Modelling Language (EML), for example, seeks to provide a means to formalise and describe both the content and processes within units of learning (Koper & Manderveld, 2004). EML provides a framework that acknowledges different forms of learning object, and defines a structure for their content and behaviours.

Reusable Learning Designs

When a teacher plans a learning environment, the process of planning involves some form of specification of the activities learners will undertake. Often teachers use lessons as the basis of their planning. They plan discrete sets of activities tasks for each of the lessons that comprise the course of study. In authentic learning settings, lessons no longer form the basic unit of learning (instruction). Authentic learning settings are built around authentic tasks that provide structure and form to the learning experience.

While there are a number of discrete learning designs that can be used to support task-based learning, there are a multitude of forms and variations among these designs. Jonassen (2000) suggests 11 forms of tasks/problems that can support the forms knowledge construction sought in authentic learning environments. Oliver, Harper, Hedberg, Wills and Agostinho (2002) argue that these 11 forms can be further organised across four types of problem/task specification: rule-based, incident-based, strategy based and role-based. The use of this form of classification and categorisation provides a means for describing learning designs and as such, a means for providing forms and descriptions that are reusable.

The notion of formalising and describing reusable learning designs was the aim of a large *Australian Universities Teaching Committee* project completed in 2002 which resulted in the development of an online resource providing access to reusable learning designs supporting high quality learning outcomes (e.g., Harper & Oliver, 2002). The majority of the learning designs described in this project support authentic learning outcomes and have strong prospects for reusability (*ICTs and their role in flexible learning*, 2002).

There is still, however, work to be done to provide teachers with learning designs in the form of reusable digital resources. In their current forms, there is descriptive material providing teachers with guides and suggestions as to potentially useful forms of learning design, but teachers are still required to apply these ideas and to develop their own digital resource forms. Buzza, Bean, Harrigan and Carey (in press) describe a Canadian project that is currently looking to develop a model for describing learning designs that will facilitate their storage and discovery as resources in digital repositories. Recognising the limitations of all existing approaches to this activity, they are seeking to develop a usage-centred controlled vocabulary to facilitate the description and labelling of learning designs.

One project that has actually delivered the capacity to promote the reuse of learning designs is the Learning Activity Management System (LAMS) (Dalziel, 2003), an open-source Web-based tool. LAMS provides a means for teachers to design and implement planned learning sequences that comprise various forms of learner engagement using such Web-based activities as discussion boards, file sharing and collaboration. The frameworks that are created to support these activities can be stored in the form of reusable templates for subsequent activities.

It is likely that we will see much more work and research exploring reusable learning designs. For many, the learning design is the most important aspect of any learning environment and the prospect of teachers one day having access to reusable learning frameworks and instructional strategies into which content resources are placed is an outcome many are seeking. Allert, Richter and Nejdl

(2004) argue that reusable learning objects can be considered as one of two types, first order and second order. They propose that First Order Learning Objects (FOLO) are resources with specific learning objectives while Second Order Learning Objects (SOLO) are resources, which are themselves learning strategies. At the moment there are plentiful supplies of FOLOs and very few SOLOs and many projects are seeking to redress this imbalance.

Designing Digital Resources to Support Reusability

The previous sections have described the forms of digital resources that are needed and can be reused by teachers of authentic learning environments. With this need in mind, it is useful to consider approaches that designers of learning materials might use to ensure that any resources they create have the greatest prospect for reuse. Whilst there has been considerable effort and energy given to the development of technical standards for developing reusable digital resources for learning objects, there is less information and guidance in relation to aspects of instructional design for these entities. The following section suggests strategies that can support this aim and argues the following design characteristics as important components supporting reusability.

- Instructional segregation;
- Context independence; and
- Modularity.

Instructional Segregation

The topic of instructional neutrality as a requirement for reusability is the topic of much debate (e.g., Friesen, 2004). When many teachers develop learning materials to support student-centred environments, they will often use a series of instructions tied to some subject matter. For example, imagine a teacher creating some materials explaining to students how to use a Web-based search engine. A very common strategy is to create a document where the teacher's voice is used to describe and comment on content, in very much the same way as a teacher explaining what materials would do in a classroom setting. Learning materials that combine a teacher's voice with the content being discussed are limited in their reusability. The teacher's voice is the problem. When designing for reuse, it is a better strategy to place the instructional elements separately from the content. In this way, the content is reusable in its original form. The same content can then be used for many different purposes and is not tied to the original instructional setting. This separation of learning design from the underpinning content provides some recognition for the FOLO and SOLO concept as proposed by Allert, Richter and Nejdl (2004) and suggests possible forms which SOLOs might take.

Context Independence

Wiley (2003) describes the notion of "using a learning object" better described as "placing an object into an instructional context." In order for resources to be able to be used freely in a variety of instructional contexts, they cannot afford to have internal contexts that might impede this action. Resources that can be reused need to be able to be removed from their original contextual setting and to stand alone once removed. Reusable resources are enhanced by a lack of specificity in their internal contexts. In the design of learning materials, teachers often create resources that are linked to particular notions and themes. To facilitate reuse, the internal contexts need to be limited. This can be an impeding feature where contexts are seen as important to learning. Decisions about context specification for reuse are very difficult for developers to make when they appear to limit the application of the resources in their initial setting. For authentic learning settings, limited contexts are an advantage since the context is usually provided within the task specification.

Modularity

Modular design forms for resources are very effective in encouraging prospects for reuse. The use of modules reduces the grain size of the various components, a factor which is clearly linked to reusability (e.g., Hodgins, 2002). At the same time, a modular approach encourages design that uses information and content considerations as organisational forms. One important factor in supporting reusability is being able to discover relevant materials. The smaller the grain size of the resource and the more cohesive the content and instructional purpose, the more likely the materials can be used outside the original context. Such approaches provide the teachers and students considering reuse with increased flexibility and choice in how the resources can be re-employed.

Development Strategies Supporting Reusability

Apart from the instructional design that necessarily informs the planning of reusable learning resources, the way in which they are built, the development strategies, also plays a large part in ensuring their successful reuse. Development strategies that support reusability include:

- Developing for interoperability;
- Developing discoverable resources; and
- Ensuring scalability.

Developing Interoperability

The term *interoperability* describes the technical capability of a resource to be used by other delivery media beyond its original context. Typically people take interoperability to mean the capability of a resource to be used within different learning management systems while retaining all aspects of its functionality. Within the IEEE context, interoperability is seen as "the ability of two or more systems or components to exchange information and to use that information" (IEEE, 1990). Interoperability forms a large part of the specification within ADL SCORM, since one of the key components of training materials is an ability to record aspects of the user's progress and performance within a resource. It also enables resources to be concatenated and sequenced together so that they don't appear disjointed and disconnected. In authentic learning settings, learning resources rarely need this level and form of delivery requirement. Authentic settings provide resources for learners often as discrete and disconnected entities and the need for interoperability and connectedness is not usually important. By its very nature the Web provides very high levels of interoperability and most authentic learning environments are able to employ resources from a variety of developmental origins.

Discoverable Resources

The discovery of a resource is the first step that needs to be taken on the road to its reuse. The strategy that ensures resources are discoverable is the use of metatags in the description of the resource. There are now a number of metadata standards that can be applied to ensure resources have adequate descriptions to be discovered. The IEEE Learning Object Metadata scheme (LOM) is becoming the most widely used standard for this purpose. Whilst there are standards that are now readily employable, too few developers seem to have the capability to apply the metadata tags accurately and efficiently (e.g., Brownfield & Oliver, 2003). For many, the addition of metadata is a task that has a low priority and is often not given the attention it deserves. It is not uncommon when searching digital repositories to find many resources with identical metadata descriptors, an outcome of an inability to accurately apply the descriptors and a lack of attention to this stage of the development process.

Ensuring Scalability

Scalability is an attribute of learning resources which is needed to ensure that when they are applied in other contexts, they have the ability to be used in the changed setting as efficiently as they were used in their original context. In particular, scalable resources have the capacity to support additional, or fewer, users without any major alteration to the operation of the resource. Scalability is an important feature in the design of reusable learning resources because the size of a learning cohort can vary so dramatically from one setting to the next. With information resources, scalability is less important than with resources that have been designed to support group work or collaborative use. In authentic learning settings where group work and distributed learning settings are quite common, it is important in the design of the resources and supports to ensure that there is adequate flexibility to cater for cohorts which are bigger, or smaller, than those for which the original planning and development has been done.

Summary and Conclusion

Learning objects and reusable resources are the focus of many current projects and activities in institutions and organisations throughout the world. The principal aim of these activities is to create learning resources that will support e-learning activities. For those teachers seeking to create authentic learning settings, the outcomes from this work offer many advantages and opportunities. We are now seeing standards and specifications emerging that will facilitate the development and storage of large numbers of resources, which can be readily discovered and used by teachers. Whilst many will argue that the focus of the activity is towards learning resources more suited to conventional forms of e-learning such as computer-based training, all of the resources can ultimately be used in authentic learning settings. One of the defining features of an authentic learning setting is its openness and flexibility in terms of the learning resources it employs. Learning objects in every form can be used in authentic learning settings regardless of their original context.

This chapter has explored current and past activities in the development of standards and specifications for learning objects and has demonstrated the useful outcomes from this work. It has described some of the unique aspects of authentic learning settings and the forms of reusable resource that are appropriately employed. It has suggested a number of design and development strategies that can be used in the development of any learning resources that will facilitate their reuse in other settings. The one area of development that appears to be less advanced than others in this field is that of reusable learning designs. Whilst there is considerable interest and activity in this area, we have yet to see the level of reusability achieved as we have seen for information and content objects. Hopefully, in the near future, we will see systems and supports providing teachers with truly reusable learning designs that will support authentic learning and promote these environments into mainstream teaching and learning.

References

Allert, H., Richter, C., & Nejdl, W. (2004). Lifelong learning and second order learning objects. *British Journal of Educational Technology, 35*(6), 701-715.

Brownfield, G., & Oliver, R. (2003). Factors influencing the discovery and reusability of digital resources for teaching and learning. In G.Crisp, D. Thiele, I. Scholten, S. Barker & J. Baron (Eds.), *Interact, Integrate, Impact: Proceedings of the 20th Annual Conference of ASCILITE* (pp. 74-83). Adelaide, ASCILITE.

Buzza, D., Bean, D., Harrigan, K., & Carey, T. (in press). Learning design repositories: Adapting learning design specifications for shared instructional knowledge. *Canadian Journal of Learning and Technology.*

Dalziel, J. (2003). *Implementing learning design: The learning activity management system* (LAMS). In G.Crisp, D. Thiele, I. Scholten, S. Barker & J. Baron (Eds.), *Interact, Integrate, Impact: Proceedings of the 20th Annual Conference of ASCILITE* (pp. 593-596). Adelaide, ASCILITE.

DLESE. (2002). *Digital library for Earth systems education.* Retrieved November 2004, from *http://www.dlese.org*

Downes, S. (2000). *Learning objects.* Retrieved June 2002, from *http:// www.atl.ualberta.ca/downes/namwb/column000523_1.htm*

Duncan, C. (2003). Granularization. In A. Littlejohn (Ed.), *Reusing online resources: A sustainable approach to e-learning* (pp. 12-19). London: Kogan Page.

Friesen, N. (2003). *Three objections to learning objects and e-learning standards.* Retrieved November 2004, from *http:// www.learningspaces.org/n/papers/objections.html*

Friesen, N. (2004). *Learning objects and standards: Pedagogical neutrality and engagement.* Retrieved November 2004, from *www.learningspaces.org/n/papers/pedagogical_neutrality.pdf*

Harper, B., & Oliver, R. (2002). *Reusable learning designs: Information and communication technologies and their role in flexible learning.* Presentation for the AUTC Reusable Learning Designs: Opportunities and Challenges Conference, UTS, Sydney, December. Retrieved from http:// *www.learningdesigns.uow.edu.au/Publications/AUTCICTProject.ppt*

Herrington, J., Oliver, R., & Reeves, T. C. (2003). Patterns of engagement in authentic online learning environments. *Australian Journal of Educational Technology, 19*(1), 59-71.

Hodgins, W. (2002). Learning by design: Future of learning objects. Paper presented at *AUTC Conference*, University of Technology Sydney, December. Retrieved May 2003, from *http://www.iml.uts.edu.au/autc/ PDF_hodgins.pdf*

IEEE (1990). *IEEE Standard Computer Dictionary: A compilation of IEEE standard computer glossaries.* New York: IEEE.

Information and Communication Technologies and Their Role in Flexible Learning, (2002). Retrieved November 2004, from *http:// www.learningdesigns.uow.edu.au*

Jonassen, D.H. (2000). Toward a design theory of problem solving. *Educational Technology Research and Development, 48*(4), 63-85.

Koper, R. (2003). Combining reusable learning resources and services with pedagogical purposeful units of learning. In A. Littlejohn (Ed.), *Reusing online resources: A sustainable approach to elearning* (pp. 46-59). London: Kogan Page.

Koper, R., & Manderveld, J. (2004). Educational modelling language: Modelling reusable, interoperable, rich and personalised units of learning. *British Journal of Educational Technology, 35*(5), 537-551.

Littlejohn, A. (2003). Issues in reusing online resources. In A. Littlejohn (Ed.), *Reusing online resources: A sustainable approach to elearning* (pp. 1-8). London: Kogan Page.

LOM (2002). *IEEE Standard for Learning Object Metadata*, IEEE, 1484, 12.1-2002, IEEE.

LTSC. (2001). *IEEE learning technology standards committee website*. Retrieved May 2003, from *http://ltsc.ieee.org/wg12/s_p.html*

Oliver, R. (1999). Exploring strategies for on-line teaching and learning. *Distance Education, 20*(2), 240-254.

Oliver, R., Harper, B., Hedberg, J., Wills, S., & Agostinho, S. (2002). Exploring strategies to formalise the description of learning designs. In A. Goody, J. Herrington, & M. Northcote (Eds.), *Quality conversations: Research and development in higher education* (Vol. 25, pp. 184-190). Jamison, ACT: HERDSA.

Rehak, D., & Mason, R. (2003). Keeping the learning in learning objects. In A. Littlejohn (Ed.), *Reusing online resources: A sustainable approach to e-learning* (pp. 20-34). London: Kogan Page.

SCORM (2001). *Sharable Content Object Reference Model, Version 1.2. Advanced Distributed Learning Initiative*. Retrieved May 25, 2003, from *http://www.adlnet.org*

Shepherd, C. (2000). *Objects of interest*. Retrieved June 2002, from *http://www.fastrak.-consulting.co.uk/tactix/features/objects.htm*

W3C SOAP (2000, May 8). *World Wide Web Consortium Simple Object Access Protocol 1.1. W3C Note, May 8 2000*. Retrieved May 2003, from *http://www.w3.org/TR/SOAP*

W3C Xquery. (2003). *World Wide Web Consortium Xquery1.0: An XML Query language. W3C Working Draft May 2 2003*. Retrieved May 2003, from *http://www.w3.org/TR/exquery*

Wiley, D. (2000). Connecting learning objects to instructional design theory: A definition, a metaphor, and a taxonomy. In D. A. Wiley (Ed.), *The instructional use of learning objects: Online version*. Retrieved May 2003, from *http://reusability.org/read/chapters/wiley.doc*

Wiley, D. (2003). *Learning objects: Difficulties and opportunities*. Retrieved November 2004, from *http://wiley.ed.usu.edu/docs/lo_do.pdf*

ZOOM. (2003). *The Z39.50 Object Oriented Model*. Retrieved May 2003, from *http://zoom.z3950.org*

Chapter XIX

Authentic Learning at Work

Lynne Hunt, Charles Darwin University, Australia

Abstract

This chapter describes models of work-based learning and outlines key features of the authentic learning pedagogy that informs its application. It contextualises work-based learning in the political and economic imperatives driving curriculum change in universities in the Western world. In so doing, it refers to curriculum development based on generic skills and notes analyses of the role of universities in contemporary society, with particular reference to the relative importance of practical and theoretical training. Innovative case studies provide practical examples of the implementation of authentic learning pedagogies through work-based university programs. The key to successful implementation is assessment, which links theory and practice. The underlying message of the chapter is that what counts are not the teaching and learning tools you have, but the way that you use them. There can be nothing more real than real, and this is the strength of work-based university learning: it offers authentic or situated learning environments that reflect the way knowledge will be used in real life.

Introduction

Work-based learning has long been a feature of professional education in Western countries. From the beginning, the professions passed on knowledge, skills and values to apprentices. Later, some areas of learning were taken on by universities, whose teachers, as often as not, were leading professionals. Links between work and university education have persisted in professions such as law, medicine and dentistry, which require on-the-job learning prior to registration. The continuing use of work-based learning by universities may be explained by its value as a learning tool. However, like any other teaching and learning tool, work-based learning is not in itself valuable. The full potential of work-based learning is only realised by the pedagogy that informs its application. In other words, it's not the resource you've got but the way that you use it that counts. This chapter describes models of implementing work-based learning and outlines key features of the authentic learning pedagogy that informs its application.

There has been an ebb and flow in the relationship between theoretical learning at universities and more practical learning at work. The outcome of this evolving relationship is that education for the professions is now inextricably linked with tertiary qualifications. Teaching and nursing provide interesting examples of the transition from training, which was at one time entirely work-based, to a model of professional education that combines theoretical, university-based elements with practical application in the workplace. Ironically, though, having distanced professional education from an apprenticeship model, universities are now adapting curricula to better suit the needs of the work force. Two key strategies have been employed to do this. One is an emphasis on generic or globally transferable skills such as written and oral communication, critical thinking, information technology skills, business acumen and teamwork. The second is the introduction of work-based learning. The two are intertwined because it is through work-based learning that students are able to demonstrate mastery of generic as well as subject-specific skills — professional knowledge. Both generic skills and work-based learning are explored in this chapter within the framework of authentic learning pedagogy.

The Significance of Work-Based Learning

In an environment in which universities compete for undergraduate students, and where university study is increasingly expensive, it is likely that the career success of graduates will become a defining feature of universities as they compete for students, fees, and private and government grants (Dearing, 1997). In this context the expansion of work-based learning may be inevitable. Indeed, the political will to produce work-ready graduates is already strong:

The changing nature of work is requiring individuals to increase their level of skills and become multi-skilled. To meet these demands, many students are looking for an education that provides a combination of elements of traditional higher education and vocational education (Commonwealth of Australia, 2002).

Employers are also declaring their hand:

In a survey of 24 major UK and international companies ... one of the main reasons for employer satisfaction with a new graduate intake was in relation to work experience. In some companies work experience is used as a specific criterion for selection. (Spiller, 2000, p. 2)

University administrators also like work-based learning because it enhances the relevance of university courses and improves retention rates. Further, it facilitates the employment of graduates. In Britain, the evidence indicates that students participating in block practicum programs of up to one year that are "sandwiched" between theoretical, university-based studies have a better chance of being employed in their field of study: "Sandwich students are more likely than full-time students to find permanent employment on graduation: 52.7% Sandwich, 41.3% full-time. Moreover, sandwich students are more successful than their full-time counterparts in finding real 'graduate' jobs (a difference of some 7%)" (Margham, 1997, p. 3). It should be noted that working in the area of their degree usually results in higher salaries for graduates. In brief, the development of work-based learning at university level represents an increasing commitment to the employability of graduates that is welcomed by employers and students alike.

Work-Based Learning

Work-based learning is a two-way street between universities and the workplace. At the undergraduate level it provides opportunities for undergraduates to gain theoretically-related, work-based experience. At the postgraduate level, it refers to the full or partial replacement of coursework or thesis preparation by research-based programs conducted within the workplace under the supervision of university-based supervisors. Examples of undergraduate work-based learning include practice in schools for trainee teachers, clinical practice for nurses and doctors, and project work for engineering students. A key, identifying feature of work-based learning is that it is an accredited, assessed and an integral component of degree programs. For this reason, it is sometimes referred to as work-integrated learning. The university, the student and the workplace typically design individual, work-based learning programs collaboratively: "It will, in general, have outcomes relevant to the nature and purpose of the workplace ... the learning achieved will include appropriate underpinning knowledge and will be tailored to meet the needs of the student and the placement" (Margham, 1997, p. 2). Work-based learning, therefore, is individualised to students' learning needs, which may be discipline-specific and include globally transferable skills. Its emphasis on meeting students' and employers' needs, and the importance of theoretical knowledge and reflective practice, distinguish it from work experience, which is not necessarily integrated into a theoretical and research-based university program.

Generic Skills

Work-based learning facilitates interaction and socialisation with professionals as critical elements in the learning process. It enhances opportunities for professional networking that may facilitate students' employment prospects: "Students are expected to play [an] ... active part in learning and the focus [is on]... making connections with various professional practices" (Roelofs & Terwel, 1999, p. 202). Most importantly, it focuses on generic skills:

These include the use of appropriate technologies for processing information (Beavan, 1996; Caudron, 1997; Leveson, 1996); verbal, aural and written communication skills (Heskin, 1994; Jones, 1995; Ward, 1996); team skills (Heskin, 1994); proficiency in solving workplace problems (Heskin, 1994); time management (Mullen, 1997); flexibility (Leveson, 1996); and ability to work under pressure (Caudron, 1997) (Taplin, 2000, p. 279).

The inclusion of generic skills, sometimes known as graduate attributes or transferable skills, in university curricula is clearly part of the "transformation of [universities] so that they operate according to market logic" (The New London Group, 1995, p. 8). As such, they become part of the "bigger, as yet unresolved, debate about the purpose of university education," (James, Lefoe & Hadi 2004,

p. 174) and the extent to which a university education is predicated on theoretical, rather than practical or vocational knowledge. However, James, Lefoe & Hadi (2004, p. 176) argue that basing curricula in generic skills "opens up a particularly interesting pedagogical space ...This is a teaching space which encourages, even demands, that our teaching practice be more than content transmission." This accords with notions of authentic learning which "better engage learners and support the effective construction of their knowledge, as well as their application of the knowledge" (Bahr & Rohner, 2004, p. 16).

Models of Work-Based Learning

Work-based learning has been implemented in a variety of ways in Australian and British universities (Hunt, 2000a). These include: recognition of prior work experience; independent work-based modules; stand-alone work experience awards; sandwich degree programs; work-based learning degree programs; corporate degrees; and graduate work-based learning.

Recognition of Prior Work Experience

One way in which universities are developing links with the workplace is to recognise prior, work-based training and experience as part of undergraduate and postgraduate degree programs. This is theorised through personal portfolios that demonstrate the higher levels of critical-thinking required in university study: "Accreditation of Prior Learning is based on the student establishing the authenticity, recency, relevance and sufficiency of the learning presented in the portfolio" (Lyons, 2002, p. 2). The kind of evidence on which students are required to reflect includes publications and conference presentations, in-service participation and personal journals. Recognition of prior learning is normally subject to a fee for portfolio assessment. The cost normally increases with the number of credit points assessed.

Independent Work-Based Modules

Independent practicum modules are usually an accredited part of university curricula. They are self-designed in negotiation with an appropriate staff member, and often supported by a workbook that structures the experience. An advantage of this approach is that students can fast-track their studies by completing a module during vacation time. It also paves the way to internationalising work-based learning because international students can complete the module, or unit of study, in their home country.

Stand-Alone, Work Experience Awards

It is sometimes difficult to integrate work placements into existing degree programs. This may be because the degree is content-heavy, affording little time for practicum work, or because staff remain unconvinced about the role of work-based learning in universities. Whatever the reason, some universities have chosen to move around the problem by establishing stand-alone work experience awards. Such programs usually focus on the development of generic, rather than subject-specific skills, developed through students' part-time and casual employment. In itself, casual employment is not enough. It is the identification of skills and analysis of work contexts that give rise to learning that can be theoretically linked. As one employer noted:

A common example is working in a pub [hotel]. We would be looking for people who could actually indicate they had learned something from that. In a pub you are dealing with people, cash and potentially difficult customers; you may be responsible for some other members of staff; you are working as part of a team. There is a lot of learning in there. It is what people are gleaning out of it, learning from it and are able to communicate to a selection panel. (Spiller, 2000, p. 2)

Stand-alone programs may be supported by a learning package, which Spiller (2000) described as encouraging reflective-thinking and skills in the development of a work experience portfolio.

Sandwich Degree Programs

"Sandwich" degree programs are so called when six months or one year in the workplace is sandwiched between university studies, normally after the second year. Thick placements refer to one continuous block of work experience in a setting relevant to the student's degree. Thin placements are described as a series of short, work experience placements to develop professional competence. Findings, published in *The impact of sandwich education* (Bowes &

Harvey, 2000), indicate that sandwich students have an early career advantage but that this is partly dependent on subject area. The career advantages are less for science and language graduates than for environment, business, engineering and social science sandwich graduates. The work placement is supervised and assessed. However, some universities make provision for work experience, without supervision or assessment, for a year after students' second year of study.

Work-Based Learning Degree Programs

Work-based learning studies, sometimes known as *Partnership Programs* (Portsmouth University, UK) or *Learning at Work* awards (Liverpool John Moores University, UK), are based largely on projects undertaken at work. Titles of such awards are generic in nature to enable the incorporation of a range of learning opportunities under one banner. Essentially, these are negotiated programs of university study that are individualised to students' needs. The students' programs of study may include work-based projects, in-service training, and modules of university study. These are, as Lyons (2002, p. 1) noted, "combined with the deeper learning that comes from reflection on professional practice." The negotiation process itself is normally structured as an assignment in which students outline prior learning, identify gaps in skills and knowledge, and suggest a program that responds to learning needs through a combination of work-based projects and university study. The outcome of the negotiation process is a learning contract that is used to monitor progress: "For quality assurance purposes the student must ... explain the coherence of the proposed study including the relationship between the parts and the connection between the new study and their accredited prior learning" (Lyons, 2002, p. 3). Quality in work-based learning degree programs is assured through formal procedures that normally include strict guidelines and a review panel comprising employer and university representatives.

Each student's program is unique and includes varying combinations of recognition and accreditation of prior learning, taught courses and work-based projects. As Lyons (2002, p. 1) observed: "The negotiated and individualized nature ... [of] the programs reflected the trends toward the diverse and multidisciplinary careers that are now the norm in industry and commerce." Students study at their own pace, often off-campus, and distance learning resource packages may be used to support learning needs. Given the sophisticated nature of such a process, Learning at Work or Partnership Programs more often feature at postgraduate level. Yet, with appropriate infrastructure, such as a dedicated university office for work-based learning to provide guidance and support, it is possible to also develop negotiated, undergraduate work-based learning programs. As an example of this, a police officer, working through Middlesex University in Britain, has combined taught courses with his experience of police work to develop a program for his degree in Work-based Learning Studies: Crime Management (Middlesex University, 2000).

Learning at Work degrees are normally taught on a full fee-paying basis. In general, fees for negotiated, work-based learning are higher than those for standard, university modules because individual tuition costs more. However, the potential for financial support of students by employers, who may benefit from the outcomes of such programs, offers significant advantages in countries where the introduction of fees for undergraduate education risks deterring students from tertiary study.

Corporate Degrees

Corporate degrees are an extension of "Partnership Programs" or "Learning at Work" awards. For these degrees, Portsmouth University, in Britain, has brokered a range of learning opportunities into a degree structure. As well as the customary combination of work projects with university study, corporate degrees accredit, as a formal part of the degree structure, learning provided in the public and private sectors. They bring to fruition the "potential of collaboration with other education and training providers and corporate universities in developing corporate degrees" (Lyons, 2002, p. 4). Corporate degrees also provide a structure for working collaboratively with international corporations and educational providers. One way to conceptualise aspects of the corporate degree structure is to envisage for universities a role in harnessing corporate in-service programs, either through providing them or through accreditation.

Graduate Work-Based Learning

Programs to bridge the gap between graduation and employment, sometimes known as graduate apprenticeships, provide opportunities for new graduates to develop skills in the workplace. This can serve as a stand-alone, work-based learning program and also provide employers with an opportunity for what is sometimes called an "extended interview," whereby they can assess the suitability of a graduate for employment.

Organisational Strategies for Implementing Work-Based Learning

Despite its demonstrable advantages, there are potential difficulties in the implementation of work-based learning. Firstly, it is sometimes suspected of detracting from the status of university qualifications by reducing the theoretical, research-based content of degree programs: "Many criticisms ... have been based on how closely the learning environment resembles, not a cognitive apprenticeship, but a traditional apprenticeship" (Herrington & Oliver, 2000, p. 24). Secondly, there remain legitimate concerns about the conservative implications of training students to work with "what is" rather than "what might be." The worry is that the visionary nature of a university education may be lost in the detail of appropriate work practice. Thirdly, there are practical difficulties. For example, universities located in small population centres may have limited opportunities for work placements, and available placements risk being over-used as more tertiary institutions develop work-based learning. In addition, risk management can become an issue because insurance is a vital concern. Finally, the cost of supervising work placements can be high and must be balanced against the cost of equivalent learning on-campus. However, the battle is largely won. Work-based learning is now accepted as part of the future of universities. The issue is not whether or not to introduce it. Rather, the question is, how?

Hunt (2002) described a community development approach to the introduction of work-based learning at Edith Cowan University (ECU), known as the Work-links project. The aim was to introduce work-based learning in an empowering and participative manner rather than imposing new curriculum ideas. The community development approach to curriculum change may be characterised as both "top-down" and "bottom-up." Policy and resources are provided from the top to foster initiative. Ideas and innovation bubble-up from "the bottom" — teachers at the coalface — in a manner that creates ownership of curriculum change at faculty and departmental level. The rationale for this approach was drawn from the experience of community projects in developing countries (Oakley, 1997), which indicate that participative and capacity building processes:

- Result in more efficient use of funding;
- Establish greater relevance;
- Build capacity to manage at the local level;
- Increase the population coverage of initiatives;
- Lead to better targeting of benefits; and
- Facilitate sustainability.

Similar principles and practice are espoused around the world. For example, the same strategies were recommended in the Ottawa Charter (1996) for the promotion of public health. These included:

- The creation of supportive environments;
- Policy development;
- Community action;
- The reorientation of organisations; and
- The development of personal skills.

The originality of the ECU Work-links project (Hunt, 2002) is that these community development strategies were adapted to work-based learning curriculum change in a university. Specific strategies used included: the development of a university-wide discussion paper on work-based learning (Hunt, 2000b); linking work-based learning to policy through the University's Strategic Plan; working with existing organisational structures to build corporate knowledge about work-based learning; staff development; the selection of key staff to model the implementation of work-based learning; the development of an employer data base; an employer launch; and the creation of a Web site to provide an ongoing resource for staff, students and employers.

In brief, the successful implementation of work-based university learning requires strong strategic direction from university management. Supported by a university strategic plan, the infrastructure to implement and sustain work-based learning can be decentralised and specific to faculty needs or centralised in a work-based learning unit. A centralised organisation provides space and time to create the vision and practice of work-based learning: "the team of staff who introduce such changes should be totally dedicated to the task" (Report on Work-based Learning Degree Programme, 1996, p. 20). The choice between a central or devolved implementation strategy reflects the universal planning dilemma associated with mainstreaming or the provision of separate services. A designated, central organisation risks marginalising work-based learning away from core teaching and learning activities in the faculties. A diffuse, decentralised structure may cause the work-based learning initiative to be lost if no one is responsible for its development. One thing is certain: successful introduction and expansion of work-based learning will not occur without appropriate organisational change in universities. This is Lyons' (2002) clear conclusion from his experiences in developing such programs at Portsmouth University: "Not only the conventional curricula but also the working procedures of the university need to change ... we have learned that collaborative partnership must involve sharing responsibility for tasks, cultural understanding and respect for separate identities" (p. 6). According to Lyons, the basis of successful collaboration lies in Wells and Barley's (2000) *High C's of Partnership*: communication; credibility; champions; commitment, and a community of learning.

The Authentic Learning Pedagogy of Work-Based Learning

To reiterate: it's not the teaching and learning tools you've got but the way that you use them that counts. Duignan (2002) endorsed this point when he noted that: A "*laissez-faire* approach will not exploit the academic potential of [work] placement" (p. 220). In itself, work-based learning will be ineffective if not embedded in an appropriate pedagogy. As Reeves (1995) observed: "Deeper, richer levels of learning and human development may be better attained via fundamental changes in our pedagogical philosophy." This means that the potential of work-based learning lies not only in the opportunities it creates for students but also in its capacity to reinvent university curricula: "Instead of being presented as a 'closed' system, subject-matter originates before the students' eyes in a process of re-invention" (Roelofs & Terwel, 1999, p. 202).

By its nature, work-based learning fits authentic learning pedagogy because it constitutes "bridging apprenticeships" (Resnick, 1987) that link the theoretical knowledge of universities with "the real-life application of the knowledge in the work environment" (Herrington & Oliver, 2000, p. 24). Authentic learning is not new: "Contemporary 'authentic pedagogy' is ... a modern form of much older ideas about 'educational reform'. Those ideas involve pedagogy in which everyday experiences, and students' interest in those experiences play a central role" (Roelofs & Terwel, 1999, p. 202). Authentic learning has a long history under different names such as experiential learning, the benefits of which were described by Stanley and Plaza (2002) as: "enhanced attitudes towards learning in general, heightened inquisitiveness, and more active participation in class discussions ... In addition, knowledge gained through experiential education seems to be 'more permanent, functional and transferable'" (Crew, 1987, p. 2).

Authentic learning is an eclectic pedagogy that incorporates elements of action learning described by Sandelands (1998) as a form of learning by doing. According to Koo (1999), it has relevance to work-based learning because, "The action learning approach suggests that people learn best about work, at work and through work, within a structure which encourages learning" (p. 89). It focuses on real-life problems and, as Keys (1994) indicated, its aim is to encourage students to ask questions rather than learn answers. Talisayon (2001) endorsed the importance of the authentic setting of the workplace to action learning noting that, "Real tasks are used as the vehicle for learning. The learning is immediately relevant and useful to the work setting. Both tacit and explicit knowledge transfers can take place more effectively" (p. 1). Tacit knowledge is assumed knowledge — if you like, the hidden curriculum of the workplace. According to Herrington and Oliver (2000) much of this is learned from the expert performances of role models: "Interestingly, some of the students commented on the incidental peripheral learning that is possible from an apprenticeship-like learning situation and revealed the 'window on practice' (Brown & Duguid, 1993), or the social or cultural insights into ... [the workplace]" (p. 36).

In encouraging students to test ideas and to reflect on outcomes, action learning is similar to problem-based learning (PBL) which is "conventionally defined as students learning new knowledge by working on the solution of a defined problem" (Taplin, 2000, p. 279). Purists argue that, "One of the commonly-accepted characteristics of PBL is that the problem is encountered first in the learning process, before any preparation or formal study has occurred" (Taplin, 2000, p. 283). However, it is commonly assumed that problem-based learning provides an opportunity to apply previously acquired theoretical knowledge and skills. This also accords with the teaching and learning processes in authentic, work-based learning.

Whilst differences in nomenclature may indicate important distinctions in aspects of pedagogy, the similarities between action and problem-based learning as they apply to work placements may be more important than the distinctions. These similarities are captured in Herrington and Oliver's (2000) definition of authentic learning, which incorporates core features of action and problem-based learning. According to them, the essence of authentic learning may be found in the features of learning that unite knowing and doing, leaning heavily on "constructivist learning principles which encourage learners to construct their own meaning for knowledge and information in the learning process" (Oliver, Herrington & Omari, 1998, p. 2). It resonates with "the kind of learning and thinking through which knowledge is transformed into personal understanding that shapes the way we see the world" (Dombey, 1999, p. 2).

Work-based learning falls within the framework of what has been described as flexible learning. It is flexible in time, in that students can complete work-based commitments in their own timeframe: vacation time, on weekends, or after hours, where possible, and during normal semester time. Work-based learning is flexible in space. Students are not tied to campus locations and can work anywhere. This is particularly useful for rural and remote students and for international students because they can return home to work in local organisations. Further, work-based learning can include online features such as the use of bulletin boards for communication with university supervisors and other students. Flexibilities such as these have equity implications because, as Elson-Green (1999) reported:

A university education continues to be an elusive dream for some of the most disadvantaged groups in Australian society despite years of equity programs aimed at giving everyone a 'fair chance'. The Equity in Higher Education study ... reveals the university system is failing indigenous students and people from rural, isolated ... backgrounds.

Indeed, the problem-based (PBL) nature of work-based assessment may be almost better suited to distance education students, as Schiller and Ostwald (1994) have suggested:

One of the ideal ways to deal with PBL is to give the students a problem and to let them work through it with their friends in their own time and at their own pace. Internally, we have difficulties with this because we have to have timetables ... Externally, the students work much closer to what would happen when they work in industry, when they enter the professions ... . (p. 220)

Learning in the workplace provides authentic contexts and activities as well as opportunities to learn from best practice. According to Herrington and Oliver (2000), these are core elements of their nine dimensions of authentic learning, which also include opportunities to experience multiple roles and perspectives, and to work collaboratively and reflectively in the construction of knowledge. The application of theoretical knowledge to real, work-place problems creates opportunities for students to recreate and scaffold knowledge flexibly, in accordance with the task at hand. This also provides for the authentic assessment of learning within tasks. Embedded in authentic learning pedagogy, work-based learning recognises the importance of interaction and socialisation among learners. It requires that teachers and students work on problems in partnership: "They become jointly responsible for a process in which all grow ... no one teaches another, nor is anyone self-taught" (Freire, 1970, p. 61). Work-based learning enhances this process by creating classrooms without borders, opportunities for networking, and the freedom for students to work in structured and unstructured ways using teachers as facilitators rather than instructors. In this way students participate in what Lave and Wenger (1991) called a community of practice, which, according to Herrington and Oliver (2000), "enables the learner to progressively piece together the culture of the group and what it means to be a member" (p. 24).

In providing a "window on practice" (Brown & Duguid, 1993), work-based learning creates a new role for teachers — one that Michael Wilding, in his satirical novel, *Academia Nuts* (2002), refers to as a window-cleaning role. Teachers, become facilitators (window cleaners) who shed light on theoretical insights arising from work-based learning. As Roelofs and Terwel (1999) noted, "authenticity is always a matter of degree ... but one of the most striking differences is the changing task of the teacher" (p. 205). Bowerman and Peters (1999) referred to this as a process of *de-expertising*:

People need to be encouraged to take responsibility for their own learning ... we call this 'expertising' as opposed to what we do as facilitators which is 'de-expertise ourselves' ... [there are] dangers posed by 'experts' in seeming to hold all the answers and taking away the ability for people to think for themselves ... Learning shouldn't be done 'to' people, it should be done with them and by them. (p. 5)

This can be liberating, as Stanley and Plaza (2002) observed: "We found that the active learning model was liberating for us as well as for our students. We did not have to regard or present ourselves as the experts; we did not always have to be in control" (p. 7). However, de-expertising can become an excuse for doing too little. As Roelofs and Terwel (1999) put it: "We do not accept the ideas behind radical constructivism — that knowledge can only be constructed by the students, that learning can only happen in complex situations, and that transmission by the teacher is impossible" (p. 221). They seek a middle road in which teachers are "cognitive guides." In any case, in work-based learning the facilitator's role also has an advocacy dimension because, without careful advocacy and university support, students can have less than satisfactory learning experiences.

Work-Based Learning and Authentic Assessment

A key role of university teachers, as facilitators, is to scaffold learning through assessment: "The task that students were required to complete and the assessment of that task were integrated seamlessly into their working practice and provided multiple indicators of whether the students were successful in completing the task" (Herrington & Oliver, 2000, p. 41). Assessment is an important means through which the practical experiences of the workplace can be theorised and integrated into university curricula. A concrete example of how this can be done may be seen in a pilot, tutorial agency which invited teacher education students, specialising in mathematics, to participate in tutor training (Hunt, Kershaw & Bana, 2003). The tutorial agency subsequently brokered paid employment for the students as tutors to primary and high school pupils. This experience was integrated into the university curriculum through mathematics education assignments, in which students reflected on matters such as how to diagnose mathematics learning difficulties, effective intervention strategies and evaluation of outcomes. It was the assignment task that encouraged critical thinking by creating an opportunity to theorise the process. Without this link, the tutoring experience would have been work experience, rather than theoretical, work-integrated university learning.

How should work-based learning be assessed? Assessment of work-based experiences encourages reflective and critical thinking about real problems in real settings. Assessment is normally based on portfolios and journals, and includes a high degree of self-direction. Portfolio assessment (Cooper, 1997; Cooper, 1999; Cooper & Emden, 2001) directs attention to learning outcomes, rather than teaching input. It forms part of what Collins, Brown, and Holum (1991) referred to as a "cognitive apprenticeship, which is a useful instructional paradigm when a teacher needs to teach a fairly complex task to students" (p. 45). Deep learning is the key. As Van Oers and Wardekker (1999), explained, truly authentic learning must "encourage a participant to become an autonomous and critical agent, not just a competent robot" (p. 232). Indeed, Newmann and Wehlage (1993) "use the word 'authentic' to distinguish significant and meaningful learning from that which is trivial and useless" (Gross & Kientz, 1999, p. 22). They established five criteria by which to evaluate the extent of depth and authenticity in assignments. These included: "(1) higher order thinking; (2) depth of knowledge; (3) connectedness to the world beyond the classroom; (4) substantive conversation; and (5) social support for student learning" (Gross & Kientz, 1999, p. 22).

Projects at work respond to employers' needs as well as those of students and universities. As a consequence, work-based tasks do not necessarily fit the neat, discipline-based structure of university awards. This requires some reorientation of thinking about the nature of assignments and the role of university departments in devising them. Authentic learning tasks at work require acceptance by universities of different kinds of processes and evidence. These might include, "industrial business style enquiry (reflection, risk analysis, prototyping, market analysis, use of the Web, etc.) as valid research" (Lyons, 2002, p. 4). Work-based learning assignments vary from traditional, university essays and reports and might include written submissions developed for the workplace, reflective diaries and logbooks. Further, "Skills and competencies can be demonstrated in practice and through the production of artefacts, or the submission of testimonials by senior professionals" (Lyons, 2002, p. 3). This requires much of students as Lyons (2002) observed because, "the additional literature and best practice research required to contextualise the project, beyond that required commercially, should not be under-estimated" (p. 3).

Generic skills are a significant feature of authentic, work-based assessment. The Dearing review (Dearing, 1997) emphasised the need for students to develop skills and capabilities suited to the workplace. In some cases, the assessment of generic skills has been structured as a separate key skills qualification. Whatever the underpinning structure, such assessment often takes the form of a portfolio of achievement. Alternatively, such skills can be integrated into a regular program of assignments and tracked through a student's degree program so that they graduate not only with a degree transcript but also a record of their acquisition of generic skills. In the context of credit point transfer, it has become increasingly necessary for universities to develop level descriptors so that students can demonstrate to prospective employers the level at which each skill has been achieved.

The action learning cycle is inherent in the reflective practice of work-based learning assignments. As McGill and Beaty (1995, p. 236) noted, action learning is a "powerful method to those who wish to bring together the world of theory and the world of practice." In this context, assessment does more than satisfy the immediate requirements of university assignments. As Koo (1999) points out: "It is likely that action learners will develop an inclination to become lifetime learners. The utopia for action learning is ... [to develop] a learning society" (p. 7). Clearly there are high expectations of authentic, action learning pedagogy, and, within that, work-based learning.

Conclusion

Work-based learning has become an imperative in the context of quality assurance because universities are increasingly being assessed on skills development and graduate employability. However, the main argument for the promotion of work-based learning is that the authentic learning pedagogy in which it is embedded produces a vibrant, diversified teaching and learning context in universities. There can be nothing more real than real, and this is the strength of work-based university learning — it offers authentic or situated learning environments that reflect the way knowledge will be used in real life. Work-based learning encourages students to reflect on their learning needs and to link these to current studies and future employment. It engages students with professional associations and enhances opportunities for networking that may facilitate employment prospects. Most importantly, it focuses on generic skills. Authentic and situated learning are particularly appropriate pedagogies for the implementation of work-based learning because "the situation largely determines the structure, content and coherence of the concepts used" (Roelofs & Terwel, 1999, p. 203). Finally, work-based learning may be described in the terms that Stanley and Plaza (2002, p. 8) applied to action learning: "what students learned was not so much a product as a process — a creative, cognitive process of offering ideas, critiquing and expanding upon them." In this sense, work-based university learning complements, rather than undermines, traditional, discipline-specific, university education because it equips students with work-relevant, key skills as well as subject-specific, theoretical outcomes that facilitate long-term innovation and flexibility.

References

Allen, M. (1991). *Improving the personal skills of graduates: Final report.* Sheffield: Personal Skills Unit, Sheffield University.

Bahr, N., & Rohner, C. (2004). The judicious utilization of new technologies through authentic learning in higher education: A case study. *Transforming Knowledge into Wisdom: Holistic Approaches to Teaching and learning. Research and Development in Higher Education, Vol. 27.* Milperra, NSW: Higher Education Research and Development Society of Australasia.

Bowerman, J., & Peters, J. (1999). Design and evaluation of an action learning program – A bilateral view. *Journal of Workplace Learning, 11*(4), 131-139.

Bowes, L., & Harvey, L. (2000). *The impact of sandwich education.* Birmingham: The University of Central England.

Brown, J.S., & Duguid, P. (1993). Stolen knowledge. *Educational Technology, 33*(3), 10-15.

Caudron, S. (1997). Hire for attitude: It's who they are that counts. *Workforce, 1,* 20-5.

Collins, A., Brown, J. S., & Holum, A. (1991). Cognitive apprenticeship: Making thinking visible. *American Educator, 15*(3), 6-11, 38-46.

Commonwealth of Australia. (2002). *Varieties of learning. The interface between higher education and training.* Canberra: Commonwealth Department of Education Science and Training.

Cooper, T. (1997). *Portfolio assessment: A guide for students*. Quinns Rocks, Western Australia: Praxis Education.

Cooper, T. (1999). *Portfolio assessment: A guide for lecturers, teachers and course designers.* Quinns Rocks, Western Australia: Praxis Education.

Cooper, T., & Emden, C. (2001). *Portfolio assessment for nurses and midwives.* Quinns Rocks, Western Australia: Praxis Education.

Crew, A. (1987). A rationale for experiential education. *Contemporary Education, 58,* 145-47.

Dearing Review. (1997). *The National Committee of Inquiry into Higher Education: Higher education for the 21st century.* London: HMSO.

Dombey, H. (1999). Use of language across the primary curriculum / information technology and authentic learning: Realising the potential of computers in the primary classroom. *Cambridge Journal of Education, 29*(1), 145-147.

Duignan, J. (2002). Undergraduate work placement and academic performance: Failing by doing. *Quality Conversations. Research and Development in Higher Education, Volume 25.* Canberra: Higher Education Research and Development Society of Australasia.

Elson-Green, J. (1999, March 31-April 6). Equity in higher education confirms inequities. *Campus Review,* p. 5.

Friere, P. (1970). *Pedagogy of the oppressed.* New York: Continuum.

Gross, J., & Kientz, S. (1999). Collaborating for authentic learning. *Teacher Librarian, 27*(1), 21-25.

Herrington, J., & Oliver, R. (2000). An instructional design framework for authentic learning environments. *Educational Technology Research and Development, 48*(3), 23-48.

Heskin, K. (1994). Generic skills requirement for stakeholders: An Australian case study. Paper presented to the *34th Annual Forum of the Association for Institutional Research,* New Orleans, LA, USA.

Higher Education Funding Council for England (HEFCE). (1997). *Undergraduate non-completion in higher education in England, No. 97/29.* Retrieved August 2003, from *http://www.niss.ac.uk/education/hefce/pub97*

Hunt, L. (2000a). *Work based learning in British universities: International study program report.* Retrieved August 2003, from *http://www.ecu.edu.au/ssa/worklinks/resources/international.html*

Hunt, L. (2000b). *Discussion paper: Towards a policy and framework for work-based university learning.* Perth, Australia: Edith Cowan University.

Hunt, L. (2002). Getting started with work-based university learning: Crossing the border between university and work. In J. Cross (Ed.), *Proceedings of the EDUCOM 2002 Conference*. Perth, Australia: Edith Cowan University.

Hunt, L., Kershaw, L., & Bana, J. (2003). The tutoring services provider: Authentic learning for an unknown future at work. *Learning for an Unknown Future. Research and Development in Higher Education, Volume 26.* Milperra, NSW: Higher Education Research and Development Society of Australasia.

James, B., Lefoe, G., & Hadi, M. (2004). Working 'through' graduate attributes: A bottom-up approach. *Transforming Knowledge into Wisdom: Holistic Approaches to Teaching and learning. Research and Development in Higher Education, Volume 27.* Milperra, NSW: Higher Education Research and Development Society of Australasia.

Jewels Bulletin. (2000, March). Issue 3. Plymouth: Plymouth University.

Jones, E. (1995). *National assessment of college student learning: Identifying college graduates' essential skills in writing, speech and listening, and critical thinking.* Final project report. University Park, PA: National Centre on Postsecondary Teaching, Learning, and Assessment.

Keys, L. (1994). Action learning: Executive development of choice for the 1990s. *Journal of Management Development, 13*(8), 50-6.

Koo, L.C. (1999). Learning action learning. *Journal of Workplace Learning, 11*(3), 89-94.

Lave, J., & Wenger, E. (1991). *Situated learning: Legitimate peripheral participation.* Cambridge: Cambridge University.

Leveson, R. (1996). Can professionals be multi-skilled? *People Management, 2*(17), 36-39.

Lyons, F. (2002). Establishing industry-university learning partnerships. Paper presented to the *EDUCOM 2002 Conference*, Khon Kaen, Thailand.

Margham, J. (1997). *A green paper on work-based learning.* Liverpool: John Moores University.

McGill, I., & Beaty, L. (1995). *Action learning: A guide for professional, management and educational development.* London: Kogan Page.

Middlesex University. (2000). *Course advertising brochure for work-based learning.* Middlesex: Author.

Mullen, J. (1997). Graduates deficient in 'soft' skills. *People Management, 3*(22), 18.

The New London Group. (1995). *A pedagogy of multiliteracies: Designing social futures.* Occasional paper 1. The NLLIA Centre for Workplace, Communication and Culture, James Cook University of Northern Queensland and the University of Technology, Sydney.

Newmann, F.M., & Wehlage, G.G. (1993). Five standards of authentic instruction. *Educational Leadership*, 8-12.

Nixon, J., & Williamson, V. (1989). *Short-term placements in first degree courses. Project Report 25.* London: CNAA.

Oakley et al. (1997). *UNDP guidebook on participation* (Draft).

Oliver, R., Omari, A., & Herrington, J. (1998). Developing converged learning environments for on and off-campus students using the WWW. In R. Corderoy (Ed.), *Conference Proceedings ASCILITE '98* (pp. 529-538). Wollongong, Australia: The University of Wollongong,

Ottawa Charter. (1996). Retrieved from *http://www.who.int/hpr/backgroundhp/ottawacharter.htm*

Reeves, T. (1995). *Reaction to 'interactivity': A forgotten art?* Retrieved August 2004, from *http://www.listserv.uga.edu/*

Report on Work Based Learning Degree Programme. (1996). Luton: The University of Luton.

Resnick, L. (1987). Learning in school and out. *Educational Researcher*, *16*(9), 13-20.

Roelofs, E., & Terwel, J. (1999). Constructivism and authentic pedagogy: State of the art and recent developments in the Dutch national curriculum in secondary education. *Journal of Curriculum Studies*, *31*(2), 201-227.

Sandelands, E. (1998). Creating an online library to support a virtual learning community. *Internet Research: Electronic Networking Applications and Policy*, *8*(1), 75-80.

Schiller, J., & Ostwald, M. (1994). Staff perceptions of implementing a problem-based approach in an external degree course. In M. Ostwald, & A. Kinglsland, (Eds.), *Research and development in problem based learning* (pp. 219-31). Newcastle, Australia: University of Newcastle.

Spiller, L. (2000). *Learning from experience: Work experience award.* Plymouth: Universities of Exeter and Plymouth.

Stanley, K., & Plaza, D. (2002). No passport required: An action learning approach teaching about globalisation. *Teaching Sociology*, *30*(1), 89-99.

Talisayon, S. D. (2001, August 21). Knowledge and people: Working is learning and learning is working. *Business World.*

Taplin, M. (2000). Problem-based learning in distance education: Practitioners' beliefs about an action learning project. *Distance Education, 21*(2), 278-299.

Van Oers, B., & Wardekker, W. (1999). On becoming an authentic learner: Semiotic activity in the early grades. *Journal of Curriculum Studies, 31*(2), 229-249.

Wells, J., & Barley, K. (2000). Sharing control: The high C's of partnership. *The New Corporate Review, 8*(2).

Wilding, M. (2002). *Academia nuts*. Glebe, NSW: Wild and Woolley.

Chapter XX

Professional Development for the Online Teacher:
An Authentic Approach

Jan Herrington, University of Wollongong, Australia

Ron Oliver, Edith Cowan University, Australia

Abstract

While telecommunications and telematics have been available in schools and universities for decades, the speed of adoption of the Internet into general use has been unprecedented. This has placed a great deal of pressure on university teachers to re-evaluate their roles in the light of new teaching and learning opportunities. The Internet has opened up possibilities beyond the simple acquisition of information, and has created teaching and learning challenges that many teachers feel ill-equipped to meet. This chapter examines the impact of the Internet on the teacher's role and explores the types of skills and strategies that teachers will need to be effective and efficient in online learning environments. The professional development needs for the new role of online teacher will be discussed within the context of a Graduate Certificate in Online Teaching and Learning designed to encapsulate authentic approaches to learning.

Introduction

The widespread adoption of the Internet in education has created new challenges for all stakeholders in the teaching and learning process, but particular challenges exist for the university teacher. In this climate of Web proliferation, professional development becomes critical, where universities must make significant investments, not only in technology infrastructure, but also in staff development (Bates, 2000).

Professional development for university teachers needs to address a widespread inertia often caused by a top-down approach to the adoption of technologies in universities (McNaught & Kennedy, 2000). Those academics who feel comfortable working with technology in online environments are rare, and there is generally little transference of expertise to their colleagues (Bennett, Priest & Macpherson, 1999), a situation compounded by an increasing number of sessional and part-time teachers (Van Dusen, 1997). Other reasons for the resistance to technology amongst university staff include: lack of experience or confidence in using technology, caution about methodologies teachers regard as unproven, and a belief that computer-based options threaten the human interaction teachers value in face-to-face teaching (Cremer, 2001; Sparrow, Herrington & Herrington, 2000). In particular, the speed of adoption of the Internet in higher education has caught many teachers unaware and unprepared to face the challenges required to succeed.

The Internet and the Changing Role of the University Teacher

The use of the Internet has risen three times more quickly than any comparable development (Economist, 1999) such as radio, the personal computer and television. All these technologies have affected our daily lives and access to information, news, and entertainment. But not all technologies have successfully made the transition from general use to educational use. In 1992, Strommen and Lincoln (1992) claimed that: "The technological changes that have swept through society at large have left the educational system largely unchanged" (paragraph 3), and prior to the widespread adoption of the Internet, this comment was an accurate reflection of the general lack of use of technologies in schools and universities at that time. For example, Cuban (2001) has pointed out that many technologies adopted with enthusiasm for classroom use have not survived there, such as radio in the 1920s, film projectors in the 1930s, and instructional television in the 1950s.

However, while those technologies have impacted only minimally on education practice, the Internet is positioned to dramatically affect the way we teach and learn. The process has been predicted by Pittinsky (2002) to be "a fundamentally transformed way of delivering and supporting the instructional process in higher education" (p. 2). Already, it has provided educators with a powerful tool to create effective and immersive learning environments (Jonassen & Reeves, 1996), and to provide efficient and collaborative means of communication for students with their teachers, and with each other (Jonassen, 1995). Despite controversial claims that the Internet could be "the ultimate isolating technology that further reduces our participation in communities" (Nie & Erbring, 2000, p. 19), it is well placed to provide opportunities for cooperation and communication that never existed with previous technologies.

While the promise of the Internet is exciting to educators, as with any new innovation, it requires a substantial rethinking of traditional approaches and roles. The rapid uptake of the technology has meant that school and university administrators are no longer content to allow the early adopters set the pace of change within their institutions. Online delivery has captured the imaginations of these administrators, who see the potential of computer-based and resource-based learning to provide low-cost teaching in times of cutbacks and reduced budgets and as a means to provide less teacher-dependent modes of learning. With much at stake in terms of strategic positioning in the marketplace, the online delivery of units and courses has now become central to universities' strategic planning. Arguably, the momentum to use the Internet has become a top-down, policy-driven push, rather than a bottom-up diffusion of good educational innovation and practice.

These trends have understandably left many university teachers uncertain and confused about their own role as teachers in an online learning environment. Many feel threatened by the move to change the traditional modes of delivery where, at present, they have a crucial and well-established role. They are threatened by the prospect of increased student numbers and workloads, while they themselves are coming to terms with the new role required of them as they teach online. What is the role of the university teacher in the age of online learning?

New Roles for the Teacher

Research derived from new learning theory is clearly showing that online delivery is no more a threat to teachers than teaching machines were in 1968, exemplified by Keller in his ironically titled article, "Goodbye teacher ..."

(Keller, 1968). Thirty years on, the role the teacher plays is still critically important to the success of student learning (Palloff & Pratt, 1999; Willis & Dickinson, 1997). However, if the traditional role of the university teacher is simply transferred to the online learning environment, an exciting opportunity will be missed.

A crucial aspect of effective online learning may hold the key to the changing role of the university teacher. Wade (1994) pointed out that the promotion of learner autonomy means increased responsibility for the student which, if it is to succeed, requires "a strong framework of *support and guidance* for the student from the outset" (p. 13). The process of redefining and developing the crucial role of the teacher in student learning is one where the teacher provides coaching and scaffolding support as a central and important pedagogical element, and as an alternative to didactic forms of teaching.

Teacher as Coach

A traditional approach to the design of learning environments proposes that the best way to deal with complexity is to simplify a topic by breaking it down into its component parts. However, Perkins (1991) suggested that the temptation to over-simplify learning environments should be resisted, and instead designers and teachers should search for new ways to provide appropriate scaffolding and support. In this situation, the teacher provides the skills, strategies and links that the students are unable to provide to complete the task. The foundation for the notion of scaffolding lay in Vygotsky's (1978) "zone of proximal development" described as, "the distance between the actual developmental level as determined by independent problem solving and the level of potential development as determined through problem solving under adult guidance, or in collaboration with more capable peers" (p. 86). Vygotsky's ideas prompted others to develop the notion of scaffolding (Wertsch, 1985), described by Greenfield (1984) as comprising five salient characteristics. According to Greenfield, scaffolding, in both the building and the educational sense:

1. Provides a support
2. Functions as a tool
3. Extends the range of the worker
4. Allows the worker to accomplish a task not otherwise possible
5. Is used selectively to aid the worker where needed (p. 118)

Many designers and administrators of online courses believe that such courses should be self-contained resources that include everything the student needs to be able to learn a particular topic. However, teachers who expect students to work individually online are not only denying them the benefits of collaboration, but also the benefits of expert assistance — providing hints, suggestions, critical questions, and the "scaffolding" to enable them to solve more complex problems. Collins, Brown and Newman (1989) point out that coaching is highly situation-specific and is related to problems that arise as students attempt to integrate skills and knowledge, a role that is still best performed by the teacher. Care must be taken to ensure that a perpetuation of traditional pedagogies in a new medium does not occur, or in the words of (Van Dusen, 1997) the teacher must avoid bringing "old metaphors and techniques from traditional classrooms into virtual space" (p. 63). Instead of providing and delivering information, the university teacher's principal function is to create collaborative, authentic and supportive learning environments within which the learner operates.

Competencies for Online Teaching

If a teacher is to be fully prepared to face the challenge of online teaching, what specific competencies are required? Gustafson and Gibbs (2000) suggested:

It clearly emerges that teaching in an online environment involves far more than simply transferring teaching skills from the classroom. The successful facilitator will need to learn strategies for developing online 'antennae', for humanizing the electronic environment, and new ways to guide students to discuss, critique and reflect together as they engage in the construction of meaning. (p. 196)

Clearly, these types of strategies are not generally to be found in the repertoire of the face-to-face classroom teacher, nor would they need to be. Shotsberger (1997) argued that online teachers need the skills to blend communication technologies to foster a sense of community. More practically, online teachers also need strategies to deal with student frustrations caused by technology failure, and other technology-related problems such as viruses, unstable software and incompatibility problems (Bennett et al., 1999).

A workshop on *Competencies for Online Teaching* in the UK, set out to list the variety of competencies and roles teachers must be able to fulfil in becoming successful online teachers (Goodyear, Salmon, Spector, Steeples & Tickner,

2001). The workshop examined online teaching from both the humanistic and cognitivist perspectives, and drew from these the identification and description of the main roles of the online teacher. Specifically, the eight roles identified were:

- *The Process Facilitator:* Concerned with facilitating the range of online activities that are supportive of student learning.
- *The Advisor-Counselor:* Works with learners on an individual or private basis, offering advice or counselling to help them get the most out of their engagement with the course.
- *The Assessor:* Concerned with providing grades, feedback, and validation of learners' work.
- *The Researcher:* Concerned with engagement in production of new knowledge of relevance to the content areas being taught.
- *The Content-Facilitator:* Concerned directly with facilitating the learner' growing understanding of course content.
- *The Technologist:* Concerned with making, or helping to make technological choices that improve the environment available to learners.
- *The Designer:* Concerned with designing worthwhile online learning tasks.
- *The Manager-Administrator:* Concerned with issues of learner registration, security, record keeping and so on. (Goodyear et al., 2001, p. 69)

For each of these roles, associated attributes were considered. For example, for the role of *Process Facilitator* six main tasks areas were identified:

- *Welcoming* (introducing, ice-breaking, helping learners articulate their expectations, familiarising learners with the environment and expected work practices, demonstrating the value of online activity)
- *Establishing ground rules* (maintaining rules, creating community, maintaining discourse)
- *Creating community* (maintaining discourse, creating community, providing positive feedback, ensuring safe environment, allocating roles, maintaining effective groups)
- *Managing communication* (sharing, listening, showing enthusiasm, establishing and maintaining motivation)
- *Modelling social behaviour*
- *Establishing own identity.* (Goodyear et al., 2001, p. 70)

In providing such an analysis, the authors of the report acknowledged that good teaching in conventional face-to-face settings would often readily transfer to the online equivalent. But they were also careful to point out that online teaching requires many new competencies that classroom teachers have never needed in the past, and that the ways in which good teaching is expressed in conventional and online settings may be very different.

Seeking Solutions to Professional Development Needs

The professional development needs of teachers moving to adopt online learning as a delivery medium for their courses are complicated by the myriad of differences and variations to conventional practices that such approaches involve. Developing the skills and expertise to deliver effective courses in online settings often demands changes to teachers' approaches to learning, changes to their roles in the learning setting and changes to the actual delivery methods themselves. As the literature has demonstrated, appropriate professional development needs to target not only the nurturing of technical skills in use of the technology, but skills in working with online students, providing scaffolding and support and providing the forms of learning engagement required to bring about the conceptual changes being sought.

We were guided in our approach to this problem by previous work we had undertaken, which had explored learning designs for online learning which involved situating learning in authentic contexts (e.g., Herrington & Oliver, 2000). Our explorations with authentic learning suggested that such an approach was well suited to the learning needs of teachers in professional development courses. Our previous research sought to identify the characteristics of learning settings that supported knowledge construction and the acquisition of transferable skills and knowledge. From this research, we developed a framework describing authentic tasks and identified critical design characteristics (e.g., Herrington, Oliver & Reeves, 2003).

There are a number of conventional settings where learning has been organised around students seeking solutions to real-world problems through exploration and interaction with information-rich contexts (Bransford, Brown & Cocking, 2000). However, few examples of successful authentic online courses exist. In the main, universities have been slow to adopt innovative pedagogical approaches in their online course offerings. Typically, this has been caused by a lack of awareness of appropriate learning designs, and has applied even to the education of professionals where authentic approaches are considered important for the application of theory to practice (Dehoney & Reeves, 1999). Frequently, when courses are developed for Internet delivery, the design emphasises the transmission of information at the expense of inquiry-based activity to promote thinking and understanding. Authentic learning offers a powerful approach that draws upon a wealth of research in constructivist and situated approaches to education.

An Authentic Approach to Professional Development for Teachers

A *Graduate Certificate in Online Teaching and Learning* was designed and developed to address the professional development needs of teachers seeking to develop the skills and expertise needed for online teaching. It was designed in a way that provided an authentic learning experience by replicating the online learning experience of students. The purpose of developing the course was to provide an avenue for teachers of adult learners wishing to develop skills and understanding in the design and use of online learning technologies. The aim of the program is to help teachers gain the confidence to design and plan effective learning environments using online technologies. It also focuses on developing teachers' abilities to teach effectively using communications technologies. However, rather than producing a course that "taught" the basic principles of online theory and practice, the program was developed to immerse the teachers in an authentic online experience.

The design of the subjects or courses has been characterised by strongly student-centred environments, with authentic and contextualised learning tasks in collaborative settings, using integrated assessment strategies and learning scaffolded by strong teacher support. The program consists of four semester courses: Online Teaching and Learning, Resources for Teaching and Learning Online, Designing Effective Online Learning Environments, and an Online Learning Project Unit. The courses are designed to be delivered online and to instantiate a variety of effective online teaching and learning strategies. In this chapter, the approach of the first subject entitled Online Teaching and Learning will be described.

This introductory subject was designed to explore issues associated with the creation of effective learning environments, and draws heavily on recent theory and research. The authenticity of the site was guided by principles of authentic learning (Herrington & Oliver, 2000), such as authentic contexts and tasks, multiple roles and perspectives, the collaborative construction of knowledge, coaching and scaffolding by the teacher, and integrated assessment of learning.

Figure 1. The main interface for the introductory subject

The course is based upon a task where the learner takes on a role in a fictitious scenario set in a university. Rather than provide the learners with a structure comprised of text-based hyperlinks, weekly content, and buttons, a metaphor for the learning environment is provided. The main interface is one that resembles a resource centre familiar to teachers (see Figure 1). Learners click on the different objects to gain access to the resources and tasks beneath. The course content is effectively encapsulated within the activities and the associated resources, rather than presented in a linear fashion in modules or chapters.

The context is one where the learner is required to evaluate a Web site that has been set up as an exemplar for a consortium of universities planning to develop a joint online course. The learner then, in collaboration with other students in the course ("representatives from the other universities"), recommends a set of guidelines for effective online learning environments, and then redesigns the original Web site according to those guidelines. While comprising a single authentic and sustained task, the activity can be evaluated at three points. The task is presented in the form of a series of memos, setting out the requirements in a realistic manner. Within this complex task, the learners choose their own method of accomplishing the requirements, rather than completing weekly tasks and assignments, quizzes or multiple-choice questions that have been mandated by the subject teacher.

The pace of the subject is very much determined by the learners completing the work, within the constraints of assignment deadlines and collaborative opportunities. The assessable assignments themselves are fully integrated with the subject content, so the learners submit group and individual work responding in stages to the memos. Rather than completing essays or tests, the assignments are complex, sustained activities that could take a number of weeks to complete. Instead of reading and "regurgitating" other peoples' ideas, the learners' cognitive activity is based on reflecting, analysing, planning, and problem solving. The subject teacher's role moves from one where content is organised and progress monitored, to one of a support person and coach. Resources are open-ended with the facility to explore beyond the immediate Web environment, rather than specific, bounded resources and reference lists. One might also argue that the result is deeper understanding and higher order learning, rather than the simple memorisation of facts and factual recall. The courses are offered only on the online mode, and thus provide prospective online teachers with the opportunity to experience learning from the student perspective.

Conclusion

The development of professional development activities and accreditation processes for online teachers is in its early days. Most teachers continue to use the successful strategies and processes that they experienced when they themselves were learners. Clearly the best opportunities for such professional development activities reside in the provision of quality courses that use authentic contexts and effectively "practise what they preach."

The *Graduate Certificate of Online Learning* described in this chapter provides a tangible model of an online course designed to promote learning through a design based on the principles of learner immersion in an authentic learning experience. The move to embrace technology as a support for learning in schools and colleges is growing rapidly, as are expectations among the stakeholders that the online experience will provide enhanced learning challenges and outcomes. In this chapter, we have described a design for such learning environments which can possibly realise these expectations. The use of authenticity in its many forms in learning settings provides powerful supports for learning and is a strategy that can be adopted with existing technologies quite easily. It is likely that as more teachers become aware of the affordances and opportunities of the Web and its associated technologies, such learning designs will become more popular and more commonplace in all sectors.

Technology and flexible learning are, according to Lundin (1998), "inexorably linked." Flexible learning has the capacity to transform university education, but only if care is taken to ensure that the new role of the online teacher is usefully informed by research, linked to new technologies, and transposed into a supportive, specialised and valued function. The consequence of ignoring this challenge will be the disaffection of a generation of students disillusioned with a university structure which is satisfied to provide content, technology and little else.

References

Bates, A.W. (2000). *Managing technological change: Strategies for college and university leaders.* San Francisco: Jossey-Bass.

Bennett, S., Priest, A., & Macpherson, C. (1999). Learning about online learning: An approach to staff development for university teachers. *Australian Journal of Educational Technology, 15*(3), 207-221.

Bransford, J.D., Brown, A.L., & Cocking, R.R. (2000). *How people learn: Brain, mind, experience, and school.* Washington, DC: National Academy Press.

Collins, A., Brown, J.S., & Newman, S.E. (1989). Cognitive apprenticeship: Teaching the crafts of reading, writing, and mathematics. In L.B. Resnick (Ed.), *Knowing, learning and instruction: Essays in honour of Robert Glaser* (pp. 453-494). Hillsdale, NJ: LEA.

Cremer, D. (2001). Education as commodity: The ideology of online learning and distance learning. *Journal of the Association for History and Computing, 4*(3). Retrieved June 5, 2003, from *http://mcel.pacificu.edu/JAHC/JAHCiv2/ARTICLES/cremer/cremerindex.htm*

Cuban, L. (2001). *Oversold and underused: Computers in the classroom.* Cambridge, MA: Harvard University Press.

Dehoney, J., & Reeves, T. (1999). Instructional and social dimensions of class Web pages. *Journal of Computing in Higher Education, 10*(2), 19-41.

Economist. (1999). The world in figures: Industries: The world in 1999. New York: Economist Publications.

Goodyear, P., Salmon, G., Spector, J.M., Steeples, C., & Tickner, S. (2001). Competencies for online teaching: A special report. *Educational Technology Research and Development, 49*(1), 65-72.

Greenfield, P.M. (1984). A theory of the teacher in the learning activities of everyday life. In B. Rogoff & J. Lave (Eds.), *Everyday cognition: Its development in social context* (pp. 117-138). Cambridge, MA: Harvard University Press.

Gustafson, P., & Gibbs, D. (2000). Guiding or hiding? The role of the facilitator in online teaching and learning. *Teaching Education, 11*(2), 195-210.

Herrington, J., & Oliver, R. (2000). An instructional design framework for authentic learning environments. *Educational Technology Research and Development, 48*(3), 23-48.

Herrington, J., Oliver, R., & Reeves, T. C. (2003). 'Cognitive realism' in online authentic learning environments. In D. Lassner & C. McNaught (Eds.),

EdMedia World Conference on Educational Multimedia, Hypermedia and Telecommunications (pp. 2115-2121). Norfolk, VA: AACE.

Jonassen, D. (1995). Supporting communities of learners with technology: A vision for integrating technology with learning in schools. *Educational Technology, 35*(5), 60-63.

Jonassen, D., & Reeves, T.C. (1996). Learning with technology: Using computers as cognitive tools. In D.H. Jonassen (Ed.), *Handbook of research on educational communications and technology* (pp. 693-719). New York: Macmillan.

Keller, F.S. (1968). Good-bye teacher ... *Journal of Applied Behaviour Analysis, 1*, 78-89.

Lundin, R. (1998). *Flexible delivery: An international perspective.* Retrieved February 17, 2003, from *http://www.tedi.uq.edu.au/conferences/flex_delivery/Lundin.html*

McNaught, C., & Kennedy, P. (2000). Developing new roles for university teachers: Grass-roots local staff development serviced by top-down investment and policy. In J. Bourdeau, & R. Heller (Eds.), *Proceedings of EdMedia 2000.* Charlottesville, VA: AACE.

Nie, N.H., & Erbring, L. (2000). *Internet and society: A preliminary report.* Stanford Institute for the Quantitative Study of Society. Retrieved March 1, 2003, from *http://www.stanford.edu/group/siqss/*

Palloff, R. M., & Pratt, K. (1999). *Building learning communities in cyberspace: Effective strategies for the online classroom.* San Francisco: Jossey-Bass.

Perkins, D.N. (1991). What constructivism demands of the learner. *Educational Technology, 31*(8), 19-21.

Pittinsky. M.S. (Ed.). (2001). *The wired tower: Perspectives on the impact of the internet on higher education.* Upper Saddle River, NJ: Prentice Hall.

Shotsberger, P. (1997). Emerging roles for instructors and learners in the Web-based instruction classroom. In B.H. Khan (Ed.), *Web-based instruction* (pp. 101-106). Englewood Cliffs, NJ: Educational Technology Publications.

Sparrow, H., Herrington, J., & Herrington, A. (2000). 'Shovelware' as staff development: A useful introduction to moving online. In M. Wallce, A. Ellis & D. Newton (Eds.), *Proceedings of the Moving Online Conference* (pp. 236-246). Lismore, NSW: SCU.

Strommen, E.F., & Lincoln, B. (1992). *Constructivism, technology and the future of classroom learning.* Retrieved from *http://www.ilt.columbia.edu/k12/livetext/docs/construct.html*

Van Dusen, G.C. (1997). The virtual campus: Technology and reform in higher education. *ASHE-ERIC Higher Education Reports, 25*(5), 1-147. [ED412815].

Vygotsky, L.S. (1978). *Mind in society: The development of higher psychological processes* (V.J.-S. M. Cole, S. Scribner, E. Souberman, Eds., & Trans.). Cambridge, MA: Harvard University Press.

Wade, W. (1994). Introduction. In W. Wade, K. Hodgkinson, A. Smith & J. Arfield (Eds.), *Flexible learning in higher education* (pp. 12-16). London: Kogan Page.

Wertsch, J.V. (1985). Introduction. In J.V. Wertsch (Ed.), *Culture, communication and cognition: Vygotskian perspectives* (pp. 1-18). Cambridge: Cambridge University Press.

Willis, B., & Dickinson, J. (1997). Distance education and the World Wide Web. In B.H. Khan (Ed.), *Web-based instruction* (pp. 81-84). Englewood Cliffs, NJ: Educational Technology Publications.

Chapter XXI

Authentic Teaching and Learning Standards That Assure Quality Higher Education

Ron Oliver, Edith Cowan University, Australia

Anthony Herrington, University of Wollongong, Australia

Sue Stoney, Edith Cowan University, Australia

Jim Millar, Edith Cowan University, Australia

Abstract

Quality assurance is becoming a necessary aspect of many institutions of higher education. Teaching and learning is a major area of scrutiny and requires institutional agreement on the benchmarks and standards by which quality will be determined. This chapter provides a framework for conceptualising the elements of teaching and learning that need to be accounted for in any quality assurance process, with particular focus on teaching activities that reflect an authentic approach to learning.

Introduction

This book is evidence of the exemplary approaches to authentic teaching and learning that are being implemented by individual teachers across all discipline areas in higher education. Over time these endeavors and their students' successes will flow on to the practices of their colleagues and the policies of their institutions. However, this effect can be facilitated by institutional policies that can guide and motivate the principal activities of teaching and learning while at the same time providing direction for secondary support structures such as professional and resource development. These institutional policies are being developed in an economic and political climate that demands transparent processes of quality assurance.

Quality Assurance in Higher Education

The movement to ascertain and assure quality in higher education appears to have grown from activities in the UK where quality assurance processes have been in place for some time. The document *Quality Assurance for Higher Education* prepared by the Quality Assurance Agency for Higher Education (QAAHE) in the UK describes the intention of the objectives of quality assurance of teaching and learning in higher education as:

a.   To contribute, in conjunction with other mechanisms, to the promotion of high quality and standards in teaching and learning.

b.   To provide students, employers and others with reliable and consistent information about quality and standards at each higher education institution (HEI).

c.   To ensure that HE programs are identified where quality or standards are unsatisfactory, as a basis for ensuring rapid action to improve them.

d.   To provide one means of securing accountability for the use of public funds received by HEIs. (QAAHE, 2001, p. 2)

The current quality activity in higher education in Australia commenced in December 1999 when the Minister for Education, Training and Youth Affairs, announced plans for the establishment of the *Australian University Quality Agency* (AUQA) with a brief to conduct regular quality audits and to provide reports on the quality assurance arrangements of self-accrediting higher education institutions in Australia. This quality audit process planned to adopt an approach that encompassed all aspects of institutions' activities including, teaching and learning, research and management and those activities that involved offshore elements.

The AUQA process was not the first quality audit undertaken among Australian higher education institutions. An earlier audit was commenced in 1992 when the Government of the day established the Committee for Quality Assurance in Higher Education to assist the Government in the implementation of its strategy for ensuring the quality, excellence and international standing of Australia's higher education system. The resulting audit was undertaken in three rounds across 1993, 1994 and 1995 with each round targeting a discrete area of activity. The second round in 1994 reviewed teaching and learning.

As with the current audit process, the approach adopted by the Commonwealth in 1992 placed responsibility for the determination of the quality processes on each institution. The resulting process saw a strategy of self-assessment being undertaken with institutions determining for themselves how they would demonstrate the outcomes and the effectiveness of their programs, policies and procedures. The Government provided no benchmarks and few guidelines and gave the institutions considerable freedom in determining how they would review themselves against their own plans, mission statements and written goals. The AUQA audits are now being conducted in similar ways. Institutions are being asked to demonstrate their achievements through self-assessment approaches and within teaching and learning. This involves a detailed examination of institutional goals and aims and resulting programs and instructional practices.

Quality in Teaching and Learning

While the AUQA audit covers all aspects of higher education from teaching and learning through research and commercial activities, this chapter is interested in the issues of determining and demonstrating quality in teaching and learning. The purpose of the chapter is to explore and discuss the notion of quality as it pertains to teaching and learning and to explore possible strategies for establishing standards and benchmarks by which institutions might be able to demonstrate quality outcomes in this area of activity.

There is an abundance of literature that has been developed which broadly describes quality in teaching and learning and this is achieved primarily through detailed examinations of discrete aspects of these activities. In determinations of overall quality, the important considerations take on far broader meanings and contexts and include activities that extend way beyond the curriculum, its implementation and student learning outcomes. In the broadest context, the following questions suggest those activities that are fundamental to underpinning a review of teaching and learning:

- What quality assurance policies and practices does the institutions have in place or in the process of development to assure the quality of its teaching and learning performance?
- How effective and how fully deployed are these?
- What processes does the institution have to evaluate and monitor the quality of its outcomes?
- What quality related indicators does the institution use and why?
- What are the institution's priorities for improvement?
- What quality initiative has the institution undertaken (since the last review) and what evidence of improved performance is there? (University of Tasmania, 2000)

Within the Australian scene, the audit model used by AUQA is the ADRI approach. This approach involves an investigation of four main activities:

- **Approach:** How does the university characterise itself? What is its vision and mission? How do these relate to its historical development, context and capabilities? What are its major strengths and areas of emphasis?
- **Deployment:** Is the approach being deployed in the best possible manner? According to whom? How does the University know this is the case?
- **Results:** What are the results in relation to each of the University's stated objectives? Does the University understand why it achieved these particular results?
- **Improvement:** Does the University know how it can improve? How does it know this? (AUQA, 2002)

The process of demonstrating quality within the activities of such enterprises as education and training is a relatively new activity for many institutions and we are now beginning to see the development of a body of knowledge and literature base that can provide guidance and assistance for those for whom such activities are important. In particular, we are now beginning to see the development of standards and benchmarks as indicators of quality against which performance and outcomes can be judged as part of the quality assurance process.

Quality Standards for
Teaching and Learning

Standards and benchmarking are important entities in higher education organisations that are being held accountable for the services they provide. Standards are defined in the context of this chapter as *levels of achievement of a benchmark that can be qualitatively or quantitatively measured.* The use of standards provides a means for the quality and scope of services to be documented and for the provision of such to be monitored against stated objectives. While standards have been applied for many years to business services, it is only recently that they have been considered in education and training, activities that for many years have paid little attention to any formal approaches to the specification of benchmarks against which standards might be measured.

A document that has been provided for Australian universities as a guide to considering standards and benchmarks for quality assurance purposes is *Benchmarking: A manual for Australian universities* (McKinnon, Walker & Davis, 2000). This guide suggests a number of key areas by which quality teaching and learning might be judged and assessed. The guide provides summary benchmarking statements for a number of quality indicators for teaching and learning that include:

- Learning and teaching plan;
- Course establishment processes;
- Scholarly teaching;
- Teaching environment;
- Effective academic review processes;
- Fitness of courses;
- Student progress ratio;
- First- to second-year retention trends;
- Equity quantitative success;
- Student satisfaction; and
- Employability of Australian graduates.

This guideline provides a very sound basis for quality assurance, although the selection of the indicators is seen as representative rather than complete. In fact, the document has little to say about what constitutes quality teaching — which is typical of most university course planning and review documents (Ellis, 1993).

Table 1. A framework describing quality teaching and learning

	Teaching	Learning
Presage Elements which describe pre-conditions for successful teaching and learning	• Course establishment and course review processes • Curriculum specifications • Course materials & resources • Teacher qualifications and currency • Strategic plan for teaching and learning • Facilities and resources for teaching and learning	• Student selection and entry into courses • Students' progression through courses
Process Elements which describe ongoing conditions for successful teaching and learning	• Provision of appropriate learning experiences • Assessment procedures • Work, community and professional engagement • Student support	• Appropriate learning strategies
Product Elements which describe post-conditions for successful teaching and learning	• Continuous improvement in teaching • Reflective practice and ongoing commitment to continuous improvement in teaching	• Graduates are employable in various ways • Graduates can demonstrate outcomes • Course satisfaction and attitudes

Standards of good teaching based on educational research have been espoused (e.g., Chickering and Gamson, 1987), however, more recent principles based on current theories of learning are lacking. This chapter illustrates a more comprehensive and up-to-date framework for describing quality authentic teaching and learning (Table 1). The framework draws its structure from the 3P model of learning proposed by Biggs (2003) that identifies *presage, process* and *product* as stages in the learning process. Presage indicates learning-related factors prior to student learning; process factors occur during learning; and products refer to the outcomes of learning. When these three stages are extended from considerations of learners themselves to the overall process of curriculum design and teaching, it provides a sound organisational structure for identifying what appear to be the critical elements supporting quality outcomes.

The framework provides the means to characterise quality teaching and learning and supports a process by which indicators and standards can be developed and assessed by either internal or external evaluators for the purpose of quality assurance.

Based on the discrete elements in the framework shown in Table 1, a series of descriptors and quality indicators for each element has been developed. Standards, by which the achievement of these elements might be measured, have also been suggested. Tables 2 and 3 show a sample of these descriptors and indicators as have been developed for the teaching presage cell shown above.

Table 2. Course establishment and course review processes for teaching presage

Course establishment and course review processes				
• The courses and units offered by the university need to have been developed through deliberate and well organised processes and strategies to ensure they are of the highest quality • The courses and units offered by the university need to be subject to stringent review and evaluation processes to ensure they retain their high quality **Quality indicators** • The university's curriculum policies set out how the need for courses is to be established and the connections with university objectives, unit descriptions set out learning objectives directly linked to assessment tasks, be intelligible to students, and clearly provide all essential information, such as course work requirements, marking, arrangements, modes of teaching and expected standards • The learning environment including access to library, audio-visual and IT support is specified, and assured proposals for courses are scrutinised by peers in the developmental stages, external and/or community/professional representatives are engaged in course development and appraisal.				
Standards 1	**2**	**3**	**4**	**5**
• *Courses stem from local initiative without a requirement for meeting other objectives.* • *Course descriptions are incomplete in some respect or not fully intelligible to students.* • *Learning environment taken for granted and not systematically supportive of courses.* • *Course developments without outside inputs. Perfunctory Academic Board scrutiny.* • *The main appraisal and reporting processes, including the standards achieved, are reviewed at long intervals through five year or longer Academic Review processes.*		• *Explicit relationship of at least 75% of courses to university objectives* • *Comprehensive course information available for students* • *Course development mostly internal with quality control processes overseen by the Academic Board* • *The main appraisal and reporting processes, including standards achieved, are reviewed at long intervals through academic review processes.*		• *Explicit relation of every course to university objectives* • *Course delivery, and support arrangements are specified and assured* • *Course development involves external peer and industry input and defined Academic Board approval and/or re-submission requirements* • *Annual or at most biennial appraisal, including industry or external review, reporting of outcomes and improvement processes* • *Demonstrable consistency of standards is established*

A similar set of elements, descriptors, quality indicators and standards has been described for teaching products. A sample of these elements is shown in Tables 4 and 5.

Perhaps the most significant component for practicing teachers, in relation to authentic approaches to teaching and learning, is that associated with the actual delivery of the programs. In the framework, this component is described as the teaching process. Tables 6 and 7 describe some of the elements of this component together with related quality indicators and standards.

Table 3. Curriculum specifications for teaching presage

Curriculum specifications
• Curriculum documentation should specify clear learning outcomes. Instructional aims, methods and assessment procedures should be made clear and explicit for all students. Learning outcomes should be specified in terms of discipline knowledge and generic capabilities described as graduate attributes. This information should be available for students at the commencement of each course unit • Curriculum documentation should refer to a range of current resources. Documentation that describes a course unit's curriculum should be made available to all students at the commencement of that unit. This information should identify learning resources that are accurate and current
Quality indicators
• Unit outlines for all courses that specify intended learning outcomes and instructional activities, Unit outlines with a specification of intended capabilities and performances • Unit outlines that specify graduate attributes and generic learning outcomes, Unit outlines that specify accurately relevant and current resources, Constructive alignment between planned learning outcomes, teaching and learning processes and assessment strategies

1	2	3	4	5
• *The majority of unit outlines describe aims, objectives and assessment but lack a student centred framework for teaching and learning and show limited coherence between stated aims, objectives and assessment procedures*		• *Consistent formats used for 75% of course descriptions and unit outlines* • *75% of course descriptions and unit outlines are stored systemically* • *75% of course descriptions specify graduate attributes* • *75% of unit outlines specify coherently intended learning outcomes, instructional activities, assessments and necessary resources*		• *Consistent formats used for 100% of course descriptions and unit outlines* • *100% of course descriptions and unit outlines are stored systemically* • *100% of course descriptions specify graduate attributes* • *100% of unit outlines specify coherently intended learning outcomes, instructional activities, assessments and necessary resources*

Teaching and learning standards are now being trialed in various Schools at Edith Cowan University as part of the quality assurance process. The standards which have been described for each component have been created with the view that the middle level, level 3, corresponds to a minimum acceptable standard and one below which we would anticipate no school or teaching unit might fall in any quality audit. The trialing process is seeking to examine the benchmark figures that have been set to determine their suitability both as standards and their capacity to be measured in some objective fashion. The framework is a work in progress and is intended to be reviewed and improved and a final decision taken in the future as to how it might be implemented in a strategic fashion as a core component of the university's quality assurance process. The trial period that will be used to implement and review the framework will see programs and courses of all forms being assessed through the standards that have been developed. It will be important to explore the success of the framework and the standards

Table 4. Continuous improvement in teaching for teaching product

Continuous improvement in teaching

Continuous improvement in teaching

- Quality teaching needs to be informed by feedback loops that provide measures of success and proactive measures to overcome difficulties that are identified
- A University needs to have some formalised processes to judge the quality of teachers' performances
- The measures need to be well documented and with a strong basis for determining quality measures
- Teachers need to have formal feedback processes to gather information from students concerning their perceptions of the teaching quality
- Teachers need to be able to demonstrate how the feedback has been used to inform their subsequent teaching practices
- Teachers need to be able to demonstrate acceptable levels of constructive criticism from students

Quality indicators

- Formal feedback processes are used to gather information on outcomes from all teachers and tutors
- The feedback data is reviewed and acted on in ways that improve the teaching processes
- Students are satisfied that they have a voice and that their feedback is used in productive ways to improve teaching quality
- There are processes in place that address the issues arising from feedbacks in formal and deliberate ways

1	2	3	4	5
• *The University has few formal processes in place that monitor teacher performance.* • *Little evidence exists that teaching quality in courses and units is monitored and used to improve performance*		• *The University has established formal processes in place that monitor teacher performance* • *Student feedback is obtained from 75% of the units at least once per year* • *Formalised processes demonstrate that this feedback informs subsequent delivery of 75% units*		• *The University has well established formal processes in place that monitor teacher performance.* • *Student feedback is obtained from 100% of the units at least once per year* • *Formalised processes demonstrate that this feedback from all units measured informs subsequent delivery of all units*

described as generic descriptors of teaching and learning in general and to ensure that they have direct application to all teaching and learning activities.

Summary and Conclusion

This chapter has described a quality framework as a means to describe standards for authentic teaching and learning that can provide some objective measures of performance as part of the quality assurance process. The framework has been developed in a way whereby all forms of teaching and learning for example, online teaching and learning might be assured through a similar process. The

Table 5. Reflective practice and ongoing commitments to continuous improvement in teaching for teaching product

Reflective practice and ongoing commitments to continuous improvement in teaching				
• Quality teaching is demonstrated when teachers reflect and act on their teaching experiences. Teachers need to reflect critically upon their own teaching using information from a variety of sources to ascertain to what extent they are being successful in helping students learn. Action resulting from reflection can result in improved teaching and learning • Teachers should show a willingness to develop and share their own learning. Many opportunities arise for teachers to share their expertise in the design and development of courses. Research and communication into the processes of teaching and learning are important aspects of professional scholarship **Quality indicators** • Teachers will demonstrate reflexivity in their approaches to teaching • Teachers will share their successes with peers and associates through appropriate communication channels. Teachers share their knowledge, experience and expertise of teaching and learning with their colleagues through such activities as seminars, forums, professional development and publications				
1	**2**	**3**	**4**	**5**
• *Few staff in the University demonstrate reflective practice in their teaching activities* • *Few staff in the University participate in formal activities associated with inquiry into effective teaching* • *Few staff in the University maintain portfolios of their teaching*		• *At least 50% of staff in the University demonstrate reflective practice in their teaching activities* • *At least 50% of staff in the University participate in formal activities associated with inquiry into effective teaching* • *At least 50% of staff in the University maintain portfolios/evidentiary samples of their teaching*		• *At least 80% of staff in the University participate in formal activities associated with inquiry into effective teaching and sharing of outcomes* • *At least 80% of staff in the University maintain portfolios/evidentiary samples of their teaching*

framework is now being implemented and reviewed and significant challenges we expect to face include:

- Establishing quantifiable and meaningful metrics for all elements so that they an be assessed and recorded in an objective and reliable fashion;

- Discovering strategies for assessing those elements which are hard to quantify rather than discarding them because they are difficult to assess;

- Coming to a common agreement and common understanding on minimum standards that might be applied across teaching and learning in the whole university;

- Having staff and schools take ownership of the process and the standards and seeing them as agents for quality assurance and continuous improvement and not simply instruments for monitoring and checking; and

Table 6. Provision of appropriate learning experiences for teaching process

Provision of appropriate learning experiences
Teachers should provide students with learning experiences appropriate to unit aims: • Learning experiences should challenge and motivate students to learn and continue learning. Students learn when they are challenged and motivated. Deep learning of discipline knowledge in the form of information, concepts and skills occurs when tasks stimulate students to employ higher order thinking skills in such contexts as problem solving and research • Learning experiences should be meaningful and encourage action and reflection. Meaningful learning occurs when students connect new learning to existing knowledge and experiences. Integrated and extensive understanding occurs when links are made across different representations and domains of knowledge. Students learn and apply discipline knowledge and graduate attributes such as decision making when they are challenged with rich, complex tasks that offer a multiplicity of perspectives, strategies and resources and result in a range of achievable outcomes. Enabling students to reflect on their learning allows students to develop important metacognitive skills necessary for independent, self-regulated learning • Learning experiences situate learning in contexts in which learning will be applied. Students learn, retain and transfer learning when learning occurs in contexts that reflect tasks they will encounter in society and their professional practice • Learning experiences should accommodate differences in learners' cultural and educational backgrounds. Students enter university with a variety of prior knowledge and experiences, and from varied cultural backgrounds. Students also vary in the rates and approaches they use to learn • Where appropriate, learning experiences should allow for individual endeavour and collaborative engagement. Independent learning through individual effort is important, however, graduate attributes such as problem solving and communication, and values such as service and teamwork, are socially constructed in contexts that foster cooperation, collaboration and community • Learning experiences should involve appropriate technologies. Information and communication technologies (ICT) are essential tools for teaching and learning. Technologies such as multimedia and the Internet enable students to access a range of resources and participate in learning communities. Purposeful use of digital media resources (such as videos), and software tools (such as word processors, spreadsheets and graphic packages) facilitate important technological literacies such as planning, recording, displaying and communicating information
Quality indicators • Students are engaged in learning activities that are engaging and stimulating • Students are engaged in learning activities that accommodate their prior learning, experiences and abilities • Students are engaged in rich learning tasks and activities that promote reflection • Students are engaged in authentic learning activities • Students are engaged in collaborative learning activities • Learning activities use technology as information sources and productivity tools

1	2	3	4	5
• *The majority of students are engaged in passive modes of learning based on the transmission of facts and procedures*		• *50% of students are engaged in courses which provide rich learning tasks that include such elements as: opportunities for student-centred learning, collaborative learning, authentic contexts, use of technology as an instructional aid and flexibilities that cater for individual needs*		• *80% of students are engaged in courses that provide rich learning tasks that include such elements as: opportunities for student-centred learning, collaborative learning, authentic contexts, use of technology as an instructional aid and flexibilities that cater for individual needs*

Table 7. Assessment procedures for teaching process

Assessment procedures
Where assessment tasks rest with the responsibility of the teacher they should be: • Valid: Assessment tasks should be valid, explicit, and fair. Students should be assessed with valid tasks that reflect the outcomes described for the course. These tasks should enable students to demonstrate a deep understanding of discipline knowledge as well as application of higher order thinking skills and graduate attributes. Assessment tasks and procedures should be made explicit to all students. Assessments should be varied in ways that will enable all students to demonstrate their achievements. • Educative: Assessment tasks should be educative, authentic and integrated with learning tasks. Assessment tasks should enable students to identify learning achievements and deficiencies and provide directions for further learning. Outcomes should be assessed with tasks that are authentic and set in the context of their future use. Assessment should be integrated with instructional activities rather than viewed as a separate process. • Comprehensive: Assessment should be comprehensive, using multiple sources of evidence. Assessment tasks should be comprehensive enough to enable a range of outcomes to be measured. These outcomes should be assessed in a variety of ways providing evidence that is built up over time

Quality indicators
• Assessment tasks match intended learning outcomes • Assessment tasks are authentic and integrated with instructional activities. • Assessment approaches are varied and measure a range of learning outcomes • Assessment tasks are contextualised • Assessment tasks are designed to measure a range of learning outcomes • Assessment include collaborative tasks • Assessment tasks measure deep understanding of domain knowledge • Assessment tasks measure higher order thinking skills • Forms of moderation are used within assessment processes to enable standards to be monitored and maintained

1	2	3	4	5
• *The majority of courses involve assessment tasks that are "end on" to instruction and rely on student repetition of facts and procedures.*		• *50% of courses involve assessment tasks that are integrated with instruction and involve tasks that demonstrate higher order thinking skills, deep understanding and graduate attributes.*		• *80% of courses involve assessment tasks that are integrated with instruction and involve tasks that demonstrate higher order thinking skills, deep understanding and graduate attributes.*

- Establishing the degree to which the use of such a system actually contributes to the improvement of teaching and learning in the university.

The process is an interesting and challenging activity for the university and is a process that many others will be facing and dealing with. We hope to track our experiences carefully and to ensure that the institution gains whatever advantages and opportunities it can from participation in the quality review process. The use of a formalised framework as described above seems one means by which that could help to ensure this.

References

Australian University Quality Agency (2002). *The Audit Manual v1.* Retrieved August 2004, from *http://www.auqa.edu.au/qualityaudit/auditmanual_v1*

Biggs, J. (2003). *Teaching for quality learning at university* (2nd ed.). Buckingham, UK: The Society for Research into Higher Education & Open University Press.

Chickering, A.W., & Gamson, Z.F. (1987). *Seven principles for good practice in undergraduate education.* American Association for Higher Education, March Bulletin.

Ellis, R. (1993). Quality assurance for university teaching: Issues and approaches. In R. Ellis (Ed.), *Quality assurance for university teaching* (pp. 3-15). Buckingham, UK: The Society for Research into Higher Education & Open University Press.

McKinnon, K., Walker, S., & Davis, D. (2000). *Benchmarking: A manual for Australian universities.* Canberra, ACT: Department of Education, Training and Youth Affairs.

Quality Assurance Agency for Higher Education (QAAHE) (2001). *Quality assurance in higher education.* Gloucester, UK: QAAHE. Retrieved August 2004, from *http://www.hefce.ac.uk/pubs/hefce/2001/01_45.htm*

University of Tasmania (2000). *Quality audits and the Australian University Quality Agency.* Retrieved August 2004, from *http://www.admin.utas.edu.au/academic/acservices/meetings/talc/Appendix/6_00D.doc*

About the Authors

Anthony Herrington is associate professor in both adult education and IT in education in the Faculty of Education, University of Wollongong, Australia. He has a long history of teaching in schools and universities, nationally and overseas. His initial teaching focus was mathematics education. However, with the impact of technology his interests have broadened to include adult, and information and communications technology education. Tony has won national teacher development grants resulting in award winning publications that have focused on the professional development of teachers using technologies such as video, CD-ROM-based multimedia and the Internet. He is currently engaged in researching the benefits of online communities of practice for beginning teachers.

Jan Herrington is associate professor in IT in education at the University of Wollongong, Australia. She is a member of the Research Centre for Interactive Learning Environments (RILE) at the university. Recent research and development interests have focused on the design of Web-based learning environments for higher education and the use of authentic tasks as a central focus for Web-based courses. She was awarded the *Association of Educational Communications and Technology (AECT) Young Researcher of the Year Award* in Houston Texas in 1999 and won a Fulbright Professional Award in 2002 to conduct research at the University of Georgia, USA.

* * *

Shirley Agostinho is a post doctoral fellow in the Faculty of Education at the University of Wollongong, Australia. She has been involved in teaching in the Master of Education (IT) program and her current research focus is the use of learning objects within a "learning design" framework. Shirley was the project manager for an Australian nationally funded project (2000-2002) that investigated the redevelopment of effective technology-based learning designs (implemented in higher education) into more generic forms. She also has worked as an instructional designer on multimedia CD-ROM educational programs. Shirley completed her doctoral dissertation titled: *Examining Interactions in a Web-based Learning Environment: Creating an Online Learning Community* in 2000.

Karen Anderson is senior lecturer in archives and records management at Edith Cowan University in Western Australia, where she has taught distance education courses for professionals since 1990. She has been president of the International Council on Archives, Section for Archival Educators and Trainers for 2000 - 2004, is vice president of the Section for 2004 - 2008 and is a member of the Australian Society of Archivists' Education Committee. Her interests in archival education include development, delivery and evaluation of distance education for information service professionals using online technologies. In 2003, she won the Edith Cowan University Vice-Chancellor's Excellence in Teaching Award.

Sue Bennett is a senior lecturer and researcher in the Faculty of Education at the University of Wollongong, Australia. She is an active member of the Centre for Research in Interactive Learning Environments. Sue's interest in use of online technologies to support collaboration stems from her research into authentic learning environments and her experiences as a tertiary teacher of on-campus and distance students.

Brian Cambourne is currently associate professor in the Faculty of Education, University of Wollongong Australia. He began teaching in 1956 when he was 19 years old, and spent 15 years teaching in a mix of one-room schools, and primary classrooms K-6 for the New South Wales Department of Education. He completed his PhD at James Cook University, and was subsequently a Fulbright scholar and a post-doctoral fellow at Harvard. He has also been a visiting fellow at the Universities of Illinois and Arizona. Since 1980 Brian has been researching how learning, especially literacy learning, occurs.

Di Challis is senior lecturer with the Teaching and Learning Support Unit within Learning Services at Deakin University, Geelong, Australia. Her research interests are in the areas of academic discourse, most especially tertiary teaching, and the mediation of technologies on teaching and learning with a recent focus on the management of information technologies within the University sector. She has co-authored a federal government report on information technology, consulted internationally on e-learning and contributed to scholarly literature in this area.

Brian Ferry is associate professor in education at the University of Wollongong, Australia, associate dean (Graduate) and coordinator of RILE Research Group. His research interests include the use of interactive learning environments in educational settings. In 2003 he was awarded an Australian Research Council (ARC) Discovery Grant to conduct research about the use of online simulations in teacher education. Brian has written more than 20 refereed journal articles and more than 80 refereed conference papers. His awards include: the Illawarra/ South Coast Regional Group award for outstanding service to education 1995, Vice-Chancellor's Award for Outstanding Teaching 1996 and the University Teaching Fellowship 1998.

John Fitzsimmons (BA, Honors; PhD, Adelaide - John Howard Clark Scholar; Grad Cert Online Learning, ECU) teaches literary and cultural studies in the School of Humanities at Central Queensland University in Australia. His research interests include online learning and post-modern fiction.

Evan Glazer is director of the Roanoke Valley Governor's School, USA, a regional program for secondary students who are talented in mathematics, science, and research. Some of his work can be seen in his books *Using Internet Primary Sources to Teach Critical Thinking* and *Everyday Use of Mathematical Concepts: A Reference Guide*. During his post graduate work, Evan taught courses on instructional design, research methods, and using computers in the classroom. His research examined social and environmental factors that influence professional learning as teachers integrate technology into their classrooms.

John Hedberg is professor and ICT Millennium Chair at Macquarie University, Australia. John is currently editor-in-chief of *Educational Media International*, a refereed journal for those interested in the application of media and technology in learning contexts throughout the world. He currently serves on the editorial advisory boards of the *Journal of Interactive Learning Research*,

ALT-J and *Distance Education*. His teaching and research interests focus upon cognitive strategies, interface design for learning with information and communications technologies, and implementation and evaluation of technology-based learning. He has also written widely on policy aspects of new technologies in education.

Lynne Hunt is a professor (leader teaching and learning) at Charles Darwin University, Australia. She is the recipient of three university awards for teaching excellence and the 2002 Australian Award for University Teaching in the Social Science category. She also won the 2002 Prime Minister's Award for *Australian University Teacher of the Year*. She publishes in the fields of women's health and tertiary teaching and is a Higher Education Research and Development Society of Australasia (HERDSA) Fellow. Lynne is also a member of the board of the Carrick Institute for Learning and Teaching in Higher Education.

Jennifer Jamison has been involved in chiropractic education for some 25 years. After completing her medical degree in South Africa she migrated to Australia where she obtained her PhD and EdD. She holds the position of professor of primary care in the School of Chiropractic at Murdoch University. She has published more than 185 articles in peer reviewed journals, has chapters in several books and has written six textbooks.

Cate Jerram taught with the management information systems program at the University of Western Sydney in Australia for four years and is now teaching in social psychology. Originally an adult educator working in drama, employment relations and life skills, Cate took undergraduate studies and honours in adult education. Cate is interested in inter-disciplinary research and practice, and the synergies created by bringing diverse fields of knowledge together. Twenty years as an adult educator and four years working with university undergraduates have aroused an intense interest in applying principles of adult education to challenge current undergraduate attitudes and approaches to learning, and tertiary teaching methods.

David Jonassen is a distinguished professor at the University of Missouri. He is the author of more than 20 books, 130 journal articles, 30 book chapters, 20 book reviews and several hundred conference papers. His research interests include: knowledge representation, technologies, and instructional design and learning. He is a member of more than 20 professional associations and has received numerous awards for his work in the field in information technology in education. David is also a consultant for a wide variety of bodies including: IBM computers, hospitals, libraries, credit corporations, the US Air Force, the State Police, and the National Weather Service.

Sandra Jones is associate professor of employment relations and the director of higher education programs in the School of Management at RMIT. She combines her significant practical experience as a practitioner and industry consultant with her considerable educational experience to design, develop and implement experiential learning environments in which students can combine their practical experience with their theoretical knowledge. With the introduction of a distributed learning system within the university to which all students are connected, she has augmented the experiential learning activities using the virtual learning environment.

Mike Keppell is principal lecturer and head of the Centre for Integrating Technology in Education (CITIE) at The Hong Kong Institute of Education. The centre focuses on online learning, media production, IT competencies and research. His institute-wide role encourages staff and students to utilise educational technology to enrich the teaching and learning process. His research interests cover four areas: student-centred learning, multimedia design, processes involved in optimising the instructional designer-subject matter expert interaction and knowledge management. His current interests at the Institute focus on technology-enhanced authentic learning environments, online communities, problem-based learning and learner-centred assessment.

Lisa Kervin lectures in language and literacy and educational research in the Faculty of Education, University of Wollongong, Australia. She has taught across the primary grades and has been responsible for both the literacy and numeracy curriculum areas within schools. She has been employed in consultancy roles within New South Wales education systems. Her current research interests are related to the literacy development of children, the use of technology to support student learning and teacher professional learning.

Annette Koenders is senior lecturer in the School of Natural Sciences at Edith Cowan University, Australia. Annette has a BSc (Honors) and PhD in zoology from Monash University and a Graduate Certificate (tertiary teaching) from ECU. She has lectured in undergraduate biology for over 10 years and pursues research in muscle regeneration. Annette has long-standing interests in transitional issues for first year students and in the application of technology to enhance learning in the biological sciences, having developed a virtual dissection of the garden snail.

Richard Ladyshewsky is senior lecturer at the Graduate School of Business, Curtin University of Technology, Perth, Western Australia. He is an associate fellow of the Australian Institute of Management and an inaugural fellow of the Higher Education and Research Development Society of Australasia. He teaches in the area of organisational behaviour and managerial effectiveness and conducts research in the area of coaching and professional development.

Marilyn Laiken is professor of adult education in the Workplace Learning and Change specialisation at OISE, University of Toronto, Canada, and director of the OISE/UT Certificate Program in Adult Training and Development. Marilyn combines an interest in adult education and organisational change through research, teaching and field development in such areas as organisational learning and change, system redesign, work team development, participative leadership, and experiential, transformative adult education. Marilyn has been honoured with the prestigious OCUFA award for Excellence in Teaching, and the Canadian Society for Training and Development President's Award for her contributions to the field of Adult Education.

Joe Luca is senior lecturer at Edith Cowan University, Australia, in the School of Communications and Multimedia. He lectures in both the undergraduate and postgraduate courses, with a focus on e-learning, project management and industry liaison. Research interests include creating online learning environments that promote the development of generic skills as well as deep and meaningful learning experiences. Joe's qualifications include a PhD, Master of Education (instructional multimedia), Graduate Certificate in computer based instructional design, Graduate Diploma in computing, Graduate Diploma in science education (computing), Diploma of Education and a Bachelor of Science.

Catherine McLoughlin is associate professor and head of the School of Education, Australian Catholic University, Canberra, Australia. Her publications attest to extensive research and development in flexible and online learning, innovative pedagogy in higher education, curriculum design and assessment strategies. Current research interests are the development of e-learning environments to support self-direction, online assessment, evaluation of learning environments and models for the integration of information technology in teacher-education programs. Catherine is editor of the *Australian Journal of Educational Technology* and a member of the program committee of the World Conference on Educational Multimedia and Hypermedia, organised by the Association for Advancement of Computing in Education.

Jim Millar gained a doctorate in physics from Monash University and then lectured in mathematics and science in NSW. An interest in computer education grew and led to a shift to Perth, Western Australia, lecturing in computer science and software engineering at Edith Cowan University, Australia. A diploma in tertiary education along the way provided a new focus onto learning. He has taught large first year classes and boutique post-graduate units, and filled service roles from course coordinator to chairperson of department, and associate dean teaching and learning. Currently he is director of *Learning and Development Services* and interested in policy development and planning in teaching and learning.

Ron Oliver is professor of interactive multimedia in the Faculty of Communications and Creative Industries at Edith Cowan University, Australia. He has a background in multimedia and learning technologies and currently leads a research team at ECU in these fields. He has extensive experience in the design, development, implementation and evaluation of technology-mediated and online learning materials. Current projects in which he is involved include investigations of authentic settings for online teaching and learning, the reusability of e-learning resources, and the modelling and specification of high quality generic learning designs for online learning.

Greg Parry has been a lecturer in economics at Edith Cowan University, Australia since1998. Greg's main teaching responsibilities are in first year economics and in managerial economics. His research interests include franchising and the economics of innovation, in addition to an interest in authentic learning and the application of wireless technology in tertiary education.

Sarah Puglisi is an education student at the University of Wollongong, Australia who graduated in 2004 with first class honours. Her minor thesis focused on investigating the role of an online simulation in supporting the pedagogical development of first year pre-service teachers at the University of Wollongong.

Thomas C. Reeves is professor of instructional technology at the University of Georgia, USA, where he teaches program evaluation, multimedia design, and research courses. Since receiving his PhD at Syracuse University in 1979, he has developed and evaluated numerous online and interactive multimedia programs for education and training. His research interests include: evaluation of instructional technology for education and training, socially responsible research goals and methods in education, cognitive tools, and applications of instructional technology in developing countries. He is a former Fulbright lecturer in Peru, and has been an invited speaker in many countries including Australia, Brazil, Bulgaria, China, England, Finland, Malaysia, Russia, South Africa, Sweden, and Taiwan. He is a former editor of the *Journal of Interactive Learning Research*, and in 2003, he was awarded the inaugural *AACE Fellowship Award* from the Association for the Advancement of Computing in Education.

Clive Reynoldson is former head of the School of Finance and Business Economics at Edith Cowan University, Australia, and director of the WA Management Development Centre. His current position is director of graduate studies at the Faculty of Business and Public Management, ECU. Clive teaches economics and business strategy to post-graduate students at the university. His current research interests include reform of service delivery in the public sector, quality assurance in higher education and economics education.

John Ryan is an experienced manager and management consultant from a broad range of areas. After 12 years with Ford Australia (Graduate Trainee to National Sales Distribution Manager), he joined PA consulting in Melbourne in late 1967, and transferred to Perth in 1968. He became a principal consultant, PA's highest grade. He retired to freelance in 1991. Since receiving a Doctorate in Business Administration in 2001, he has assisted with the Peer Coaching project, continued consulting and undertaken sessional lecturing. Until November 2001 he was chairman of ITIM, a national non-profit company, which offers a range of employee assistance programs throughout Australia.

Sue Stoney is senior lecturer in management information systems at Edith Cowan University, in Western Australia, and has had a wide experience of both teaching and business. She has been a tertiary educator for over 20 years and has had 15 years experience in start up businesses in the primary industry sector. The main focus of her recent research has been the usability of various Internet environments, legal aspects of the Internet, and online communities, particularly in learning environments. Sue currently teaches a first year introductory business computing course, as well as Web usability courses for both undergraduate and graduates.

Jan Turbill is currently the director of primary education in the Faculty of Education, University of Wollongong, Australia. She began teaching for the Department of School Education in New South Wales, teaching primary children for 12 years, working as a Literacy Consultant for nine years before moving to the academic world of the University in 1985. Jan's research ranges from early literacy development to the professional development of teachers. More recently she has been researching the use of technology as a support for literacy learning in the early years of schooling and as a medium for professional learning for teachers. She is the author of many books and articles and is presently president of the Australian Literacy Educators' Association (ALEA).

Index

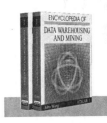